T0355078

An Anthology of Poems by Buddhist Nuns
of Late Imperial China

An Anthology of Poems by Buddhist Nuns of Late Imperial China

Translated by
Beata Grant

OXFORD
UNIVERSITY PRESS

Oxford University Press is a department of the University of Oxford.
It furthers the University's objective of excellence in research, scholarship,
and education by publishing worldwide. Oxford is a registered trade mark of
Oxford University Press in the UK and in certain other countries.

Published in the United States of America by Oxford University Press
198 Madison Avenue, New York, NY 10016, United States of America.

Library of Congress Cataloging-in-Publication Data
2023915084

ISBN 978-0-19-758631-0

Printed by Sheridan Books, Inc., United States of America.

Contents

Acknowledgments

I have been most fortunate to have had not one but four experienced translators of Chinese poetry look over this manuscript at various stages. First, I am greatly indebted to Wilt L. Idema, who very patiently read over the early drafts of many of these translations and was of great assistance in solving grammatical conundrums and identifying obscure allusions when I found myself at wit's end. I am also most grateful to the series editors, Lucas Klein and Wiebke Denecke, for meticulously going over the later drafts of the manuscript and generously offering suggestions for improvement, and to "house poet" Eleanor Goodman for helping to make the translations read more smoothly. I would also like to express my great appreciation to Stefan Vranka, the executive editor of Oxford University Press, who always responded patiently to my queries, and who, after reading the final draft, offered some particularly useful suggestions designed to make it more accessible to English readers who might not be familiar with the larger cultural and religious contexts of these nuns' poetry. Last but by no means least, I wish to express my heartfelt thanks to Daniel Gill, Alan Thwaits, Katherine Fearn and all those who patiently worked to ready this manuscript for final publication. I, of course, take sole responsibility for any errors, omissions or infelicities that may still remain.

Most of the poems in this anthology are here translated into English for the first time. However, there were a number of previously published poems that, because they are either the sole extant work of a particular nun-poet or are particularly representative of her work, begged to be included. With the kind permission of the publisher, I have used, with minor modifications, the following poems from my *Daughters of Emptiness* (Wisdom Publications, 2003): Jueqing, "Poem Inscribed on a Convent Wall"; Wuwei, "Deathbed Gāthā"; Jingming, "Improvised Dharma Instructions to My Disciples"; Dumu Jin'gang, "Gāthā" (see pg 37); Xiang'an Yinhui, "Gāthā: Eating Bamboo Shoots"; Daoyuan, "Seated Meditation: Reflections"; Shenyi, "A Dream Journey to Mount Tiantai"; Jingwei, "The Emerald Sea"; Chaoyan Miyin, "Encomium to Myself"; Yuanduan Yufu, "My Study: An Impromptu Verse"; Miaohui, "Dawn, Sitting at Bo're Convent"; Shiyan, "Recalling a Dream"; Wanxian, "Inside the Convent: Reflections"; Lianhua Kedu, "Gāthā"; Yinyue Xinglin, "In the Mountains"; Qiyuan Xinggang, "The First Month of Summer Retreat: A Song of Leisure"; Yikui Chaochen, "Five Gāthās: Sitting in Meditation (To a Previous Tune)" and

"Deathbed Gāthā"; Zukui Xuanfu, "Song of the Twelve Hours of the Day"; Jizong Xingche, "Living in the Nanyue Mountains: Miscellaneous Verses" (10 verses); Mingxiu (Mingben), "My Inscription for a Painting of West Lake Requested While Staying at My Convent in Jingzhou"; Wuqing, "Feelings"; Lianghai Rude, "Poems of the Pure Land"; and "Untitled Verses" (4 verses). University of Hawai'i Press and Brill Publishers have also kindly given permission to use, again with slight modification, the following poems: Ziyong Chengru, "Thoughts in the Bingzi Year (1696)," previously published in my *Eminent Nuns* (University of Hawai'i Press, 2008); Yizhen, "Living in the Mountains among Falling Leaves" and Jingyin, "Going to See Huang Yuanjie, but Not Finding Her In," which were published in *The Inner Quarters and Beyond: Women Writers from Ming through Qing*, edited by Grace Fong and Ellen Widmer (Brill, 2010).

Introduction

Poetry and poetry writing have always been held in very high regard in Chinese culture. One of the oldest literary texts was an anthology of 305 poems dating from the eleventh to the seventh centuries BCE, which came to be known as the *Classic of Poetry* (*Shijing* 詩經) owing to the fact that it was cherished and promoted by none other than the great sage Confucius (551–479 BCE) himself. For much of China's history, the ability to write poetry was a sine-qua-non for any educated man. Poems were used to demonstrate one's qualifications for civil service, conduct diplomacy, cultivate relationships of all kinds, and, of course, to express one's innermost thoughts and feelings. It is not surprising, then, that as Indian Buddhism gradually became assimilated into Chinese culture, poetry would become an important vehicle for the expression of some its core teachings. Buddhist monks and laymen over the centuries, while by no means as prolific as their Confucian counterparts, wrote hundreds of poems, and are well represented in collections and anthologies compiled and circulated in premodern China. Many of these Buddhist poets, perhaps the most well-known being Han Shan 寒山 (Cold Mountain), have also been translated into other languages, including English.[1]

The observant reader will have noted that all the persons referred to in the previous paragraph have been male. As was true of much of the premodern world, writing poetry, and the education required to do so well, was regarded as a largely (elite) male prerogative. While women, even of the gentry class, might acquire enough basic literacy to teach their children, they were largely discouraged from writing poetry and faced even more obstacles in having it printed. There were always exceptions, of course. China's most famous woman poet, Li Qingzhao 李清照, lived in the Song dynasty (960–1279). But it was not until the late imperial period (1368–1644) that we find a significantly greater number of educated women not only writing poetry but also having it printed and even circulated for others to read.

What is true of women in general was also true of Buddhist nuns in particular, even though the female monastic tradition in China is as long and as continuous as that for males. For example, fifty-five of the sixty-five eminent nuns whose accounts appear in the *Biographies of Nuns* (*Biqiuni*

---

1 For just a few examples, see Seaton and Maloney 1995; Egan 2010; Pine and O'Connor 1998; and Rouzer 2017.

zhuan 比丘尼傳), compiled by the sixth-century monk Baochang 寶唱 (466–518?), came from upper-class backgrounds and are often described as being both eloquent and educated. However, only one four-line verse, by the nun Huixu 慧緒 (431–499), is actually cited, with Baochang noting that it was originally a longer poem but that the rest had been lost.[2] And in the *Complete Tang Poems* (*Quan Tang shi* 全唐詩), a massive collection compiled by imperial command in 1705 comprising 49,000 poems by more than 2,300 Tang dynasty poets, we find, by one calculation, 2,913 poems by 115 monk-poets.[3] There is, however, just one single poem written by a nun: "On a Boat at Night" ("Zhouye" 舟夜)", attributed to a nun named Haiyin 海印.[4] This scarcity of preserved poems by Buddhist nuns continues through the following two dynasties, the Song (960–1279) and the Yuan (1272–1368). The few poems that we do have were for the most part composed by nuns affiliated with the great Buddhist teacher Dahui Zonggao 大慧宗杲 (1089–1163). One of the most famous of these was Wuzhuo Miaozong 無著妙總 (1095–1170), who spent most of her life as a married laywoman before taking ordination later in life, and who was known for her literary talents as well as her spiritual achievements. Although most of her writing has been lost, forty of her *songgu* 頌古, or "verse commentaries" on classical stories of past Chinese masters, have been preserved. Wuzhuo Miaozong would later serve as an important religious and literary model, as demonstrated by the fact that almost five hundred years later, the two seventeenth-century nuns, Baochi Xuanzong 寶持玄總 (p. 227) and Zukui Xuanfu 祖揆玄符 (p. 183), would put together a collaborative collection comprising forty verses of theirs, along with Miaozong's original poems.[5]

There are only two poems by nuns from the short-lived Mongol Yuan dynasty that are included in most traditional anthologies of poetry, and one of them may actually be from the Song. The first is a verse by a nun named Miaozhan 妙湛 said to have been written as an inscription for a painting of her convent rendered by the renowned woman artist Guan Daosheng 管道昇 (1262–1319).[6] The second is a poem attributed to an otherwise unknown author referred to as simply as the Plum Blossom Nun. This poem has come to be regarded as the iconic expression of a nun's religious awakening and has repeatedly been anthologized.[7]

2   For a translation of this poem, see Grant 2003, 22.

3   See Watson 1992, 30.

4   For a translation of this poem, see Grant 2003, 28.

5   This collection was titled *The Mutual Echoes Collection of Poems in Praise of Ancient Cases* (*Songgu hexiang ji* 頌古合響集). For a complete English translation, see Grant 2017.

6   For a translation of this poem, see Grant 2003, 48.

7   Chen Zhuo 1873, 100:35. One of the earliest appearances of this poem is in a Ming dynasty edition of *Helin yulu* 鶴林玉露 (*Jade and Dew from Crane Forest*), a collection

The entire day I searched for Spring,
   but saw no sign of it
As, in straw sandals, I poked around
   the clouds on the mountain peak.
Then back home, I laughingly caught
   the scent of the blossoming plum.
There on the branch tips was Spring,
   already completely in bloom!

This all changed in the Ming (1368–1644) and Qing dynasties (1644–1911), often referred to as the late imperial period, an era that coincided with a remarkable efflorescence of women's culture in general and writing in particular. This was due in large part to important economic and commercial developments beginning in the late Ming, as well as the emergence of publishers and publishing houses eager to take advantage of a growing readership among the largely urban elites, which now included merchants and women as well as the traditional literati.[8] Perhaps the most vivid illustration of this is the fact that we have the titles of nearly five thousand collections by Ming-Qing women poets, including almost every one of the sixty-six Buddhist nuns in this anthology, though unfortunately less than a quarter of these works survive today. During this period we also see the printing of anthologies dedicated exclusively to women's poetry, such as *Classic Poetry by Famous Women* (*Mingyuan shiwei* 名媛詩緯), compiled by the woman poet and editor Wang Duanshu 王端淑 (1621–1685?). This anthology, published in 1667, contained several thousand poems by women, including Buddhist nuns. Fortunately, several of these anthologies still exist today, thus ensuring the preservation of at least a few examples of the poetry of women writers whose work would otherwise have been completely forgotten.

This period also saw the publication of *The Jiaxing Chinese Buddhist Canon* (*Jiaxing dazang jing* 嘉興大藏經) (CBETA J), compiled and printed with private funds (unlike most editions of the Buddhist canon, which were court-sponsored) between the years 1579 and 1677. *The Jiaxing Chinese*

of miscellaneous writings compiled by the Southern Song dynasty scholar Luo Dajing. The editors of most anthologies, however, refer to her as a Yuan dynasty nun. In the seventeenth-century *Song Yuan shihui* 宋元詩會 [*Collection of Poetry of the Song and Yuan*] (Chen Zhuo 1873), the poem appears as the very last poem in the very last chapter of the 100-chapter work.

8 Recent decades have seen an outpouring of excellent scholarship on women's writing in China. For annotated anthologies, see Idema and Grant 2004; and Chang and Saussey 2000. For good introductory studies of late imperial women writers, see Chang and Widmer 1997; and the classic Ko 1994.

Buddhist Canon is special in that it contains many hundreds of works by Buddhist monastics not found elsewhere, including, most notably, a few collections of poetry and other writings by eminent female masters of the seventeenth century.

The majority of the poems in this anthology, arranged in roughly chronological order and accompanied by brief biographical accounts of the authors, have never before been translated into English.[9] As such, they offer a rare glimpse into the poetic worlds of Buddhist nuns living during the last two dynasties of imperial China.

The Religious Background

The nuns whose poems are translated in this volume were all practitioners of one or more forms of Chinese Buddhism, especially Chan (Zen in Japanese) and Pure Land. While it is impossible to do justice to these extremely rich religious traditions here, a brief and necessarily very general overview may help the reader to better appreciate both the lives and the writings of these nuns. Buddhism arrived in China from India and Central Asia from around the first century CE, bringing with it a plethora of different texts, teachings, and practices. Of these, those of the Mahayana or "Great Vehicle" school, which appears to have first taken shape in India around the first century BCE, would become dominant in China, as well as the rest of East Asia. "Mahayana" is best thought of as an umbrella term that covers an immense variety of ideas and doctrines. One can, however, point to a few of the most important shared characteristics. The first thing to note is that proponents of Mahayana did not reject the core tenets of early Indian Buddhism: that all things are impermanent; that the self or personality so many of us identify with is neither unique, permanent, nor independent; and that although life is intrinsically suffering, by seeing through the mistaken perceptions that impel us to crave permanence and cling to deluded notions of self and other, one can get off the unending wheel of life and death (*samsara*) and achieve liberation from all suffering (nirvana). Even as believers fully accepted these ideas, Mahayana also introduced new interpretations, perspectives, and practices, which came to be elaborated on in new religious scriptures. These scriptures, though not accepted as canonical by many adherents of early mainstream Buddhism (today often referred to by the name of one of its more important schools, Theravada), exerted a profound influence on Chinese literature, culture, and art. Examples of just a few of the Mahayana texts cherished by our nun-poets are the Diamond Sutra

---

9 Grant 2003 offers a selection of poems by nuns from the earliest down to the modern period. It includes a few of the poems in this anthology, but most of the poems in the present volume have never been translated before.

(Skt: Vajracchedikā Prajñāpāramitā Sūtra; Ch: Jin'gang jing 金剛經), the Flower Garland Sutra (Skt: Avatamsaka Sūtra; Ch: Huayan jing 華嚴經), both first translated into Chinese in the fifth century, and the Heroic March Sutra (Skt: Surangama Sūtra; Ch: Lengyan jing 楞嚴經), which appears to have been translated a couple of centuries later. In addition, there were texts that, while traditionally said to be of Indian origin, may in fact have been composed in China. One of the most famous of these is the Heart Sutra (Xinjing 心經), accepted by all East Asian Mahayana schools and the most widely studied, copied, and recited of all Buddhist scriptures.

One of the many diverse ideas elaborated upon in these sometimes very lengthy texts is the notion that there is not one but rather countless worlds, and that while the historical Buddha known as Sakyamuni, who lived in India over 2,500 years ago, might be no longer around, there exist many other otherworldly Buddhas, some of whom can be appealed to for succor by suffering sentient beings. Perhaps the most well known of these is Amitabha Buddha, who presides over a celestial "Pure Land," into which devotees can aspire to be reborn and where the conditions for transformational awakening are ideal.

Also central to Mahayana are the ideals represented by the figure of the bodhisattva, a being whose quest for enlightenment is motivated primarily by the compassionate desire to be of benefit to all suffering sentient beings. While all Buddhists are enjoined to embark on the bodhisattva path, they can find inspiration in advanced spiritual figures such as the bodhisattva Guanyin, sometimes referred to in the West as the Goddess of Compassion. Although most often represented as female, Guanyin can assume many different forms, in accord with which form will allow for the most effective assistance to those in need (an adaptability referred to in Chinese as *fangbian* 方便 or "skillful means").

Philosophically, one of the most important ideas is that of emptiness (*sunyata* in Sanskrit, *kong* 空 in Chinese). The word "emptiness," which appears repeatedly in Buddhist poetry, is notoriously difficult to define. Generally speaking, it enlarges upon the early Buddhist claim that there is no independent and unchanging self or personality, and applies the idea to *all* phenomena. Emptiness is by no means equivalent to nihilism, nor does it imply the negation of form. In fact, emptiness itself is said to be empty. In the words of the Heart Sutra, "form is empty, emptiness is form." Ultimately, however, all phenomena exist in dependence on everything else, and nothing possesses any independent or permanent reality.

Another Mahayana Buddhist doctrine that many Chinese found particularly congenial insisted that all beings contain within themselves the virtues and wisdom of an enlightened buddha or *tathāgata*, but that these were obscured by a veil of dualistic and deluded thoughts, concepts, and attachments. Awakening to this inherently pure essence was compared to, among other things, a destitute man discovering a treasure hidden away beneath the floorboards of his own house. A related concept speaks of "buddha-nature," or the potential for Buddhahood found within all beings. In our nuns' poems, we find this basic idea expressed in a variety of terms, including One Mind, Suchness, and the Unborn, all of which point to an inherently awakened state that can be achieved primarily by cutting through the false perceptions of reality that are the primary cause of all our suffering. While these ideas can be found in many Chinese Buddhist schools, they are central to Chan Buddhism, the school to which many of the nuns in this anthology adhere.

The character *chan* 禪 (pronounced Zen in Japanese) was originally a Chinese transliteration of the Sanskrit word *dhyāna*, which means meditation. While meditation is very important in Chan Buddhism, as it is in other Chinese Buddhist schools, even more significant is its emphasis on the direct and unmediated experience of religious awakening, whether attained through formal sitting or not. Traditionally, such awakening is an experience usually, though not always, facilitated and ultimately verified by an already enlightened master—often, as we shall see, by means of an exchange of verse. The history of the origin and development of Chan Buddhism from the sixth century on is complex and complicated and continues to be the subject of scholarly study and debate.[10] There are however, a number of stories, some of which are clearly more legend than fact, that continue to play a central role in its traditional narratives. One of the most well known of these traces the origins of Chan Buddhism back to India and the historical Buddha himself. According to this story, one day the Buddha, instead of delivering a sermon, wordlessly held up a white flower. Among the many gathered to listen to him, only one, the Buddha's senior disciple Mahakasyapa, grasped the significance of this gesture and smiled in response. This story is often referred to as the first wordless mind-to-mind transmission of a special teaching claimed to be "outside of the scriptures."[11] The transmission of this teaching continued through an unbroken line of Indian "patriarchs," the twenty-eighth of whom was Bodhidharma (fl. c. 480–520).[12] Bodhidharma, a figure clothed

10 Readers interested in this debate may want to refer to McRae 2004.
11 This popular description of Chan Buddhism as a transmission outside the scriptures that does not rely on words but rather points directly to the mind, as its way of leading to the attainment of Buddhahood, is traditionally attributed to Bodhidharma, even though scholarship has determined otherwise. For a succinct scholarly discussion of these oft-quoted lines, see Welter 1996.
12 The metaphor often used to describe this transmission is that of the flame of a lighted lamp used to ignite another lamp, and so on down the line.

in myth and legend, is said in some accounts to have been the son of an Indian prince. He traveled to China and would later come to be known as the First Chinese Patriarch of Chan Buddhism. Many popular stories about Bodhidharma appear repeatedly in Chinese literature and painting, including many of the poems in this anthology.

Although the Tang dynasty has traditionally been thought of as the golden age of Buddhism (and indeed, of Buddhist poetry), this view is in large part a creation of the Song dynasty, which is when a great many of the stories of the lives and teachings of the great Tang masters were actually compiled and printed. The Tang was also a period when Chan Buddhism underwent a tremendous expansion, in terms of both numbers of monks (including monk-poets) and the number of temples and monasteries. It is in the Song dynasty as well that we see the emergence of what is referred to as literary Chan (*wenzi Chan* 文字禪). Associated primarily with the Buddhist monk-poet Juefan Huihong 覺範惠洪 (1071–1128), literary Chan refers generally to the idea that Chan religious practice did not necessarily conflict with more secular-seeming pursuits, such as poetry, painting, and scholarship.[13] It is also in the Song dynasty, as we saw earlier, that we find a master in the Linji Chan lineage, Dahui Zonggao, insisting that when it came to the highest truth, distinctions between male and female were irrelevant, and officially bestowing dharma transmission on his female disciples—a fact that Linji Chan masters of the late imperial period would note and emulate.

If the Tang and Song have been traditionally regarded as the golden age of Chan Buddhism, by the late imperial period there was a widespread perception that Chan had lost its way and become corrupt—a suggestion found in poems by seventeenth-century Buddhist nuns such as Jizong Xingche 繼總行徹 (see p. 243). In reaction to this perception, Linji Chan masters such as Miyun Yuanwu 密雲圓悟 (1566–1644) and their later dharma successors were particularly keen on returning to a form of Chan practice that, in their view at least, more closely adhered to the ideals and practices of the great teachers of the Tang and Song dynasties.[14] One of the earlier teachers they looked to for inspiration was Dahui Zonggao, and following the precedent set by that great Linji master, many (though by no means all) seventeenth-century male Linji masters also gave dharma transmission to some of their female students. There are several examples of such women

---

13 For an excellent study of this important period of Chan history, see Schlütter 2008. For an insightful and informative look at the place of poetry in the lives of Song dynasty monks, see Protass 2021.

14 For more on the complexities and contradictions of this seventeenth century Chan revival, see Wu 2008.

Chan masters in this anthology, including Qiyuan Xinggang 祇園行剛 (see p. 149). While most of these women Chan masters received dharma transmission from male masters (and were not allowed to have male disciples themselves), Qiyuan Xinggang was an exception in that she was a female master who bestowed dharma transmission on a number of her female disciples, including Yigong Chaoke 義公超珂 and Yikui Chaochen 一揆超琛 (1625–1679). Unfortunately, however, her lineage did not survive, largely owing to lack of support by male monastics and laypersons. By the end of the seventeenth century, we find fewer and fewer mentions of Chan Buddhist nuns, and much less of female Chan masters, the one exception being Ziyong Chengru 子雍成如, who enjoyed the respect and patronage of the Qing dynasty Kangxi emperor (1661–1772).

While Chan Buddhism was central to the lives of many of the nun-poets in this anthology, for others it was Pure Land Buddhism. Although it would develop into a distinct school in Japan, Chinese Pure Land Buddhism is perhaps best thought of not so much as a school, like Chan, but rather as a distinct tradition of practice. According to this tradition, there are numerous so-called "pure lands" situated outside of ordinary reality, each of which has been created by the merit of beings who have become Buddhas. These pure lands are envisioned as places offering the most pleasant and propitious conditions for sentient beings to attain final awakening. The most popular of these pure lands was the Western Pure Land of the Amitabha Buddha, and the primary aspiration of his devotees was to be reborn there after death, largely by means of the single-minded focus on, and recitation of, the phrase "Namo Amituofo" or "All homage to the Amitabha Buddha."[15] Interestingly, we find even some of our Chan nun-poets advocating Pure Land practices over what they saw as the corruption in the world of Chan monasticism. In the late imperial period, we also see the growing popularity, among lay devotees as well as monastics, of so-called dual cultivation (*shuangxiu* 雙修) of Chan meditative practice and Pure Land devotions. One of the ideas found in this type of practice, and in the poetry of the mid-nineteenth-century nun Lianghai Rude 量海如德 (fl. mid-1850s), is that by purifying the mind (through both Pure Land devotional practices and Chan meditation), one can realize the Pure Land in this very world, this very body, and this very lifetime.

---

15 According to many texts, there are no women in the Pure Land, perhaps because a woman's body was traditionally identified with suffering and the Pure Land was a land of bliss. In any case, female devotees aspired to be reborn as males in the Pure Land.

Lives and Times

For many of the Buddhist nun-poets in this anthology, what we know of their lives is largely limited to short accounts appended to their poems found in such anthologies as Wang Duanshu's *Classic Poetry by Famous Women* (1667). Other sources include *shihua* 詩話 or "notes on poems" devoted to women writers, most notably *Notes on the Poetry of Famous Women* (*Mingyuan shihua* 名媛詩話), compiled by the woman poet Shen Shanbao 沈善寶 (1808–1862), first published in 1846 and then reprinted with a sequel in 1879. For other nuns, especially those who rose in the ranks to become Chan masters, bits of biographical information can be found in Buddhist compilations such as *The Complete Books of the Five Lamps* (*Wudeng quanshu* 五燈全書) (Chaoyong 1697), a collection of accounts of Buddhist monastics of the Chan school who lived in the seventeenth and eighteenth centuries. Another important source is the biographical (and sometimes even autobiographical) accounts appended to these nuns' recorded sayings (*yulu* 語錄), a term used to refer to collections of a Chan master's sermons, accounts of exchanges with students, letters, funerary sermons, and poetry, usually compiled by the master's disciples to be printed and circulated for the benefit of all.

The brevity of most these biographical accounts (some are no longer than a line or two long) do not allow for a truly in-depth knowledge of these women's lives. However, when read in conjunction with their poems, these biographies do suggest a significant range and diversity of backgrounds and experiences. On one end of the spectrum were women who devoted themselves exclusively to religious devotions carried out in a small cloister near or even within the family compound, or in times of political turmoil, who fled to the mountains where they took up residence in small hermitages. Many times, these women shaved their heads, as did Buddhist nuns, but sometimes it is not clear whether they were formally tonsured or ordained. In fact, in a few cases, Daoyuan (p. 45) for example, editors and anthologists differ as to whether a particular woman should be regarded as a Buddhist nun or a Daoist nun. At the other end are the nuns whose biographical accounts explicitly state that were officially tonsured and ordained by known (male) Buddhist masters. Among these were those who embarked on intensive periods of study with these masters and even went on to become their dharma successors, and thus became officially recognized Chan masters themselves.

Not surprisingly, there were also different reasons why a woman would decide to become a nun. A view popular in premodern China, with its strong Confucian valorization of the family and of women's "natural" roles as mothers and wives, was that the only reason a woman would become a nun was that she was obliged to do so. And indeed, a great many of the nuns in this anthology entered the religious life only because ill-health or difficult family circumstances precluded a successful marriage, or after having lost husbands or fiancés. This was particularly true of women living through the often violent and extremely traumatic social and political upheavals of the Ming-Qing transition in the mid-seventeenth century. Zaisheng 再生 (p. 55) and Shenyi 神一 (p. 51), for example, fled into the mountains to escape soldiers or bandits, after which they lived as nuns in a small countryside hermitage. There were also women who had been inducted into the Inner Palace, the quarters deep within the palace reserved for women associated with the court, especially the consorts and concubines of the emperor, and who, with the fall of the Ming court in 1644, had no alternative but to become nuns. And finally, there were courtesans, many of whom were women of considerable literary talent, who found refuge in the convent. As the reader will see, often the poems of these women are marked as much by expressions of sorrow and even bitterness as they are by calm spiritual transcendence of suffering. However, not every woman who entered the religious life did so only because she had no other alternative. In many cases we find women who are said to have been drawn to the religious life from an early age and went so far as to refuse to marry so that they could pursue their spiritual aspirations. There were also women who, while they may have entered the religious life due to unfortunate life circumstances, went on to pursue authentic religious careers both as practitioners and even as eminent teachers.

By the close of the seventeenth century, the new Qing dynasty had been firmly established, and there was a return to more traditional Confucian notions of proper female behavior, embodied by the so-called "Three Followings" (sancong 三從), which stipulated that as a daughter, a woman should follow and obey her father, as a wife, her husband, and as a mother, her son. We also find fewer and fewer examples of extant poetry by Buddhist nuns in general, the one major exception being the mid-eighteenth-century nun Lianghai Rude (p. 319), best known for her poems of the Pure Land.

Texts: Content, Form, and Genre

Unlike the scriptures of early Buddhism, which were relatively short and designed to be transmitted orally, many Mahayana Buddhist texts, such as the Flower Garland Sutra, were very long and clearly meant to be read and savored. They were usually composed in a combination of prose and un-rhymed verse known as gāthā (ji 偈 or jisong 偈頌 in Chinese), the purpose of the latter being to summarize or reiterate, often in quite beautiful and expressive language, the contents of the former. When these were translated into Chinese, readers were struck by the language and imagery of these texts, and by the fourth century, we find Chinese Buddhist poets beginning to write their own Buddhist poetry, including gāthā. In doing so, however, rather than imitate the original Indian texts, they drew upon the indigenous poetic tradition with which they were intimately familiar. For example, this tradition stipulated that all verse should rhyme, and so poets began to write rhymed gāthā. From the beginning, nature imagery, although not always used allegorically, has often played a role in Chinese poetry. The fourth and fifth centuries, when more and more poets were beginning to write their own Buddhist poetry, was a period when landscape poetry and painting flourished, and from then on we find Buddhist poets making rich use of natural images to embody Buddhist ideas, such as drifting white clouds to suggest impermanence and constant change. They also began to make increasing use of traditional Chinese genres. As we saw earlier, the *Complete Tang Poems* includes nearly 3,000 poems by monk-poets, the great majority of which were written in the style of regulated verse or *lüshi* 律詩. One of the most important of all forms of classical Chinese poetry, and one that all educated men sought to master, regulated verse was made up of eight lines of five, six, or seven characters, each of which had to adhere to prescribed rules of tonal parallelism and rhyme.

Already in the Tang dynasty, the line between Buddhist poetry and secular mainstream poetry was often a tenuous one, so much so that, in the minds of some, writing poetry was not something that those committed to the spiritual life should engage in. An example is Jiaoran 皎然 (730–799), often referred to as one of the three greatest monk-poets of the Tang, who gave up writing poetry for several years before being persuaded that poetry-writing could be regarded as a form of "skillful means," that would draw readers to Buddhism. This uneasiness continued into the Song when, even with the popularity of literary Chan, there were still many (including Dahui Zonggao) who questioned it. And in the seventeenth-century, we find the references to monks and nuns who gave up writing poetry after entering the religious life, or like the nun Shangxin 上信 (see p. 111) foreswearing the use of mainstream Chinese poetic genres such as regulated verse, continuing to compose gāthās and hymns. By the same token, some traditional Chinese readers and critics were also acutely aware of a distinction, and some went so far as to claim that Buddhist religious poetry, especially gāthās which were often explicitly didactic, should not be considered poetry at all. Another example is the commentaries in verse such as those composed by Dahui Zonggao's woman dharma-successor, Wuzhuo Miaozong. During the Song and Yuan dynasties, this type of verse (*songgu* 頌古) was collected separately, and normally not included in poetry collections. However, in many anthologies from the late imperial period, including Wang Duanshu's *Classic Poetry by Famous Women* (1667), verse commentaries by nuns appear together with other genres of Chinese poetry.

The poems in this volume are of many kinds and served many purposes.[16] Some were designed to be used in a ritual context, others were composed for the purposes of instruction or edification, and still others were written to express feelings of friendship or appreciation of natural beauty. Examples of ritual verses include poems written on the occasion of an experience of awakening or spiritual realization. Often embedded in the official record of a particular nun's religious training, such verses were traditionally composed to show the master, who would presumably be able to gauge the authenticity and depth of their experience from their contents. Deathbed verses, on the other hand, were traditionally composed by a realized teacher just before death as a final "summing up" of his or her spiritual insight and left as both instruction and inspiration for their immediate disciples as well as to future practitioners. Often such verses are composed in the form of gāthā, which although technically not required to adhere to specific rules of composition, are usually rhymed and comprised of four lines of five or six characters.

Given that many of these nuns had roles as religious teachers, with lay as well as monastic disciples, we also find them composing popular songs or other kinds of verses largely designed for the purpose of edification. These songs are readily identifiable by their use of simple language and well-known allusions, and are usually addressed more to a lay audience than a monastic one. An example of this are the verses by the nun known as Dumu Jin'gang 獨目金剛 or One-Eyed Diamond Sutra, which celebrate the efficacious power of the Diamond Sutra. Although the primary subject of the Diamond Sutra, one of the most popular of all Buddhist scriptures, is the notoriously subtle Mahayana Buddhist notion of "emptiness," there was a popular belief that just reciting (or copying) this sutra, even without understanding its content, would bring, among other things, the blessings of a long life.[17] Another example of a poem clearly directed at a more popular audience is Zukui Xuanfu's "The Road Is Hard" (p. 213) which devotes one verse each to the sufferings of birth, aging, sickness, and death, describing them in ways that are largely formulaic and easily understood.

These types of popular and largely didactic works are quite different from the poems, often consisting of only four rhymed lines, that were designed as dharma instructions for more advanced followers, both monastic and

---

16 Jason Protass's categorization of the various types of poetic writings made use of by (male) monastics of the Song dynasty has been very helpful in considering the types of poems composed by nun-poets of the later Ming-Qing period. See Protass 2021.

17 The oldest known dated printed book in the world is a copy of the Diamond Sutra. An edition printed in 868 can be viewed at the British Library.

lay. These verses are often poetic, sometimes abstruse, and usually ad-
dressed to a named recipient, which provides an invaluable glimpse into
the larger religious community with which a particular nun interacted,
and which included not only laywomen but also laymen. Yet another type
of verse, used especially often by women Chan masters, was the *zan* 讚,
or encomium. These are verses written in descriptive praise of religious
figures past and present and often designed to be inscribed on paintings
and portraits, in some cases one's own. Chan masters such as Zukui
Xuanfu wrote a great number of these sorts of verses, many more than
are included in this anthology.

While most of these types of poems are associated with the Chan Bud-
dhist school, we also find examples of Pure Land poems. Like the verse
commentaries, during the Song dynasty these types of poems were regarded
as hymns primarily for use in a ritual context. However, by the late imperial
period, they had come to be thought of as the poetry of the Pure Land.[18]
While many Chan Buddhist nuns refer to Pure Land practices in their po-
ems, it is only with the mid-nineteenth century nun Lianghai Rude that we
find an extended series of forty-eight Pure Land poems, a representative
sampling of which have been translated for this anthology.

This brings us to occasional verse, the type of poetry most commonly
written not only by our nun-poets, but by monastics in general. Occasional
verses, which are also ubiquitous in mainstream, non-Buddhist poetry, are
of many kinds. In the Buddhist monastic context, events or experiences
that might elicit an occasional verse include visiting a temple or pilgrimage
site, conveying birthday greetings to a fellow monastic or lay follower, and
sending a fellow monastic off on a journey. There are also many poems
mourning the death of a beloved teacher or a fellow nun, which provide a
glimpse into the close personal ties among many of these women. Some
of these nun-poets also traveled extensively, sometimes out of a need to
search for safety from a political situation, but also for religious purposes
to visit eminent Chan masters or pilgrimage sites of religious significance.
Nuns such as Jizong Xingche and Ziyong Chengru, for example, left their
home convents in the north and traveled hundreds of miles to visit Buddhist
sites and teachers in southeast China, often penning poems to record their
experiences. Jizong Xingche lived for extended periods in the Nanyue 南
嶽 mountains of Hunan and wrote many poems describing its scenic spots,
as well as the joys of living a life in tune with the natural world. In the cat-
egory of occasional verse, we also find poems expressing more personal

18 Protass, citing the work of Liao Chao-heng, notes that only beginning with Chan Master
Chushi Fanzi (1206–1370) did "Pure Land verse depart from didactic ritual hymns and
instead approach a poetry of the Pure Land." See Protass 2021, 67.

reflections and thoughts, as well as poems sent as missives or letters to lay students, fellow monastics, and often distant family members.

It is important to note that all these types of poetic verse were written by male monastics as well. Some, like poems on "Living in the Mountains" (*shanju* 山居), were particularly popular with male monastics and can often found in their collections of recorded sayings. One can even say that by composing her own extended series of verses on this topic, the woman Chan master Jizong Xingche could write herself even more firmly into what was still primarily a patriarchal tradition. Nun-poets could also write themselves into the tradition by composing poems matching those of well-known monk-poets. An example of this is the series of ten poems titled "Cloud-Dispelling Terrace," by the Song dynasty Chan monk Cishou Huaishen 慈受懷深 (1077–1132), who spent his later years on Mount Lingyan 靈巖山, outside of Suzhou, Jiangsu province; the Cloud-Dispelling Terrace is one of the scenic sites on this mountain. In 1119 his series of ten verses was inscribed on a stone stele and later inspired many poets, especially monastic poets, to write their own series, matching its rhyme sequence. In 1654 this stele was rediscovered, and many contemporary Chan masters and their students wrote their own poems to commemorate the find. The poets writing poems included at least three of our nun-poets: Baochi Xuanzong (see p. 229), Yikui Chaochen, and Zukui Xuanfu. Another example is the series of poems titled "Ode to the Honeybees" (*Mifeng song* 蜜蜂頌), composed by the Song dynasty Linji Chan master Tianfeng Foci 天封佛慈. This famous series of verses, which indirectly compare the industry and devotion of the honeybee to the industry and devotion of the religious practitioner, was inscribed on a stone stele shortly after being composed. This stele too had been lost and was then rediscovered in the mid-seventeenth century, after which many eminent Linji masters of the day wrote their own series using the same rhyme, as did at least two of their female dharma heirs, Zukui Xuanfu (p. 183) and Weiji Xingzhi 維極行致 (p. 89).

As for poetic forms, many of our nuns appear to have been particularly adept at composing five- and seven-syllable regulated verse, a technically demanding form that, as we have seen, was most often used by the monk-poets of the Tang dynasty. Our nuns also wrote old-style (*guti* 古體) verse and songs (*ge* 歌), both forms allowing for greater narrative flexibility in terms of tones and rhymes, as well as length. Perhaps the most interesting example of flexibility in length is "The Song of the Twelve Hours of the Day," which was originally the title of a popular vernacular song but was adopted early on by Chan Buddhist monastics and applied to the daily routines of monastic life. We also find the nun Lianghai Rude using the four-syllable per line verse form found in the *Classic of Poetry* (many of the poems of which appear to have been of largely popular origin), as well as certain forms of old-style verse to retell the story of a filial girl who commits suicide after the death of her parents.

A mainstream poetic form largely eschewed by both male and female monastics was the song lyric (*ci* 詞), which was traditionally associated with rather un-Buddhist themes of love, romance, and sentiment in general. As it happens, this was also the genre most closely associated both with the feminine and with female writers—another reason perhaps for religious women, anxious to disassociate themselves from gender markers, not to write lyrics. There are, however, a few examples of song lyrics in this volume; see for example those by the nun Shuxia 舒霞 (see p. 309) who came from a family of well-known lyricists and appears to have continued to write lyrics even after entering the religious life. It is important to note that the song lyric originated in the late Tang dynasty as a popular form written to specific musical "tunes." In time the musical tunes became tonal and rhyme patterns, and lyrics were composed by respectable literati poets, even though in general they retained their emotional, if not erotic, subject matter. The popular origin of the song lyric is reflected in Zukui Jifu's poem "The Road Is Hard," mentioned earlier, which makes use of the song lyric tune "Immortals by the River," (Linjiang xian 臨江仙) but is not the slightest bit romantic or sentimental in nature.

Reception

In premodern China, Buddhist poetry, and in particular Buddhist monastic poetry, has traditionally had a very mixed reception, especially in mainstream literary circles. However, especially from the Tang dynasty onward, the writings of many Buddhist monk-poets were appreciated and often admired. Indeed, many lay literati counted such monastics as friends and acquaintances and often exchanged poems with them. Representative works of these monk-poets were also included in male-edited poetic anthologies, even if they were sometimes placed in chapters or subchapters located at the end. With the flourishing of women writers and the appearance of anthologies of women's poetry in the seventeenth century, we find a greater appreciation of poetry by Buddhist nuns as well, especially since, as noted earlier, many of them had acquired literary reputations even before entering the religious life. Wang Duanshu's editorial comments on these nuns and their poems reflect an understanding and often a real sympathy with not only their life situations but also their religious concerns and aspirations as well. This is not altogether surprising, given that her own sister, Wang Jingshu, had become a nun. As Wang Duanshu would later write, "My elder sister possessed the karmic roots of intelligence and sublime realization, and she took refuge in the Dharma King.[19] She was fond of living among the famous mountains and rivers, and had no taste for such things as acquiring a glorious reputation."[20] Wang included several of her sister's poems in her own anthology, noting that her sister "in her leisure time would write little poems. She did not seek to make them artful; she transcended both things and feelings, and simply followed her elevated mood."[21] While her own claims for her sister's poetic talents are modest ones, Wang Duanshu also records the editorial opinion of an unnamed appreciative reader who comments very favorably on Wang Jingshu's poems and, interestingly, notes, "It has been difficult enough for women to write poetry; how much more difficult for them to [gain renown] for both their Chan and their poetry."[22]

As noted earlier, although all but a handful of the recorded sayings of women Chan masters of the late imperial period have now been lost, many were in circulation during their own eras, thus allowing readers a fuller appreciation of their writings. Wang Duanshu, for example, appears to have read the poems included in the recorded sayings of Chaoyan Miyin 超衍密印, from which she selected a few for inclusion in her anthology. In her editorial preface to her selection of Chaoyin Miyin's verses (see p. 105), Wang Duanshu wrote the following:

> It has been said that in the heart of those who have mastered the study of texts, there is not a single word, and that also in the heart of those who are skilled at reading books, there is not a single word. In the beginning, the Eminent Master did not read books and did not harbor a single word in her breast, but then she arrived at the state where hearing a single sound would elicit a total enlightenment, like the torrential flow of streams and rivers, such that even those who have mastered the study of texts cannot equal it.[23] The poems in her recorded sayings are like fish leaping in the vast sea and birds soaring in the spacious sky. She neither gets entrapped by words, nor is she hindered by them. How could she have achieved this unless she had the roots of wisdom from a previous lifetime?[24]

The recorded sayings of the seventeenth-century poet and Chan master Mingxiu 明修 (see p. 303) was also apparently received with particular

---

19 The Buddha.
20 Wang Duanshu 1667, 15.5b.
21 Wang Duanshu 1667, 15.5b.
22 Wang Duanshu 1667, 15.5b.
23 The "Eminent Master" is Chaoyin Miyin.
24 Wang Duanshu 1667, 26.3a–b.

appreciation. Wang Qishu 汪啓淑 (1728–1799), in his 1773 anthology of women poets titled *Collected Fragrances* (*Xiefang ji* 擷芳集), included not only several of her verses, but also quotes from two prefaces introducing her recorded sayings. One of these prefaces was written by the scholar-official and poet Jiang Lian 蔣漣 (1675–1758), who appears to have met Mingxiu after she had returned from her pilgrimage to Mount Wutai and settled in the Beijing area. He noted that she showed him a section from what would become the collection of her recorded sayings, possibly in the hope that he would write a preface for it, which he did. Jiang Lian devoted much of this preface to a description of Mingxiu's well-known filial piety toward her mother and her subsequent religious attainments, all of which led him to conclude that as long as one possesses sufficient determination, "whether male or female, there is none who will not be able to advance" to the shores of liberation. He also wrote appreciatively of Mingxiu's literary skills:

> Whenever she had social dealings with others, she would quickly pen a verse. She never just followed the set style of writers from the past, but instead would spontaneously come up with something extremely elegant and lively. She had no need to "cull phrases and cite passages," and I could see how fine her writing was.[25]

The second preface quoted by Wang Qishu was written for a different collection of Mingxiu's writings by someone who appears to have been a Manchu woman associated with the Qing court.[26] Here too, much of the preface is devoted to a description of Mingxiu's extraordinary devotion to her mother, whom she "served with as much care as if for the Buddha himself," as well as the strong impression she made on members of the court after she arrived in Beijing. But like Jiang Lian, this preface writer also explicitly comments on Mingxiu's writing, which, perhaps a little surprisingly, she compares to that of the famous Tang Daoist priestess-courtesan Yu Xuanji:

> In the intervals between time spent quietly on the meditation cushion, she would write poems and verses to give expression to her spirit. The lines she produced were for the most part tranquil and

---

25 Wang Qishu 1773, 72:20a.

26 I have been unable able to identify the author of this preface, but the name Tongmen Nara 佟門那拉氏 can be translated as a woman from the Nara clan married to a man of the Tong lineage. Both Nara and Tong are Manchu family names.

spontaneous and can be compared with those of other women who have renounced the world, such as Yu Xuanji.[27]

Yet another example of an appreciative reader, this time of the nun Weiji Xingzhi (see p. 89), is the Chinese Muslim poet Ding Peng 丁澎 (1622–1686), who even went so far as to compose a song lyric in honor of Weiji's birthday. Of Weiji's poems, many of which appear to have been song lyrics, Ding is said to have remarked that her spontaneous and unforced writing style established her in "the uppermost ranks of the Pure Land." According to Pure Land beliefs, the most advanced practitioners would be born as lotus flowers that would transform into spiritual beings upon blooming. Here, of course, Ding is referring both to Weiji's religious accomplishments and to her superlative literary skills.[28]

It is worth noting that some readers of women's poetry were acutely aware of the relative scarcity of poems by nuns. One example is the poet and editor Shen Shanbao 沈善寶 (1808–1862), who in her *Remarks on Poetry by Famous Women* (*Mingyuan shihua* 名媛詩話) (1845), provided biographical information as well as her own commentary on 500 women poets, including herself. She mentioned around a dozen well-known nuns and noted the titles of several collections of recorded sayings, but also remarked on the relative scarcity of poems by women monastics.[29] We see a similar awareness of this absence of poems by nuns by the editors of an 1872 anthology titled *Pure Land Poems by Disciples of the Fourfold Sangha from Suzhou* (*Wumen sizhong dize jingtu shi* 吳門四眾弟子淨土詩). It seems that the publication of this anthology was delayed for some time because, while they had poems by three of the four major groups of the Buddhist community—laymen, laywomen, and monks—they could not find any poetry by Pure Land nuns. Fortunately, a manuscript copy of the *Shadows and Echoes Collection* (*Yinxiung ji* 影響集), by the nun Lianghai Rude, was discovered in the home of a lay follower, thus completing the quartet. The Buddhist layman Jiang Yuanliang 蔣元亮, who assisted with compilation, wondered why it had been so difficult to find such poems:

> Of the four categories of Buddhist followers, we found ourselves lacking only writings by nuns. The gentle beauties of heaven and earth are not judged according to which category they belong to.

27 Wang Qishu 1773, 72:20a. The text refers to her as Yu Yuanji 魚元機, as during the Qing the character *xuan* 玄 was taboo, as it was in the name of the Kangxi emperor Aisin-Gioro Xuanye 愛新覺羅玄燁.

28 Quoted in Xu Qiu, *Ciyuan congtan* vol. 4, 9:24a–b.

29 Shen Shanbao, *Mingyuan shihua*, 12:3a.

How much more should this be true of the different categories of Buddhists? Moreover, those who belong to a given category should be the ones to inspire others from the same category. How can it be that nuns should teach only by way of example and not by words?[30]

The fact that often only a single poem or a handful of poems by individual Buddhist nuns can be found in many traditional anthologies suggests a persistent reluctance to fully acknowledge the value of these women's writings. Today there is a growing appreciation of the poetry of these nun-poets, both in China and in the West, to which, I hope, this new anthology will further contribute.

A Note on the Texts

There are two major sources for the poems translated in this volume: Chinese anthologies of Ming-Qing poetry compiled during the Qing and early Republican periods and texts found in the Chinese Buddhist canon. Thanks to the user-friendly online database and archive Ming-Qing Women's Writings, it has been possible to access some of the earliest known sources for many of the poems translated in this volume, as well as a certain amount of biographical information and critical commentary. One of the most important of these is Wang Duanshu's *Classic Poetry by Famous Women* (1667), mentioned earlier. Many of the poems included in Wang Duanshu's anthology are also included, along with other poems in the *Anthology of Correct Beginnings by Talented Women of the Present Dynasty* (*Guochao guixiu zhengshi ji* 國朝閨秀正始集), compiled by the woman editor Wanyan Yun Zhu 完顏惲珠 and printed in 1831. This anthology, comprising 1,736 poems by 933 poets, was followed in 1836 by a sequel edited by Wanyan Yunzhu's granddaughter, Wanyan Miaolianbao 完顏妙蓮保 and consisting of 1,229 poems by 593 poets. Many of the poems by nuns contained in these two collections, along with others from sources that appear to be no longer extant, can also be found in the voluminous *Anthology of Poetry of the Late Qing* (*Wanqing yishihui* 晚清簃詩匯), compiled by Xu Shichang 徐世昌 (1858–1939), who apart from being a noted writer, scholar, painter, poet, and calligrapher, briefly served as president of the Republic of China between 1918 and 1922. In this compilation, chapter 199 of the 200-chapter anthology is dedicated primarily to the poetry of Buddhist nuns, along with a few poems by women Daoists. The other primary source for the poems translated in this volume is the Chinese Buddhist canon, which is now easily accessed online thanks to the Chinese Buddhist Electronic Texts Association (CBETA). Here the main sources are *Complete Books of the Five Lamps*

---

30 Zhiguan, *Xiuxi wenjian lu*, CBETA X78, no. 1552, p. 398c17–20.

(*Wudeng quanshu* 五燈全書) (Chaoyong 1697), a collection of accounts of Chan Buddhist monastics who lived in the seventeenth and eighteenth centuries; the recorded sayings of the seventeenth-century women Chan masters found in *The Jiaxing Chinese Buddhist Canon* (CBETA J); and poems found in *Supplement to the Chinese Buddhist Canon* (*Xuzang jing* 續藏經).

A Note on Names

Many, if not most, women in premodern China, if known at all, are known only by their family surname (*shi* 氏), for example, Liu *shi*, or the woman née Liu. Others were known by their personal name (*ming* 名), given to them by their parents and determined largely by family tradition. Educated women might, like their male counterparts, choose one or more literary or style names (*zi* 字) for themselves, which they could append to their writings and which would often be used by close friends when addressing them. Dharma or religious names were usually given by a senior monk at the time of a person's formal entry into religious life, whether as a monastic or layperson. The characters making up dharma names—characters such as *dao* 道 (the way or path), *zhi* 智 (awareness), *hui* 慧 (insight), *kong* 空 (emptiness), wu 悟 (awakening), etc.—usually reflect basic Buddhist ideals or doctrines. In most cases they were selected according to a set pattern and were not necessarily tailored to the individual. In the case of the dharma names of Chan monks and nuns, the characters in their names sometimes indicated the particular lineage to which they belonged, as well as their generational standing. For example, the names of all of the immediate female disciples of the female Chan master Qiyuan Xinggang contain a character pronounced *yi*. Thus we have Yigong 義公 (Righteous and Just) and Yiquan 義全 (Righteous and Complete). A third disciple, whose name appears in the texts as Yikui 一揆 (Single or Unified Principle), may have originally been called Yikui 義揆 (Righteous Principle). While some nuns have only one dharma name, others may have more than one. In addition, more eminent Chan masters were also often referred to by the names of the temple with which they were primarily associated. Qiyuan Xinggang, for example, is sometimes also referred to in texts as Fushi Qiyuan 伏獅 祇 (qi). 園, or Qiyuan from Fushi (Crouching Lion) Convent. One important thing to note about dharma names is that they are for the most part non-gender-specific. Thus, unless a name is followed by the character for nun (*ni* 尼) or other contextual material is provided to indicate gender, there is no way of knowing whether the name refers to a monk or a nun. Although the dearth of biographical information makes it difficult to know for certain, it would appear that some of the nun-poets in this anthology may have adopted the monastic way of life without being formally ordained. In these cases, it may be that they simply chose their own dharma names, just as they would choose their own style names. An example is the nun known as

Deri 德日 (Virtuous Sun), whose sister, when she also became a nun, chose the name of Deyue 德月 (Virtuous Moon). Moreover, a committed practitioner (a non-monastic firmly committed to Buddhist practice, including a layperson) might also be referred to as a person of the way (*daoren* 道人) or a person of Chan (*chanren* 禪人).

A Note on the Translations

In translating the poems in this anthology, my goal has been that of most translators: to strike as elegant a balance as possible between fidelity to the original and readability. I have made no effort to reproduce such elements as rhyme and tonality, as central as they are in the original. I have, however, endeavored to retain at least a suggestion of the original rhythm of the lines. Many of the poems in this anthology, for example, are in the form of regulated verse, which requires eight lines of either five or seven syllables each. In such cases, while I have not tried to duplicate the number of syllables per line, I have attempted to keep each line the same approximate length. In the case of pentasyllabic verses, each line of the original is represented by a line in the English translation; in the case of heptasyllabic verse, I have generally divided the original Chinese line into two English lines, the first corresponding approximately to the first four Chinese words or syllables, and the second to the last three Chinese words or syllables. I have also made efforts to preserve some sense of the technical characteristics of the original, such as alliteration and parallelism, although only when this does not interfere with the overall readability of the poem.

While I have endeavored to select poems for this anthology that are not overly laden with technical Buddhist terminology, there are times when an understanding of the meaning or significance of certain Buddhist terms is essential to a full appreciation of a poem. Many of these terms, such as "Emptiness" or "The Unborn," recur often and may be familiar to some readers. For other terms or allusions, I direct the reader to footnotes, which I have tried to keep as simple and straightforward as possible. I have made a conscious effort not to rewrite or "re-create" an English version of a poem that might sound better to a non-Chinese-language speaker, as tempting as that might be. For example, Buddhist nuns within the same monastic family would refer to each other used male kinship terms such as "elder dharma brother" (*faxiong* 法兄) or "younger dharma brother" (*fadi* 法弟). While modern sensibilities might prefer terms such as "dharma sister," this would ignore the fact that, theoretically at least, most traditional Buddhist nuns saw themselves, if not having transcended gender altogether, at the very least no longer exclusively identifying with the female sex.

Many of these poems make use of Buddhist, and especially Chan, imagery and terminology that can sometimes seem a bit obscure. While footnotes may help in these cases, many times the ambiguity or paradox is part and parcel of the original poem and cannot always be explained away. Similarly, because one of the primary goals of this anthology is to demonstrate the great variety of nuns' poems, many of which have never been translated into English or any other language, I have selected many different types of poems, including ones that may not necessarily fit readers' notions of what a Buddhist poem should look like.

Finally, I should note that for most of these poems by nuns, unlike poems by their more famous male counterparts, there are virtually no Chinese annotations providing reliable information about the meaning of words or the sources of allusions. Whenever necessary, I have indicated that my translation is tentative. This lack of secondary sources leaves open the very real possibility of mistakes or misinterpretations, despite my most conscientious efforts and best intentions. I hope, however, that this will not detract from the value of making these poems accessible to an audience that their authors could not have imagined ever reading them at all.

The Poems

悟蓮

雨晴

海棠初種竹新移
流水潺潺入小池
春雨乍晴風日好
一聲啼鳥過花枝

1   See Wang Duanshu 1667, 1:13b.

Wulian

Wulian was the religious name of Xia Yunying 夏雲英 (1395–1318), who hailed from Juzhou 莒州 (present-day Rizhao 日照) in Shandong province. She is said to have been a precocious child who learned to read at the age of four, and by the age of six could recite Buddhist sutras from memory. Apart from being quite beautiful, she was also musically talented and known for her fine needlework. She was inducted into the Inner Palace at the age of twelve, where she served first as a palace lady before becoming a consort of the distinguished playwright Zhu Youdun 朱有燉 (1379–1439), a grandson of the Hongwu emperor. She suffered from ill health, however, and at the age of twenty-one, she requested permission to take the tonsure and become a nun. She died just two years later. Despite her youth, she left four collections of writings, the most important of which was a collection of nearly seventy poems titled *Poems of the Placid and Pure Studio* (*Duanqing ge shi* 端清閣詩), and several dozen gāthās and encomia on the Lotus Sutra, Apart from of handful of poems, however, no other works of hers remain extant today.[1]

After the Rain

The crab apple has just been planted,
    the bamboo has just been newly moved,
And the running water babbles
    as it flows into the pond.
Then the spring rain suddenly clears,
    and the weather turns fine:
A bird chirping
    through the flowering branches.

秋夜即事

西風颯颯動羅幃
初夜焚香下玉墀
禮罷真如庭院靜
銀缸高照看圍棋

An Autumn Night: Written in the Moment

The west wind soughs and sighs,
 stirring the gauze screen,
As evening falls, I light the incense
 and descend the palace stairs.
After I bow to the Buddha.
 the courtyard is still.
The silver candlestick is held high
 to allow us to watch a game of *go*.

介石

朝來

朝來剩得好春陰
芍藥屏花歲歲心
解作流連是啼鳥
一行茅屋綠陰深

清明

桃花雨過菜花香
隔岸垂楊綠粉牆
斜日小樓新燕子
清明風景好思量

---

2   See the biographical note in Wanyan Yun Zhu 1831, 1836, *fulu* 9a. Jieshi's poetry collection, titled *Remnant Drafts from the Spring River Boat* (*Chunshuifang cangao* 春水舫殘稿, is no longer extant.

3   My translation here is tentative.

4   There would appear to be a contrast here between the peonies, which wither away quickly after blooming, and the birds who manage to stay past the springtime.

Jieshi

Jieshi was from Shangyuan 上元, Jiangsu province. Her secular name was
You Ying 尤瑛, and her style name Zhongyu 鍾玉. Before becoming a nun,
she was a courtesan known for her musical talent, as well as her ability to
write beautiful letters. She left one collection of poetry.[2]

Early Morning

Morning leaves in its wake
    a fine spring coolness.
Peonies bloom, like flowers on a screen,
    and each year the same desire;[3]
The ones that stay on
    are the twittering birds,[4]
And a row of thatched cottages
    deep in green shade.

Qingming[5]

Peach blossoms after the rain,
    the fragrance of rapeseed flowers,
Weeping willows on the other bank
    turning white-washed walls green,
A setting sun over the small tower,
    and swallows just out of the nest—
The scenery on this Qingming day
    is something to remember!

5   The Qingming festival, sometimes translated as Tomb-Sweeping Day, is celebrated on
    the 15th day after the Spring equinox, which falls in early April. On this day, it was tra-
    ditional for families to visit the tombs of their ancestors, sweep the tombs, and make
    ritual offerings. It is a time of family celebration, however, rather than one of mourning,
    especially since it coincides with the beginning of Spring and new life.

妙霓

春夜

新篁風韻夜窗幽
好夢驚回惹舊愁
一瞬春光歸去也
子規啼月下西樓

Miaoni

Miaoni was from Wujiang 吳江 (Suzhou), Jiangsu province. Little is known about her, apart from her family name of Jiang 江 and the fact that she apparently entered the convent when she was just a young girl.[6]

Spring Night

The graceful charm of new bamboo
    and the seclusion of a night window.
When startled awake from a good dream,
    an old sorrow begins to stir.
In an instant, the spring radiance
    has left and gone away.
The cuckoo calls in the moonlight
    as I descend the western tower.[7]

---

7   This line is borrowed from a famous lyric by Li Yu 李煜 (937–978), the last emperor of the Southern Tang, who was captured by the invading Song in 976 and two years later died in exile in the northern Song capital of Kaifeng. His poems are often interpreted as laments over his lost kingdom and his homesickness for the south. Since we do not know exactly when Miaoni lived, it is not clear whether she is alluding to the fall of the Ming, or whether her sorrow is due to a more personal loss. The call of the cuckoo is thought to sound like *burugui* 不如歸, or "better to go home."

尼燕女

偈

業緣休認是姻緣
一念真空已了然
迷時與你為媳婦
今日身居天外天

8   See Wang Duanshu 1667, 26:10a.
9   That is, a single moment of fully understanding the nature of ultimate reality.

The Girl Nun from Yan

This otherwise nameless young woman from Yan (another name for Bei-jing) was said to have come from a poor and most likely lower-class fam-ily. As a girl, she was very lively and intelligent. She would accompany her pious aunt in her Buddhist devotions, her memory so good that she remembered the words of all of the religious texts she heard recited. She continued with her Buddhist practices even after the death of her aunt, and even went so far as to vow that she would never marry. She apparently was also an attractive young woman, and her mother pressured her to accept an offer of marriage from a local rich man who wanted her as a wife for his son. Her mother worried about his paying off the bride price, but the girl predicted that not only would it be provided, it would turn out to be unneeded. It was at this point that she is said to have composed the gāthā below. It was delivered along with the repayment of the bride price, which was subsequently stolen by thieves. Many in the area came to regard the girl as a "living Buddha" with powers of prediction and came to worship her and offer incense. Her acuity also led to accusations of witchcraft, which landed her in prison. She was then ordered to marry, but passed away before the wedding could take place.[8]

Gāthā

I don't believe that our karmic conditions
   point to a predestined marriage.
With a single thought of True Emptiness,[9]
   my realization is complete.
In a moment of delusion I was promised to you
   as a daughter-in-law.
But on this day, my body resides
   in a heaven beyond the heavens.[10]

---

10 In Buddhist cosmology, there are many heavens; the higher the heaven, the more spirit-
    ually purified the beings who dwell there.

性空

自感

斷俗入禪林
身清心不清
夜來風雨過
疑是叩門人

Xingkong

Xingkong was from a wealthy family and became a nun at the well-known Mingyin 明因 Convent in Hangzhou. She appears to have started out with the best of intentions, but her beauty attracted numerous male suitors, and before long her reputation was lost. In her anthology of women writers, Wang Duanshu includes Xingkong in the section on nuns serving as a negative example.[11]

Reflecting on Myself

I've left the world and entered the convent.
My body is pure, but my heart is not.
During the night the gusts of wind and rain
Sound like someone knocking at the door!

摩淨

經虎丘

鹿走蘇臺春寂寂
江花江草傷心碧
行人不見古今愁
指點青山王珣宅

---

12   Xu Shichang 1990, 9178. Mojing's collection of works was titled *Drafts of Poetry of Tongli* (*Tongli shicao* 桐里詩草).

13   Su Terrace refers specifically to a magnificent terrace said to have once stood in this area, which in the sixth century BCE were the palace grounds of the king of the southern state of Wu. He built it for the beautiful Xi Shi, and his infatuation with her led to his eventual downfall. This terrace is often used as a symbol for the inevitable fall of the rich and powerful. Here it refers to Suzhou in general.

Mojing

Mojing, whose family name was Ren 任, was from the town of Zhenze 震澤, today part of Suzhou, Jiangsu province. She was known for her poetic abilities, but she apparently destroyed all her poetry after becoming a nun, and so only one poem survives.[12]

Going by Way of Tiger Hill

The deer run along the Su Terrace,[13]
   which in springtime is lonely and still.
The flowers and grasses by the river
   are all a heartbreaking green.
The travelers don't seem to notice
   this perennial melancholy,
Pointing out instead the green hill
   where Wang Xun had his villa.[14]

14 Tiger Hill is a famous scenic site in Suzhou. The celebrated calligrapher Wang Xun 王珣 (349–400) and his younger brother Wang Min 王珉 (351–388) donated the villas they built there, which became the basis for its main Buddhist temple. Most of the temple was destroyed during the Second Sino-Japanese War, but the ruins that remain, including the Yunyan Pagoda (Yunyan sita 雲岩寺塔), are still popular scenic sites.

覺清

庵壁詩

急忙簡點破袈裟
收拾行囊沒一些
袖拂白雲歸洞口
肩挑明月遠天涯
可憐松頂新巢鶴
卻負籬根舊種花
再四叮嚀貓與犬
休教流落俗人家

15 See Wang Duanshu 1667, 26.8a.

Jueqing

Jueqing appears to have been a nun from a small convent in Nanjing who was forced to flee during the anti-Buddhist campaigns of the Jiajing era (1522–1566). Buddhist nuns were especially targeted during these persecutions, perhaps because they most clearly exemplified how Buddhism could work to undermine traditional Confucian notions of proper female behavior. In 1527 nearly six hundred nunneries in Beijing were destroyed, and a decade later, under the direction of Board of Rites Secretary Huo Tao 霍韜 (1487–1540), approximately 140 nunneries in the Nanjing area were destroyed, and about five hundred nuns were forced to return to lay life.[15]

Poem Inscribed on a Convent Wall[16]

In haste we gather up
    our tattered monastic robes.
We pack up our traveling bags,
    though there is not much to take.
Sleeves brushing white clouds,
    we seek refuge in caves;
Bright moon on our shoulders,
    we travel to faraway places.
I will miss the new cranes' nests
    on top of the pine trees,
And am sorry to leave the flowers
    planted along the fence.
Over and over again I admonish
    my cat and my dog:
"Don't go hanging about
    other people's homes!"

---

16 While it was not uncommon for poets to inscribe poems on the walls of temples or ruins, often they were verses about the beauty of nature or thoughts inspired by a day's excursion in the mountains. During the last years of the Ming dynasty, when people were often forced to flee invaders, poems written on walls by women in desperate straits became more common.

無為

偈

六十四年活計
今朝撒手歸西
得箇菩提三昧
依然明月清風

Wuwei

Wuwei, whose family name was Lai 來, was from Xiaoshan, Zhejiang province. When very young, she vowed to remain unmarried, kept to a vegetarian diet, and engaged in the practice of reciting the name of the Amitabha Buddha (*nianfo* 念佛). At the age of twenty, she shaved her head and built herself a rustic hut, where she engaged in Pure Land devotional practices. A few years later, she set out to visit various masters to deepen her religious understanding. Along the way, she cared for the hungry and destitute. This brought her to the attention of the court, which bestowed upon her the title of Chan Master Weixin 為心禪師. She then returned to her old residence, where she lived to the end of her days. Numerous relics were said to have been found among her cremated remains, a traditional sign of advanced spiritual attainment.[17]

Deathbed Gāthā

After sixty-four years of working with my hands,
This morning, I'm letting go and returning West.[18]
My mind perfectly still, my liberation won,
The bright moon and clear breeze are as before.

18   That is, to the Western Pure Land.

濟印

上堂偈

松林月冷霜威遠
梅嶺香生春意回
意氣不從天地得
英雄豈藉四時推

---

19 See Wang Duanshu 1667, 26:4b. A few of Jiyin's dharma talks, but no poems, can be found in Chaoyong 1697, 479b9–20. The collection of her recorded sayings was titled *Recorded Sayings of the Nun Chan Master Renfeng from Lingzhi on Yufeng* (*Yufeng Lingshi ni Renfeng chanshi yulu* 玉峰靈崎尼仁風禪師語錄).

Jiyin

Jiyin's secular name was Gu Renfeng 顧仁風, and she was from a well-known scholar-official family from Kunshan 昆山 (in present-day Suzhou), in Jiangsu province. She is said to have had a distaste for worldly life even as a young girl and was permitted to enter the religious life of her own volition. She eventually received dharma transmission from Linji Master Jiqi Hongchu 繼起弘儲 (1605–1672) and served as abbess of Lingzhi 靈崎 Convent on Mount Yufeng 玉峰 in Kunshan. Her official recorded sayings has not been preserved.[19]

Dharma Hall Gāthā

Above the pine trees, the moon is cold,
    and the heavy frost recedes.
From Plum Mountain, a fragrance rises
    as spring begins to stir again.
Inner spirit isn't acquired
    from Heaven and Earth,[20]
So how can the actions of heroes
    be swayed by the seasons![21]

---

20 In other words, each person is responsible for their own inner development.

21 This is a couplet found in many Chan texts. The meaning appears to be that if one aspires to be a hero, or an authentic realized person, one must be the master of oneself and not be subject to externalities.

德隱

新秋晚眺

山中多晚涼
清風屬秋節
遙瞻四五峯
壁立皆奇絕
修竹傍林開
喬松倚巖列
黃菊散芳叢
清泉凝白雪
對此懷素心
千里共明月
願保幽貞姿
歲寒雙皎潔

22 Wanyan Yun Zhu, 1831, 1836, *fulu* 16a. Deying's collection of poetry was titled *Drafts of Living with the Clouds* (*Lüyunju gao* 侶雲居稿).

23 My translation of this couplet is tentative. The poet may be saying that the bamboo are slender enough or have lost enough leaves to allow one to see the pine trees that were hidden before.

Deyin

Deyin, whose secular name was Zhao Shao 趙昭 (style name Zihui 子惠), was born in Changzhou, Jiangsu province. Her father was the artist and calligrapher Zhao Huanguang 趙宧光 (1559–1625), her grandmother was the well-known poet Lu Qingzi 陸卿子, and her mother, Wen Chu 文俶 (style name Duanrong 端容, 1595–1634), was a famous painter. Not surprisingly, Deyin herself also gained an early reputation for both her painting and her poetry. She married Ma Zhongzi 馬仲子 from Pinghu 平湖, but was left a destitute widow when both her husband and father-in-law perished in the turmoil of the Ming-Qing transition. After her husband's death, she built herself a hermitage in the Western Hills of Dongting Lake, where she lived as a nun for over twenty years.[22]

Early Autumn: A Distant Evening View

The mountains are filled with an evening chill,
And the clear wind bites, as it does in autumn.
I gaze afar at the four or five mountain peaks
That rise precipitously in unsurpassable splendor.
The woods are opened by slender bamboo at their border,
And rows of tall pines lean against the cliffs.[23]
Scattered clumps of fragrant yellow chrysanthemums,
And a clear spring turning to ice under the white snow—
Facing these, I hold on to pure intention,
As over a thousand *li* we share a radiant moon.
I vow to preserve this pure secluded form,
Both of us brilliantly pure in deepest winter.[24]

---

24 Here the poet appears to be comparing herself to the moon, a symbol of the universal Buddha nature, everywhere the same. The pine and the bamboo remain green even during the coldest time of the year, thus symbolizing the adversity that allows her to demonstrate her moral mettle.

種竹歌

南山南
北山北
其中有竹人不識
託根數莖臨嚴霜
虛心願并幽溪柏
秋深草木零落盡
此竹亭亭終不易

皆令黃夫人過寓山閨即事

吟得新詩子夜殘
銀釭點點照花欄
須臾小婢來相報
深竹烏啼月滿灘

25 There is an allusion here to the Eastern Han scholar and recluse Fa Zhen 法真 (100–188), who, when asked to come out of seclusion and take up a government post, responded that he would rather "go farther north than the northern mountain and farther south than the southern mountain."

Song of Planting Bamboo

South of Southern Mountain,
    North of Northern Mountain,[25]
There grows a bamboo
    that nobody knows.
When its trunk and branches
    face the heavy frost,
It aspires empty-hearted to accompany
    the secluded streamside cypress.[26]
In deep autumn, when other trees
    are completely bare,
This bamboo stands gracefully tall
    and is always the same.

Lady Huang Jieling[27] *Came to Stay at My Mountain Boudoir, Written in the Moment*

We composed new verses
    into the midnight hours,
With flickers of light from the lamp
    shining on the painted railing.
Suddenly the little maid
    came in to let us know
That there was birdsong in the deep bamboo
    and moonlight on the strand.

26 The word *xuxin* 虛心 literally means "empty- or open-minded," and is an indirect allusion
    to the hollowness of the bamboo, as well as to the Buddhist notion of "no-mind." The
    cypress, whose leaves remain green, is often used as a symbol for those who maintain
    their integrity in the face of hardship.
27 The woman painter and calligrapher, Huang Yuanjie (see n. 35).

德容

惜籠中鳥自喻

　　千里朝凰唱和遥
　　誰憐孤鷔禁樊牢
　　貞心甘守籠中日
　　再世齊鳴共九霄

28　See Wanyan Yun Zhu 1831, 1836, *fulu* 15b.

Derong

Derong, also known as Zhu Youzhen 朱又真, was from Jiashan 嘉善, Jiangsu province. Said to have been a good, filial daughter, at the age of 15 she was married to Zhang Wopu 張我樸. The marriage appears to have been a happy one. Zhang passed the highest presented-scholar exams in 1652, but in 1657 was implicated in a major scandal related to the Jiangnan provincial examinations. Found guilty of taking bribes as an examination official, he was beheaded, and his family sent into exile. After a memorial she submitted to the emperor requesting that she be allowed to commit suicide to expiate for her in-laws was denied, she became a nun. Youzhen was known for her poetic talents, and although only a handful of her poems remain, there are four titles of poetry collections associated with her name. Of particular note is an autobiographical poem of 130 four-syllable lines titled "Weeping" (*Qihuai* 泣懷). This long poem begins with a reference to the virtue of her parents and her own upbringing as a cherished daughter born to a family of ten brothers when her father was already middle-aged, then describes her marriage to Zhang and his rise to success, and finally tells of the tragedy of his execution and her decision to become a nun as a way of expiating for the shame brought upon her and her family.[28]

Pitying the Caged Bird Who Is Just Like Me

Across the vast expanse, the female phoenix
    sings in harmony from afar.
Who pities the lonely duck
    locked inside her cage prison?
True-hearted, she willingly endures
    her days inside the cage,
And in the next life, they'll sing together
    up in the highest heavens.

梅花

蝶夢三春淚落花
風飄餘粉謝鉛華
天生玉色菩提片
疏影幽窗獨自誇

The allusion here is to the famous story about the Daoist figure Zhuangzi, who dreams
that he is a butterfly, and, upon waking, wonders whether he is a man who dreamed of
being a butterfly or a butterfly now dreaming of being a man. Here the poet may be re-
ferring to the three years since the death of her husband, during which the line between
reality and illusion seemed blurred.

Plum Blossom

Three springs of a butterfly dream,[29]
  weeping over fallen flowers.
The leftover powder drifting in the wind
  is free of any rouge.[30]
It is by nature the color of jade—
  a piece of Supreme Wisdom.
Scattered shadows on the hidden window,
  it sings its own praises!

30 Although "powder" and "rouge" may conjure up images of a woman's toilette, here they
  describe the pure white plum petals scattered by the wind.

鏡明

口占示徒

庭中卓剎竿
懸旛更懸鐙
鐙明大千界
旛引最上乘
門外河之水
照面復照心
真面何虞皺
道心須要深

---

31 See Xu Shichang 1990, 9179.

32 The universe referred to here includes the billion worlds that together comprise the Buddha's domain. The Great Vehicle refers to the Mahayana school of Buddhism (see the Introduction, p. xviii).

Jingming

Jingming, whose family name was Chen 陳, was from Renhe 仁和 (present-day Hangzhou). She was said to have been a very sickly child, which is presumably why at the age of six, her parents entrusted her to the care of the nuns in Xiaoyi Convent 孝義菴 in Hangzhou, which was where Tang Taisu 湯太素, the second wife of the great Ming dynasty Buddhist Master Yunqi Zhuhong 雲棲袾宏 (1535–1615), had pursued her devotions after he left her to become a monk. Jingming grew up in the convent and was ordained at the age of nineteen. She eventually became the convent's abbess, and over time added several buildings to the nunnery, including a lecture hall, a meditation hall, and a stupa garden. The girl who had been so sickly as a child that no one thought she would survive did not die until the age of eighty-one.[31]

Improvised Dharma Instructions to My Disciples

In the center of the hall is a stately pole
From which hang lanterns and banners:
Lanterns that illumine the entire universe,
And banners that welcome the Great Vehicle.[32]
Outside the gates are the river's waters,
Which reflect face and mind.
The true face need not worry about wrinkles[33]
If the mind is intent on profound awakening.

33 The true face refers to the original nature of the mind, that is, one's inherent Buddha nature.

靜因

訪黃媛介不遇 / 訪黃皆令不遇

遙聞佳客至
雙槳度江風
道侶原相結
禪心孰與通
雲翻寒袖影
花落小池紅
不見孤舟返
愁予暮色中

34 See Wang Duanshu 1667, 26.11a.
35 Huang Yuanjie was famous for her poetry, as well as her calligraphy and painting, which she sold to support herself and her family. She also traveled, often without her husband, to meet with other gentry women poets, with whom she exchanged poems. This poem refers to one of these visits, likely to stay with Shang Jinglan.

Jingyin

Jingyin, also known as Master Gusu 谷虛, was from Nanjing and married into the well-known Shang 商 family from Shaoxing. Widowed at a young age, she became a nun. Wang Duanshu speaks very highly of her spiritual attainments and praises the quality of her few extant poems. Recent scholarship suggests that Jingyin in fact started out in life as a Nanjing courtesan known for her intelligence and poetic skills before becoming a concubine in the Shang family. After her husband's premature death, she became a nun, probably taking up residence in a small nunnery established by a sister of Qi Biaojia 祁彪佳, whose wife was the famous woman poet Shang Jinglan 商景蘭 (1604–ca. 1680). As a nun, she continued to mingle socially with many local gentry women poets and painters, including Shang Jinglan and Huang Yuanjie 黃媛介.[34]

Going to See Huang Yuanjie, but Not Finding Her In[35]

I hear from afar of the honored guest's arrival,
Crossing the river wind with her boat's double oars.
Companions of the Way have always been linked;
With whom else can I share the mind of Chan?[36]
The clouds move, casting my cold sleeves in the shade.
The flowers fall, turning the little pond crimson.
Her solitary boat returns without my seeing her,
Leaving me melancholy in the fading light of day.

36 That is, a pure mental state free of distractions and defilements.

獨目金鋼

偈

佛說金剛妙出羣
一言了悟絕聲聞
有人解得金經旨
四八何須逐段分

---

37 See Zhou Kefu, n.d., 553a13–b10.

38 In Mahayana Buddhism, a voice-hearer or *śrāvaka* refers to a Buddhist follower who, although diligent in basic practice, lacks the insight and compassion of those embarked on the (higher) Bodhisattva path.

Dumu Jin'gang

Dumu Jin'gang's story is found in *Anthology of Diamond Sutra Miracle Tales of Successive Generations* (*Lichao Jingangjing chixian ji* 歷朝金剛經持驗集), a collection of anecdotes or "miracle tales" attesting to the religious efficacy of the Diamond Sutra, compiled by the Qing dynasty Buddhist layman Zhou Kefu 周克復. According to this account, she lived in Shuijing Convent, located outside the city of Guidefu, Henan province. She is said to have been a woman of honest and straightforward character who lived simply and would often give away any donations that she received to other monks and nuns. She was best known for her complete devotion to the Diamond Sutra, which she read and recited so often that she ended up losing sight in one eye, giving her the name Dumu Jin'gang, which means "One-Eyed Diamond Sutra." She was also known for her sermons, which attracted both laypeople and monastics. She died at over seventy years old, having predicted the day of her death, which was accompanied by the most auspicious of signs.[37]

Gāthā

The Buddha's Diamond Sutra
    is sublime and peerless:
Those who grasp even a single phrase
    cannot be mere voice-hearers.[38]
Once a person attains an understanding
    of the Diamond Sutra's essence,
What need is there to go through
    its thirty-two separate sections?[39]

---

39 The Diamond Sutra is traditionally divided into thirty-two (four times eight) major sections. According to Zhou Kefu, this verse was composed after an exchange with a member of the local gentry who asked about this traditional division. Dumu Jin'gang replied to his question by first quoting the famous line by Confucius regarding his teachings: "My Way has a single thread running through it." Similarly, there was a single principle running through the Buddhist text, and thus the question of the number of sections was irrelevant.

偈

男女何須辯假真
觀音出現果何人
皮囊脫盡渾無用
試問男身是女身

偈

荼毗一去永歸空
著處尋空便不空
我去我來仍是我
電光泡影一般同

---

40 Guanyin, commonly known as the Bodhisattva of Compassion, can assume thirty-
three different forms, both male and female, to skillfully respond to the different needs
of suffering beings.

Gāthā

Male or female—what need
    to argue over which is fake or real
When Guanyin manifests
    what kind of person there will be?[40]
Peeling away that sack of skin
    would also be of no use.
I ask you, is it the body of a man
    or is it that of a woman?[41]

Deathbed Gāthā

Once the body has been cremated,
    it returns forever to Emptiness.
But if you search for this Emptiness,
    it will no longer be empty.
Whether "I" come or "I" go,
    it is still the same "I."
Lightning, bubbles, and shadows—
    the "I" is just like all of that![42]

41 One day someone asked Dumu Jin'gang why, since she had such a profound understand-
    ing of the Buddha's teaching, she did not manifest in a male body. "When it comes to
    one's physical form, there is male and female. However, when it comes to one's essential
    nature, there is no this or that. Do not view things in terms of differences and degrees."
    She then composed the gāthā translated here. Note also that Guanyin, while primarily
    venerated in her female manifestation, can manifest in many shapes and forms.
42 The allusion here is to a well-known Diamond Sutra verse that compares all phenomena
    to dreams, illusions, bubbles, shadows, dew, and lightning.

象菴隱慧

食筍偈

久隱深山保聖胎
一聲電動出頭來
層層剝盡蒸來喫
不負親嘗者一回

德山托鉢

當頭一問豈尋常
撥轉鋒芒暗裏藏
父子各人彈別調
聲聲猿叫斷人腸

43 See Chaoyong 1697, 619a8–13.

44 The sacred womb that both contains and nourishes the developing bodhisattva, or more generally, the embryonic beginnings of Buddhahood.

45 This poem can perhaps be read as an analogy for the process of spiritual cultivation, especially in retreat. The layers of "self" are peeled away until one finally gets to taste the Buddha nature within.

46 This verse is a commentary on case 13 of the collection of koans titled *The Gateless Gate* (*Wumen Guan* 無門關). The story involves a comment made by Yantou Quanhuo 巖頭全豁 (828–887) to the effect that his teacher Deshan Xuanjian 德山宣鑒 (782–865), while

Xiang'an Yinhui

Xiang'an Yinhui, whose secular family name was Zhuang 莊, hailed from Hangzhou, Zhejiang province. She is said to have had her initial awakening experience while reading a passage from the recorded sayings of Linji Chan Master Hanyue Fazang 漢月法藏 (1573–1635), after which she composed the verse translated below. She then went to study with Hanyue Fazang's second-generation student Huotang Zhengyan 豁堂正嵒 (1597–1670) and eventually became his sole female dharma successor. She was associated with Jun Convent in Hangzhou.[43]

Gāthā: Eating Bamboo Shoots

Hidden away in the deep mountains,
    the bamboo watched over its sagely embryo[44]
Until, stirred by a flash of lightning,
    it finally stuck out its head.
I will peel away layer after layer,
    boil it, and then eat it.
I will not miss this opportunity
    to taste it once for myself![45]

Deshan Carries His Bowl

How can Yantou have asked
    just an ordinary question?[46]
He was unfolding the cutting edge
    of a deeply hidden treasure.
The father and the son each play
    a different tune,
As cry after cry, the gibbon's calls
    breaks people's hearts.[47]

seemingly quite advanced in his practice, did not understand the "last word." When he heard this, Deshan sought out Yantou, who confirmed that he had indeed criticized him in this way. Deshan said nothing, but the next day when he went up to preach, he did so differently from before. Yantou was delighted and laughingly confirmed that Deshan had now come to understand the last word. This story is a good example of the teacher learning from the student.

47 In Chinese literature, the gibbon's call is thought to sound like the cries of a grieving person.

妙慧

過馬十娘墓

南國容華謝
西陵松柏蕃
妍媸終有盡
修短復何言
舞態翔歸鶴
歌聲哽夜猿
傷情同伴女
時一吊高原

花月人千古
乾坤土一杯
霜疑鉛粉剩
苔認翠鈿留
孤塚埋幽恨
寒烟愴暮愁
相看憐病骨
清淚灑松楸

48 See Wang Duanshu 1667, 24:19b (where she appears under the name of Ma Ruyu) and
    Wanyan Yun Zhu 1831, 1836, *fulu* 19b (where she appears under the name of Miaohui).

49 That is, the once-beautiful face of the deceased, who came from the southern part of the
    country.

50 Pine and cypress trees were often planted on tomb sites.

Miaohui

Miaohui was the religious name of the famous courtesan Ma Ruyu 馬如玉 (style name Chuyu 楚嶼) from Nanjing. She was known not only for her beauty, but also for her deep immersion in the Chinese poetic tradition and her own considerable writing skills. A devout Buddhist, she ended up taking ordination from Chan Master Cangxia 蒼霞 of Qixia Monastery in Nanjing. Soon thereafter, Ma Huifang 馬蕙芳 (the Tenth Daughter Ma in the poem below), who ran the courtesan establishment in Nanjing where Miaohui worked, also took the tonsure with Chan Master Cangxia and died not long afterward. After going on pilgrimage to the sacred Buddhist site of Mount Jiuhua, Miaohui planned to take up residence in a thatched hermitage on the banks of Mochou Lake just outside of Nanjing when she fell ill and died at the age of thirty-seven.[48]

Passing by the Tomb of Tenth Daughter Ma

On the southern face, the flowers have withered;[49]
On the western tombs, the pines and cypresses thrive.[50]
The beautiful and the homely both come to an end,
Willowy or squat, who will ever speak of them again?
The circling, whirling dance of the homing cranes,
The choked-up wailing of the night-time gibbons.[51]
My heart breaks for this woman, who was my friend,
As over and over my lament reaches the high plains.

Flowers and moon: she rests in eternity;
Heaven and earth: now a handful of dirt.
Frost like bits of scattered silver,
Moss like stray beads of kingfisher feathers.
A lonely tomb and a hidden resentment,
A cold mist and a twilight melancholy.
Casting looks of pity at my wasted frame,
I shed tears over the catalpas and pines.[52]

---

51 Cranes traditionally symbolize immortality; the cry of the night gibbon often symbolizes deep, if sometimes inarticulate, grief.
52 Catalpa trees were also often planted on tomb sites.

飲雨花臺賦得落葉

登眺台千尺
論心酒一尊
青霜侵樹抄
丹葉舞江村
逐浪同浮梗
隨風欲斷魂
榮枯何足嘆
此日幸歸根

---

53 The Chinese idiom "Falling leaves settle on the roots" (*yeluo guigen* 葉落歸根) is used
primarily to refer to a person who returns to his ancestral home after having been away
for an extended period. In Buddhism, however, returning to one's roots refers to a return
to one's original nature, that is, one's Buddha nature.

When Drinking on Flower-Raining Terrace, I Was Assigned
"Falling Leaves" as the Topic for a Poem

I climb up to gaze from the thousand-foot platform,
A jug of wine serving as confidante.
Clear frost invades the treetops
And red leaves dance in the river hamlets,
Floating on the waves like driftwood
And tossed by winds, they crush the spirit.
Why sigh over flourishing and decay?
Fortunately, I've now returned to the root.[53]

道元

禪坐書懷

碧雲靜鎖梵王宮
猶似明霞拱禁中
玉樹舊枝歸淨業
內家新調擅宗風
三千里外腸堪折
十二年前淚暗紅
欲悟無生何處是
禪燈移照鏡臺空

---

54 See Wang Duanshu 1667, 26.9b.
55 A Brahma Palace (*Fanwang gong* 梵王宮) is another term for a Buddhist monastery.
56 The emperor's private quarters, forbidden to outsiders.
57 "Lineage airs" is a reference to the practice associated with a particular Chan Buddhist lineage. Here the contrast appears to be between the secular melodies that Daoyuan had been used to in the inner palace, and those of her new life in the convent, where the sounds were more likely to be those of sutra recitation or chanting.
58 That is, the fall of the Ming court in the northern city of Beijing.

Daoyuan

Daoyuan's family name was Wang 王, and she came from Chenliu (pres-
ent-day Kaifeng), Henan province. She was, it seems, inducted into the
Inner Palace during the last years of the Ming dynasty and fled south with
the court when Beijing fell to the Manchus in 1644. Not long afterward,
she entered Mingyin Convent in Hangzhou.[54]

Seated Meditation: Reflections

The high floating clouds quietly lock in
    the Brahma Palace,[55]
Just as a glistening haze once encircled
    the Forbidden Palace.[56]
I am an old branch from a jade tree,
    aspiring to unworldly purity.
The new melodies of the Inner Palace
    are replaced by lineage airs.[57]
Three thousand *li* away from home
    is enough to break one's heart.[58]
What happened twelve years ago
    brought tears of darkest red.[59]
I wish to awaken to the Unborn,
    wherever it is to be found.
In the flickering of the temple lamps,
    the mirror stand is empty.[60]

---

59 Her grief was so intense that she wept tears of blood.
60 This may be an allusion to the famous story recounted in the *Platform Sutra* of an ex-
    change of verses between Shenxiu 神秀 (606?–706) and Huineng 惠能 (638–713), who
    would eventually become as the Sixth Patriarch of Chan Buddhism. In his poem, Shen-
    xiu compares the mind to the stand upon which is placed of a bright mirror (which at
    this time was usually made of bronze and had to be constantly polished so that it did
    not collect dust). There are several versions of the poem that Huineng is said to have
    composed in response, but the gist of his argument was that both mirror and stand are
    inherently clean (or in one version, nonexistent or empty) and thus there is nowhere for
    dust to accumulate. This reflects the Chan notion that awakening is to be acquired not
    by polishing away afflictions, but rather by realizing one's innate purity, the "Unborn."

僧鑒

初夏

落盡紅芳入夏初
槐陰繞屋竹扶疏
清風一室閒鐘磬
疏雨幽窗自看書

---

61 This biography is based on the account found one of the earliest available references to Sengjian, in Wu Dingzhang 1745, 85:32. Her poetry collection was titled *Sengjian's Poetry Drafts* (*Sengjian shichao* 僧鑒詩鈔).

Sengjian

We know very little about Sengjian, apart from the fact that she was associated with Hanshan Convent in Wuxian (present-day Suzhou) and that she left a collection of poetry, apparently no longer extant.[61]

Early Summer

The red blossoms have all fallen
    as we move into summer.
Shading my hut are locust trees
    and clumps of lush bamboo.
The room is filled with fresh breezes
    and sporadic sounds of bells.
A light rain falling on the window
    lends itself to quiet study.

秋海棠

紅甲垂垂白露姿
薜蘿牆下最堪宜
不教鸚鵡呼肥婢
肯與蓮花作侍兒
幾處閉門秋雨後
何人立月晚香時
愁腸欲斷非關汝
續命無煩葉底絲

62 This image here may possibly be that of the red scales of fish shimmering like dew in the water.

63 This may be a reference to Yang Guifei 楊貴妃 (719–756), the favorite consort of the Tang dynasty emperor Xuanzong 玄宗 (685–762) known for her voluptuous beauty. She was later blamed for the disastrous An Lushan rebellion and strangled by the emperor's soldiers as he fled the capital seeking safety in the south. The plump maidservant might also be the tree personified, or perhaps a reference to the poet's earlier life as a palace lady. Court ladies often kept parrots as pets.

The Autumn Flowering Crab Apple Tree

Its blossoms dangling like red scales
    and glistening with white dew,[62]
It is perfectly suited to where it grows
    at the foot of the mossy wall.
It has no need of a parrot to call out
    for that plump maidservant,[63]
But would rather be with the lotus
    and serve as an attendant.[64]
Behind the closed gates
    after the rain has stopped,
Who is there under the moon
    in this season of late fragrance?[65]
A grieving heart about to break
    has nothing to do with you.
May your life not be disturbed
    by the threads below the leaves.[66]

64 Here there may possibly be an allusion to the fictional nun known as Red Lotus, who plays an important role in several Ming dynasty stories and plays. The idea seems to be that the tree prefers to be the hermit-poet's attendant rather than a palace lady.
65 The reference here is possibly to the poet herself.
66 The silken threads (*si* 絲) dangling from the crab apple tree may perhaps refer to the lingering thoughts (*si* 思) of the past that threaten to continue to haunt the poet.

神一

67 See Wanyan Yun Zhu 1831, 1836, *fulu* 9b. There is also a more detailed account in Wang
Chang 1802, 44:36b–37b.

Shenyi

Shenyi (d. 1662), whose secular name was Xia Shuji 夏淑吉 and style name was Longyin 龍隱, was born in Huating (present-day Shanghai), Jiangsu province. Her father, Xia Yunyi 夏允彝 (1596–1645), was a well-known poet-official, and Shenyi became known early on for her talents in poetry and calligraphy. Shenyi's husband, Hou Xuanxun 侯玄洵, died from an illness when Shenyi was only twenty-one and their son just a toddler. Nearly a decade later, her father and beloved younger brother, both fervent Ming loyalists, perished in the resistance against the Manchus. A few years after that, her only son also fell ill and died. Having lost everything, Shenyi fled southeast to the village of Caoxi, located in the mountainous region of Jiangxi province, where she took up residence in a small rustic hermitage and adopted the style name Longyin. At some point she decided to become a nun and took the dharma name of Shenyi. Eventually she would be joined by other bereaved women, two of whom also became nun-poets (Zaisheng 再生 and Jingwei 靜維) and took Shenyi as their religious mentor. There are no less than four collections of writings attributed to Shenyi.[67]

夢游天台

　　石梁飛度接花茵
　　殿閣經行覩勝因
　　香氣入衣初不觸
　　鐘聲到耳迥無塵
　　木童石女賓中主
　　翠竹黃花覺後身
　　憶舊臨風三歎息
　　碧潭明月影磷磷

重過橫雲山懷靜維

　　翠竹丹崖倚碧流
　　輕橈重撥意悠悠
　　山靈未許同招隱
　　畫棟飛雲鎖上頭

68　The Stone Bridge, which spans a waterfall, is still one of the most famous scenic sites of
　　the Tiantai Mountains in Zhejiang province. Legend has it that this natural rock bridge,
　　which is very narrow at its far end and perilous to cross, leads to a land of paradise. The
　　bridge features in a number of famous literary works, including the famous "Rhapsody
　　on Roaming on Tiantai," by Sun Chuo 孫綽 (ca. 310–397), which describes a Daoist
　　mystical journey.
69　The supreme cause 勝因 refers generally to whatever will lead to a good effect, in this
　　case, perhaps enlightenment.

A Dream Journey to Mount Tiantai

Across the Stone Bridge I flew
    onto a carpet of flowers;[68]
Wandering through the great halls,
    I witnessed the supreme cause.[69]
A fragrance suffused my clothes,
    and for once I felt cleansed;
I heard the sound of a bell
    and felt instantly purified.
Wooden lads and stone maidens,
    the host within the guest;[70]
Green bamboo and yellow flowers,
    I now see what they mean.[71]
Remembering, I lean into the wind
    and let out three long sighs.
The bright moon on the blue sea
    is like a shimmering jewel.

Again Crossing Mount Hengyun, Thinking of Jingwei[72]

Emerald bamboo and vermilion cliffs
    lean into the azure stream.
The oars slap lightly again and again
    as my thoughts drift far away.
The mountain spirits are not yet willing
    to let you join me in seclusion.
So you still find yourself locked inside
    the tall painted towers.

70 Wooden lads and stone maidens, metaphors for the paradox of form and emptiness, can be found in many Chan Buddhist writings. The various positions of host and guest (host as host, guest as guest, host within guest, and guest within host) are often used to illustrate the relationships between subject and object, noumenon and phenomenon.

71 There is possibly an allusion here to an argument made by the Tang dynasty Chan master Dazhu Huihai 大珠慧海 (fl. 788) that unless one is truly enlightened, one should not glibly equate bamboo with the Dharmakaya (the body of the Buddha or ultimate reality) and luxuriant clusters of yellow flowers with *prajñā* (realized wisdom). In other words, unless one truly understands the emptiness of both the Dharmakaya and *prajñā*, there is a danger of seeking out and clinging to external forms, such as green bamboo and yellow flowers, in the false conviction that to do so is equivalent to having achieved an ultimate understanding of reality.

72 Mount Hengyun is a mountain outside of present-day Shanghai.

再生

73 There are two collections of writings associated with Zaisheng: *Zaisheng's Posthumous Drafts* (*Zaisheng yigao* 再生遺稿) and *Zaisheng's Miscellanea* (*Zaisheng yushi* 再生餘事).

Zaisheng

Zaisheng, secular name Yao Weiyu 姚嫣俞 and style name Lingxiu 靈修, was from Changzhou (present-day Suzhou). She was a granddaughter of the well-known literatus-official Yao Ximeng 姚希孟 (1597–1636), who had served as minister of culture in the Ming court. Weiyu's husband, Hou Xuanyan 侯玄演 (1620–1645), committed suicide with his brother and father in 1645 rather than submit to the invading Manchu troops. After an unsuccessful attempt to commit suicide herself by swallowing needles and drinking mercury, she joined Shenyi (see p. 51), to whom she was related by marriage, in her hermitage in the Jiangxi countryside and eventually shaved her head and became a nun. There are two collections of writings associated with Zaisheng, although few of her poems remain. She appears to have been especially noted for her seven-syllable regulated verses.[73]

早春卽事

煙鎖虛窗展素緗
微風吹到落梅香
孤懷待月惟枯坐
餘恨添眉卻晚妝
舊事不堪重省憶
新詞漫自費平章
黃粱一夢從今覺
願息塵機禮法王

---

74 In her previous life, the poet would have readied herself for an evening spent with family or friends.

75 This is an allusion to a well-known Daoist story about a young scholar who stopped for the night at an inn on his way to the capital to sit for the imperial exams. While waiting for his evening meal of yellow millet to cook, he fell asleep and dreamed that he had passed the exams, established a family, and risen up in the ranks of officials to become prime minister. However, his success attracted the jealousy of others, and he was wrongly

Composed in Early Spring

A mist locks in the empty window;
    books bound in yellow silk.
A gentle breeze brings in its wake
    the scent of fallen plums.
Solitary in the light of the moon,
    I sit with nothing to do.
Leftover sorrows on my brows;
    my evening toilette abandoned.[74]
Things that happened in the past
    do not bear dwelling upon.
Fresh poems bubble up naturally;
    no need to judge them!
From now on, I have awakened
    from the Yellow Millet Dream.[75]
Vowing to end my worldly concerns,
    I bow to the Dharma King.[76]

accused of malfeasance and lost his post. His wife left him, his children died, and he became destitute and homeless. At this point, he woke up to find the yellow millet still cooking on the fire. Persuaded by his dream of the vanity of worldly success, the young scholar decided instead to cultivate the way of transcendence. For an English translation of one of the earliest versions of this story, see Neinhauser 2002.2010.

76 The Buddha.

冬日

坐擁烏皮倚隱囊
且翻梵夾静焚香
淒淒庭院悲風急
漠漠江天朔雁翔
一段旅懷還磊落
百年心事付蒼茫
登樓望遠迷鄉樹
又見寒鴉送夕陽

A Winter's Day

I sit wrapped in a black felt blanket
    and lean against a bolster,
Turning the pages of Sanskrit texts,
    as the incense silently burns.
In the courtyard it is sad and dreary,
    the mournful wind unsettled.
The river and sky are vast and wide;
    the geese are heading south.
The emotions of long-ago journeys
    return in bits and pieces;
A lifetime of worries lodged in my mind,
    surrender to the endless space.
Climbing the tower, I gaze into the distance,
    the trees of home now obscured.
Then I watch the winter crows
    seeing off the setting sun.

寒夜抒懷

寂寞青鐙夜未闌
半生心事獨盤桓
煙波縹緲魂非遠
人事悲涼歲欲殘
素志應同明月皎
離情還共白雲漫
良宵剪燭歌行露
松竹蕭森起暮寒

---

77 The term "misty waves" (*yanbo* 煙波) is often used to refer more generally to the rivers and lakes around the dwelling place of a hermit or recluse.

Narrating My Feelings on a Winter's Night

By the solitary oil lamp
   in the small night hours,
The worries of half a lifetime
   circle round and round.
Drifting on the misty waves,
   my soul fails to travel far.[77]
Human affairs are sorrowful,
   and the year is about to end.
My long-held aspiration should be
   as clear as the moon:
To cut off all feeling and return
   to drift with the white clouds.
Late in the night I trim the wick
   and sing "Paths with Dew,"[78]
As from the dark pines and bamboo
   there rises an evening chill.

78 An allusion to poem 17 of the *Classic of Poetry*, the speaker of which can be read as a
woman adamantly refusing to marry a man, even though he appears to be threatening
her with a lawsuit. In this case, it may perhaps be read as a protest against the usurping
Qing rulers, especially in view of the fact that her husband died fighting their troops.
For a translation of this poem, see Arthur Waley, tr. *The Book of Songs*, pp. 16–17.

靜維

碧海

碧海風濤靜不飛
凌霄高閣敝雲扉
擁書千卷無人到
翦燭三更有鶴歸
漢殿香消青鳥去
緱山秋冷玉笙微
劫灰辨得餘悲愴
獨向人間寄衲衣

79 See Wanyan Yun Zhu 1831, 1836, *fulu* 10b. Jingwei's collection of writings was titled
    Posthumous Drafts of Jili (*Jili yigao* 寄笠遺稿).

80 A tempest on an emerald sea is an image often used to refer to particularly violent or
    unsettled times, in this case, the upheavals caused by the fall of the Ming dynasty.

81 A tall pavilion is often used to describe someone's lofty ambitions. Here it is shuttered
    by clouds, thus is perhaps a symbol of broken dreams and lost hopes.

82 Usually, a candlewick is trimmed so as to be able to continue talking late into the night
    with friends. Here, however, the poet in her mountain retreat has only a crane as her
    companion.

83 An allusion to the legend that the Han dynasty emperor Wu (r. 140–87 BCE) was visited
    in 110 BCE by the Queen Mother of the West, together with her entourage of heavenly
    maidens. The emperor was alerted to her arrival by her messenger, a blue bird, which
    gave him time to prepare the palace for his mystical encounter with her on the seventh
    day of the seventh month.

Jingwei

Jingwei, whose secular name was Sheng Yunzhen 盛蘊貞 and who was also
known as Person of the Way Jili 寄笠道人, was born in Huating (present-day
Shanghai). She was betrothed to the ardent Ming loyalist Hou Xuanji 侯玄
潔, Shenyi's brother-in-law, but he committed suicide in 1645 before the
marriage could take place. Jingwei then joined Shenyi and Zaisheng and
became a nun. A collection of her writings was compiled after her death.[79]

The Emerald Sea

The tempest on the emerald sea[80]
    is no longer raging,
And the pavilion soaring into the sky
    is shuttered by clouds.[81]
I am surrounded by a thousand books,
    but no one comes to visit.
I trim the candlewick at midnight,
    yet only the crane comes home.[82]
The incense in the Han halls has dispersed,
    the blue bird has left.[83]
In the autumn chill of the Hou mountains,
    the jade pipes grow faint.[84]
In the ashes left by the apocalypse
    are remnants of sorrow,[85]
As alone I face the human world
    by finding refuge in nun's robes.

84 Legend has it that during the Jin dynasty (256–420), a famous prince retreated to the
    Hou Mountains (in Henan province), where he mounted a white crane and became a
    Daoist immortal. Here the poet may be alluding to her deceased husband.
85 According to Buddhist cosmology, the universe undergoes cycles of creation and de-
    struction by wind, fire, or flood. The Buddhist term *jiehui* 劫灰 refers to the ashes left
    after the universe has been destroyed by fire. It was also used to refer to the devastation
    left after periods of warfare, in this case, the fall of the Ming dynasty.

村居雜感

春山斜遠郭
淥水滿晴川
白鳥孤雲外
青林返照邊
風波何處少
耕鑿此中偏
莫作途窮歎
聊同鹿豕全

秋宵對月

夜靜天地涼
憑樓獨凝眺
煙樹色離離
雲山望中杳
萬籟寂無聲
數螢流木杪
青鐙照羅幕
殘葉鋪池沼

<hr />

86 There is an allusion here to a passage in *Mencius* that describes the legendary Emperor
    Shun 舜 as someone who was able to completely maintain his integrity even when living
    on his own in the mountains and "roaming alongside the deer and boar."

Random Thoughts on Living in the Country

Spring mountains extend along the distant walls,
While blue waters fill the streams under a clear sky.
A white bird is there beyond the solitary clouds,
And green trees reflect the late evening light.
Where is the turbulence of the times any less?
Better to be here, tilling land and drilling wells.
Do not lament about being in desperate straits.
For now, keep your integrity among the deer and boar![86]

Facing the Moon on an Autumn Night

The night is still, heaven and earth are chilled,
As I lean on the tower and look around intently.
The mist-enveloped trees are lush;
The cloud-covered hills are visible far away.
The ten-thousand pines are still and silent,
And scattered fireflies float among the treetops.
A blue oil lamp shines against the silk curtain,
As fallen leaves pile up along the creek banks.

悲哉今古情
乾坤徒浩渺
憂懷自蒼茫
至意漠難曉
姮娥知我愁
流影來相照
當持金石心
千秋同皎皎

夜坐

殘鐙照簾幕
樓閣有餘情
落葉堆蛩砌
涼風吹雁聲
暮蟬愁裏聽
河漢望中橫
獨坐悲秋夜
疏櫺淡月瑩

87 A mythological goddess who resides on the moon.

How sorrowful are the feelings of past and present,
The universe so vast and limitless.
My inner anxieties are also vast and boundless,
My deep thoughts silent and hard to know.
Chang'e sympathizes with my sorrow,[87]
And her light streams in to shine on me.
I must maintain a heart of metal and stone,
Sharing for eternity her gleaming purity.

Sitting at Night

The flickering lamp shines on the screen.
In this house is a surplus of feeling!
The fallen leaves pile up on the stone stairs;
The cold wind carries the sound of geese.
I listen in sadness to the twilight cicadas
And gaze at the Milky Way crossing the sky.
As I sit alone on this gloomy autumn night,
The moon shines through the latticework.

上鑒輝宗

88 See Wanyan Yun Zhu 1831, 1836, *fulu* 12a–13a., and Shen Shanbao 1846, 12:3a–b. The
titles of Shangjian's collections are *Fragrant Valley's Remnant Drafts Saved from Burning*
(*Xiangu fenyu cao* 香谷焚餘草), *New and Old Poems by Fomei* (*Fomei xinjiu shi* 佛眉新
舊詩), and *Lyrics from Suoxiang Hermitage* (*Suoxiang'an ci* 鎖香庵詞).

Shangjian Huizong

Shangjian Huizong (1644–1661), born in Changzhou, is perhaps better known by her secular name, Wu Qi 吳琪 (style name Ruixian 蕊仙). Her father, Wu Kanghou 吳康侯, held important office during the last years of the Ming and is known for his painting. Shangjian displayed a precocious intelligence as a girl and became a talented painter and skilled writer of both poetry and prose. During the turmoil of the times, her husband, the scholar-official Guan Xun 管勳, died in prison and left her destitute. She supported herself and her daughter by tutoring young women and eventually took the tonsure, adopting her religious name. She appears to have continued to write and paint and was especially close to Zhou Qiong 周瓊, a Daoist nun and one of the most well-known women painters of her day. The two women collaborated on a book of poetry. The author Shen Shanbao 沈善寶 (1808–1862) notes that Shangjian was especially fond of the landscape around Hangzhou and took many excursions with Zhou Qiong to the temples on Mount Lingyin 靈隱山. Shen Shanbao also calls Shangjian one of the three best known nun-poets of the early Qing, the other two being Shenyi and Zaisheng. There are three collections of poetry attributed to Shangjian.[88]

村居

貧家風物厭鉛華
波影浮來盡落霞
夢裏青山閒歲月
鏡中人面悟空花
秋鐙病後惟餘硯
春水愁多未浣紗
枕上片魂誰喚起
夕陽烟樹幾歸鴉

幽居志興

戢影衡門下
悠然物外身
擇林知鳥異
藏尾識龍神
山靜雲光活
溪閒草色新
廢琴兼病鶴
相與得天眞

89 There may be an indirect allusion here to a famous poem titled "Cypress Boat" from the *Classic of Poetry*, in which the speaker, often interpreted as female, compares the troubles of her heart to "unwashed clothes."

90 A more literal translation of these two lines would be "One knows the exceptional nature of birds by the way they choose their roosts; / One recognizes the divinity of dragons by the way they hide their tails." Traditionally, magical shape-shifting dragons were believed capable of hiding their long tails so that only their heads were visible. The metaphor of dragons hiding their tails was often used to refer to the elusive quality of a superior poem, in which the traces of human handiwork are hidden. Here the poet appears to be referring to her own wise decision to become a recluse.

Village Life

Living here impoverished,
    I've lost all taste for ornaments.
The shadows of the cloud waves drift in
    with the last of the sunset clouds.
The green mountains in my dreams
    idly pass the months and years.
The face of the woman in my mirror
    is a flower that knows Emptiness.
Beside the autumn lamp after an illness,
    there is only a leftover inkstone.
The spring waters bring sorrow
    that clings like unwashed silk.[89]
That fragment of my soul on the pillow,
    who will call for it to rise?
The evening light in the misty trees,
    a scattering of home-bound crows.

Thoughts on Living in Seclusion

I hide my shadow behind rustic gates,
And my body far from worldly affairs.
Rare birds know how to choose their roosts;
Divine dragons know how to hide their tails.[90]
Above peaceful hills, the cloud glow is vibrant;
Along leisurely streams, grass colors are fresh.
With the broken zither and emaciated crane,[91]
Together we will realize Heaven's Truth.[92]

91 The broken zither is an allusion to the story of Yu Boya 俞伯牙, who was known for his superb zither playing, and the woodcutter Zhong Ziqi 鐘子期, who was the only one who truly appreciated his playing. When Zhong Ziqi died, Yu Boya smashed his zither and never played again. From this story comes the term *zhiyin* 知音 (someone who knows the tone), used to refer to someone who truly understands one, a close friend. The image of the emaciated crane is often used to refer to a person of integrity in difficult and destitute circumstances.

92 Heaven's Truth (*Tianzhen* 天眞) refers to the unsullied and unchanging inherent truth or reality that underlies all phenomena.

閨友見訪感舊

蓬門來訪碧山秋
別久相逢放更幽
紅葉隱鐙疏雨亂
白雲堆榻晚風留
自埋書劍新篁寺
誰倚琴樽舊畫樓
料得百花洲畔月
年年長照水空流

---

93 Throughout Chinese history, there have been women known for their swordsmanship, which required not so much physical strength as skill and mental agility. For some seventeenth-century women, swordsmanship was a sign of refined gentility, along with painting, poetry, and other literati arts. It also became a symbolic gesture symbolizing anti-Manchu resistance.

A Friend from the Inner Chambers Comes to Visit:
Remembering Old Times

When she arrived at my rustic gate to visit,
    it was autumn in the blue mountains.
Meeting again after a long separation,
    we felt the seclusion even more.
The lamp was hidden by red leaves
    scattered by sporadic rain.
White clouds piled up on my couch,
    while the evening breezes lingered.
I am buried away with books and swords
    Here in this new bamboo temple.[93]
Who is there with zither and wine jar
    in the old painted tower?[94]
I imagine that there are white blossoms,
    and a moon over island banks,
Which every year continues to shine
    as the river flows on in emptiness.

94 Here the poet may be alluding to her friend from the inner chambers, as well as to her
own life before becoming a nun.

感懷

鶴煮琴焚事已賒
不堪回首數年華
愁來有句留殘葉
夢去無人問落花
鳥惜晚香窺檻鏡
婢憐新病鎖窗紗
柳枝剩有蘇台曲
未審春風憶若耶

<hr>

95 Literally, "The cranes have been made into soup, the zithers have been smashed."

Heartfelt Recollections

What is beautiful and precious has been destroyed[95]
   in events that happened long ago.
I can't bear to turn and look back
   at the glory of those few years.
When sadness comes, there are lines of poems
   that I can leave with the withered leaves.
When dreams depart, there is no one
   to ask about the fallen blossoms.
The birds pity the evening fragrance
   and peek in the windowsill mirror.
The servant girl worries about my health
   and closes the window screen.
In the willow branches there lingers
   the melody of Su Terrace,
And I've not yet asked the spring wind
   if it remembers Ruoye.[96]

96 The name of a river in Zhejiang province, known in the literary tradition as the place
where the beautiful Xi Shi did her washing before she was discovered by a minister of
the King of Yue. She was subsequently used to topple the rival state of Wu.

無垢

書懷（一）

青翠入簾櫳
永日駐幽閣
愁縈芳草生
靜覺桐花落
奩鏡網蟏蛸
庭柯巢鳥鵲
夢去不關愁
曉來心自惡
獨坐只書空
微雨益蕭索

---

97 See Wanyan Yun Zhu 1831, 1836, *fulu* 14a–b, as well as the later more detailed account in Xu Naichang 1909, 4.26b. Wugou's two poetry collections are titled *Indian Madder Collection* (*Ruhui ji* 茹蕙集) and *Studio of Embroidering Buddhas Collection* (*Xiufozhai ji* 繡佛齋集).

98 The falling of the snow-white blossoms of the paulownia tree is traditionally said to mark the end of spring.

Wugou

Wugou, whose secular name was Chen Jie 陳潔, was from Tongzhou, Jiangsu province. She came from a gentry family with a long tradition of scholarship and official service, and even as a young girl was known for her love of study as well as her ability to write both poetry and prose. A marriage was arranged for her with Sun Anshi 孫安石, a young scholar and scion of a local family that had been quite wealthy but was swiftly falling into decline. The marriage was not a happy one: failing to bear a son, Wugou was apparently treated like a common maidservant, and she decided to return to her natal home. She eventually became a nun, taking up residence in Hongbao Hall 鴻寶堂, which had belonged to her grandfather, a high-ranking Ming official. Her last years were filled with poverty, hunger and illness. She is said to have died by slipping and falling out a window. Wugou left two collections of poetry.[97]

Writing of My Feelings [version 1]

Verdant hills peek through my curtains.
All day I've kept to this secluded room.
Sorrows linger as sweet grasses spring up;
I come to a quiet realization as paulownia blossoms fall. [98]
Spider webs cover the toilette mirror.
Magpie nests fill the courtyard trees.
Dreams depart regardless of the sorrow,[99]
While day dawns and fills my heart with rancor.
Sitting alone, I can only inscribe the void,[100]
Drizzling rain adding to the desolation.

---

99   That is, having to wake from dreams of home or of loved ones.
100 The image of writing in the void is an allusion to the story of a fourth-century general who, after being unjustly demoted, would write words in the air. While sometimes used with political overtones, in this case it would seem to be primarily an expression of vague melancholy. For a discussion of Wugou's use of this image in some of her earlier poems, see Li Wai-yee 2014, 103.

書懷（二）

青翠入簾櫳
永日駐幽閣
愁縈芳草生
靜覺桐花落
奩鏡網蟵蛸
庭柯巢鳥鵲
夢去不關愁
沖淡心無惡
獨坐只面壁
微雨聽簌簌
何時證菩提
一笑天花落

101   This second version, found in a small collection of comments on poetry by women, compiled by Jin Yimo (1914), is of interest due to its more explicitly Buddhist ending. It is unclear whether this represents the original version, or Jin's own emendation.

Writing of My Feelings [version 2][101]

Verdant hills peek through my curtains.
All day I've kept to this secluded room.
Sorrows linger as sweet grasses spring up;
I come to a quiet realization as paulownia blossoms fall.
Spider webs cover the toilette mirror.
Magpie nests fill the courtyard trees.
Dreams depart regardless of the sorrow,
And the detached heart leaves no rancor.
As I sit meditating alone facing the wall,[102]
I can hear the sounds of drizzling rain.
When will I experience an awakening?
Heavenly flowers fall with a smile.[103]

102 Bodhidharma is said to have sat in meditation facing the wall of his cave on Mount Song for nine years.
103 In many Mahayana Buddhist sutras, flowers being cast down by heavenly spiritual beings are indications of blessing and approval.

雪後登山

滕君似妒青山翠
萬里峯巒鋪玉碎
蒼涼四望野雲低
江天靜與茅亭對
此時誰是景中人
王恭鶴氅難為繪
我愛江天積雪幽
朗吟雪賦寄中流
長江寂寞魚龍沒
坐向孤寒月影浮

---

104 The name of the mythical snow god is Teng Liu 藤六.

105 According to a story found in the fifth-century collection of anecdotes called *New Account of Tales of the World* (*Shishuo xinyu* 世說新語), the high-minded aristocrat Wang Gong 王恭 (d. 398) rode in a high carriage dressed in a cloak of white crane feathers, and people who saw him thought they were seeing an immortal. If he were riding in the snow, his cloak would, of course, have made him nearly invisible. See Mather 2002, 345.

Climbing the Mountain after the Snow

The Snow God appears to be jealous
    of the mountains' verdant colors.[104]
Ten thousand *li* of peaks and ridges
    are now blanketed in bits of jade.
I gaze about me at the cold
    and low-hanging wild clouds.
The rivers and heavens are motionless
    before the thatched pavilion.
At times like these, who is
    the person within the scene?
Wang Gong with his feathered cape[105]
    would be difficult to draw.
I love how the river and sky
    are hidden by the piled snow.
I will recite "The Rhapsody on Snow"[106]
    and entrust it to the river's flow.
The Yangzi is still and quiet,
    its fish and dragons hiding deep.
I sit and face the loneliness and cold,
    as the moon's reflections drift by.[107]

106 An allusion to what is perhaps the best known literary descriptions of snow, "Rhapsody on Snow" ("Xuefu" 雪賦), by Xie Huilian 謝惠連 (407–433). For a translation of this text, see Knechtges 2014, 21–31.

107 The reflection of the moon is often used as a symbol of the purity of the essential mind or Buddha nature.

超一

遺詩

靜中無箇事
反復弄虛空
地老天荒後
魂飛魄喪中
有師開道統
無法度愚蒙
忽底虛空碎
夕陽依舊紅

108 See Wanyan Yun Zhu 1831, 1836, *fulu* 14b. Wang Shizhen's comment is quoted in Xu Shichang 1990, 9144.

109 According popular Chinese religious belief, after death the body separates into the ethereal or yang soul (*hun* 魂), which leaves the body and ascends into the heavens, and the corporeal or yin soul (*po* 魄), which remains behind.

Chaoyi

Chaoyi, whose family name was Yin 殷, hailed from Yangzhou, Jiangsu province. There is very little information about her, but we do know that her husband died not long after their marriage, and she subsequently took the tonsure and dedicated herself to Chan meditation. Just three years after becoming a nun, she herself fell ill and passed away. She left a small collection of poems and religious verse, and was praised by her contemporary, the famous poet and literary critic Wang Shizhen 王士禛 (1634–1711), who commented that her inner realization was reflected in her poems.[108]

Deathbed Gāthā

In the midst of stillness, nothing happens.
Back and forth I frolic in the empty void.
After the aging of the earth and the fading of the sky,
Between the *hun* soul soaring and the *po* soul sinking,[109]
There are masters teaching the Confucian Way.[110]
But even they can't save the blind and deluded.
Suddenly the empty void shatters into tiny bits,
The setting sun still red, just as it was before.

---

110 The term *daotong* 道統 can refer generally to the transmission of the teachings of a particular school or lineage, but it is often used to refer more specifically to the Confucian orthodoxy. This interpretation implies a criticism of the limitations of Confucianism as compared to Chan Buddhist practice.

明萱悟真

秋夜

忽見梧桐染淡黃
更聞鶗鴂叫秋霜
不因白髮催明鏡
且抱紅心寄上方
就竹開窗通海月
當庭種桂散天香
閒來擁衲憑高坐
靜聽疏鐘萬慮忘

111 See Zha Sheng, *Zudeng Xuan dashi xinglüe*, in Shenqi, n.d. Mingxuan Wuzhen's poetry
collection was titled *Impromptu Chants of the Flower Bud Pavilion* (*Ruijian ouyong* 蕊閣
偶咏), and the collection of her recorded sayings was titled *Records of the Clear Mind
of Chan Master Wuzhen Xuan of Zudeng* (*Zudeng Wuzhen Xuan Mingxin lu* 祖鐙悟眞
萱禪師明心錄).

Mingxuan Wuzhen

Mingxuan Wuzhen, whose secular name was Jiang Yi 蔣宜, came from a well-established family in Renhe (present-day Hangzhou), Zhejiang province. Her father was the literatus-official Jiang Xinzhai 蔣心齋, known especially for his calligraphy and seals, some of which still occasionally come on the market today. Even as a girl, Mingxuan was known for her painting and poetry, as well as for her beauty. When she was nineteen, she became the concubine of the preeminent historian and painter Zha Jizuo 查繼佐 (1601–1676). Like many contemporary literati, Zha would often visit eminent monks, and Mingxuan would accompany him on many of these visits. After Zha's death in 1676, she took up residence at Zudeng Chan Monastery in Hangzhou, where she lived until her death at the age of 74. She left a collection of poems as well as a collection of recorded sayings, which would indicate that she had received dharma transmission and was an acknowledged Chan master.[111]

Autumn Night

Suddenly I notice the paulownia
    washed with a pale yellow.
I hear the large hawk-cuckoo
    calling in the autumn frost.
It is not my hair turning white
    that sends me to the bright mirror;[112]
Rather, it is with a burning red heart[113]
    that I aspire to the transcendent.
The open window by the bamboo
    invites in the sea and moon.
In the courtyard, the cinnamon trees
    diffuse their heavenly scent.
Quietly I pull my robes around me,
    and there on my dharma seat,
Peacefully listen to the sporadic bells,
    ten thousand worries forgotten.

---

112   The bright (or clear) mirror is often used as a metaphor for one's original Buddha nature.
113   Literally, with a "red heart," denoting utmost sincerity.

落葉

消瘦寒林意自悽
可憐零落任東西
妒風何苦相淩逼
眷戀枝頭不忍離

霜染千秋色不同
縱然嬌艷也成空
憑風分付東流去
耐等寒枝春不窮

題英石

寂寞東山草更萋
孤峯獨立絕恆蹊
年來不與人相見
風雨蕭蕭鳥自啼

---

114   First used by the great Song dynasty poet Su Shi 蘇軾 (1037–1101), the image of the
eastward flowing river is often used to indicate the linear passage of time in a human
life. This image is often seen to contrast with cyclical natural time, represented by the
return of spring.

Falling Leaves [two verses]

The cold trees stripped bare,
     one cannot help but feel sad;
I feel pity the falling leaves
     being tossed east and west.
How heartlessly the jealous wind
     pushes them to and fro.
Attached to their branches,
     they find leaving hard to bear!

The frost coats a thousand trees,
     each in a different manner,
But even this charming beauty
     will turn into nothing!
Ordered off by the winds,
     the river flows eastward,[114]
As patiently we wait for the winter branches
     to again show signs of spring.[115]

Inscribed on a Ying Stone[116]

In the stillness of East Mountain
     the grasses grow lusher,
And where the solitary peak stands,
     there is no thoroughfare.
Lately I've not had much to do
     with other people.
Whistling wind, pattering rain,
     birds chattering to themselves.

---

115   The blossoming plum tree is also often used as a symbol of enlightenment.
116   Ying stones are ornamental limestones quarried from Yingde 英德 in northern Guang-
        dong province. One of the four most famous types of so-called scholar stones, limestone
        was highly prized for its thin and slender shape marked with many lines and furrows,
        making it resemble a mountain landscape.

維極行致

蜜蜂頌

　千花回繞出頭時
　八面風清得意歸
　去住豈貪簷下蕊
　遊行不覺順天飛

Weiji Xingzhi

Weiji Xingzhi (d. 1672) was the daughter of a distinguished family from Yaojiang, Zhejiang province. She is said to have expressed early on a desire not to marry. Allowed to accompany her father on his visits to Master Miyun Yuanwu 密雲圓悟 (1566–1642), she later took the tonsure with Miyun Yuanwu's dharma heir Linji Chan Master Shiqi Tongyun 石奇通雲 (1594–1663) and, after some years, received dharma transmission from him. In 1646 she was invited by local Hangzhou literati-officials to become the abbess of Xiongsheng Convent 雄聖菴 in Hangzhou. Weiji, it appears, was a formidable teacher, known for her strict discipline, as well as for her eloquent poems and forceful sermons. Although the collection of her recorded sayings has been lost and only a handful of her poems are still extant, her poetry appears to have been much admired by her contemporaries.[117]

Ode to the Honeybees

I

Circling around a thousand blooms
   when they first emerge,
With a clear breeze in all directions,
   they return satisfied.
They crave neither coming nor going,
   just the buds under the eaves.
But they roam around by instinct and
   fly along Heaven's Way.[118]

---

118 As David Pattinson points out, while bees often had negative associations in early Chinese literature, by the Song dynasty they were seen as insects to be greatly admired for their industriousness, as well as for their ability to travel long distances before returning to the hive with pollen. See Pattinson 2019. In traditional Indian Buddhism, honeybees symbolize nuns and monks who, without desire or harm, collect the alms that they need. "Just as a bee / Without hurting the flower / Neither its color nor its scent / Gathers its nectar and escapes / So should the sage roam in the village" (*Dhammapada* 4:49).

傑出深叢別有涯
天然尊貴盡投衛
甘香釀就資王用
毒刺猶來驗作家

月明簾外轉身時
不涉青黃好相離
人用當前連夜脫
掀翻窩臼快心脾

參多晚蝶趁春光
傳覺無端個裏怍
放下身心高著眼
笑他遂隊亂承當

119 The relationship between bees and their "king" (actually, the queen) has often been
     used in Chinese literature as an analogy for the relationship between a king and his
     loyal followers, who both guard him and offer him the first fruits of their labor. In the
     Chan context, the analogous loyalty may instead be to the community, which works
     and lives together under the watchful eye of the master.
120 My translation here is a tentative one. In early Chinese literature, bees were feared and
     hated for the venomous stings. In the Chan context, these stings might be likened to a
     master's "shouts" and "blows," designed to jolt students out of their mental ruts.

II

Bravely emerging from deepest clusters,
   they have a different limit.
By nature, they revere royalty
   and join in his defense.
When the sweet fragrance is fermented,
   give it to the King to use,[119]
But they bring out their poisonous stingers
   as a way of testing others.[120]

III

When the moon beyond the screen is bright
   and you are tossing and turning,
Don't get caught up in your fondness
   for distinguishing yellows and greens.[121]
For when confronted with these, people
   will try escape night after night.
However, by overturning conventional ways,[122]
   you will bring joy to their hearts!

IV

Notice how many late butterflies
   take advantage of spring's splendor.
Transmission and awakening are without reason.
   Knowing this, I blush.
Lay down both body and mind,
   keep your vision high,
And laugh at those who just tag along,
   randomly accepting things.

---

121 This meaning of this line is not entirely clear. The poet may simply be advising against getting caught up in making distinctions between right and wrong, black and white— that is, in the dualities of everyday life.

122 A mortar and pestle is sometimes used as an analogy for a set pattern or established way of doing things. In Chan, kicking things over often suggests awakening to reality by getting rid of deluded, dualistic or in this case, purely conventional perceptions.

透穿籬壁耀疏桐
出入無拘四海通
忽報上林鶯語滑
當陽奪取狀元紅

山居

數椽茅屋於竹引啼鴉
爐煖自烹殘雪
扶笻終日對梅花

聽雁

擣衣聲起家家
聽不盡西澗芭蕉送雨

123 The translation and meaning of this line are not entirely clear. The term *zhuangyuan hong* 狀元紅 may refer to the red of the Top of the List, that is the top graduate of the imperial examination, but it is also a popular name for the fragrant red osmanthus flower. In either case, it is possible that what is alluded to is enlightenment, whether the "top prize" or the loveliest of pollen-filled and fragrant flowers.
124 Feng Jinbo 1805, 17:16a.

V

Passing through hedges and walls,
    shimmering amid the paulownia trees,
Going in and out without restraint,
    they pass through the four seas.
Orioles are suddenly reported,
    singing in the Imperial Park,
As there in the bright sunlight,
    they capture the top prize.[123]

Living in the Mountains

My small thatched hut in the bamboo attracts the cawing crows.
When the stove is hot, I boil clumps of snow.
Bamboo staff in hand, I spend all day facing the plum blossoms.

Listening to the Geese[124]

The sound of fulling clothes
Is such that no one can hear it all.[125]
    The plantains by the west creek bring in the rain.

125 The poet is perhaps suggesting that ordinary people are so busy with domestic chores, such as washing clothes in the river, that they do not notice the changes in the natural world around them.

靜諾超越

126   See Xu Shichang 1990, 9156. Jingnuo's poetry collection was titled *Poetry Drafts from the Hut of Laying Down One's Burden* (*Xijian lu shicao* 息肩廬詩草).

Jingnuo Chaoyue

Jingnuo Chaoyue was born into a scholarly gentry family from Renhe, Zhe-jiang province. Her father, Lin Yibai 林彝白, at one point held the position of magistrate. The family fell on hard times, and Jingnuo became a nun at Xiongsheng Convent, where she studied with Chan Master Weiji Xingzhi (see p. 89). Like her teacher, Jingnuo earned a reputation for compassion-ate but strict discipline and impeccable behavior, and attracted hundreds of followers over three decades, many of them gentry women. She was also known as Person of the Way Zixian (Zixian daoren 自閒道人). According to one anecdote, she built a grass hut on the banks of a river, and upon observing a blossoming plum tree or drifting snow, she would say, "This is where true enlightenment is to be found." Jingnuo occasionally professed shame at the pleasure she derived from words, and yet she left behind both a collection of her recorded sayings and a collection of poetry.[126]

古梅歌

閬苑瓊姿不記年
屈曲古榦如龍盤
大庾萬枝只如此
迴旋曲折空山裏
吐蕚枝枝色正妍
移來小艇泊流泉
斜枝倒浸冰魂化
狂呼游客添杯斝
我欲攜筇過隔溪
竹林主人遠相迓
莫謂韶光還久留
人生適意多偷暇

127   This lovely garden (*langyuan* 閬苑) also refers to a legendary paradise inhabited by immortals.

128   The Dayu mountain range stretches between the southern Guangdong and Jiangxi provinces.

Song of the Ancient Plum Trees

The shapely forms in this lovely garden[127]
    have a timeless beauty.
The bends in their ancient trunks
    are like those of a coiled dragon.
The myriad trees of the Dayu range[128]
    are the only ones like it,
Circling and winding, turning and bending,
    on the empty mountains.
Branch after branch send out their buds—
    truly an enchanting sight!
I've drifted to this place in my little boat,
    and moored by a burbling spring.
Their branches hang down aslant,
    as a layer of ice melts away.
Shouting wildly, the traveler pours
    more wine into her cup.
With the help of my bamboo staff,
    I want to cross the brook.
From a distance, I exchange greetings
    with the Sages of the Bamboo Grove![129]
Don't tell me that the beauty of spring
    will still last for a while.
When this life offers a bit of pleasure,
    be sure to take advantage of it!

129 The Seven Sages of the Bamboo Grove is a name given to group of third-century scholars
    and poets, perhaps the best known of which are Ruan Ji 阮籍 (210–263) and Ji Kang 嵇
    康 (223–262), who both retreated to a life of poetry, music, and wine drinking in the
    mountains as an expression of their rejection of the corrupt and dangerous politics of
    their day.

過永慶寺逢牡丹作

東風習習春將夏
寶馬香車如放假
夾道松杉滿徑陰
黃鸝坐語春風下
偏反綽約逞嬌顏
徘徊終日不知還
花王似殿東王令
好鳥枝頭箝鼓競
莫言花落不如人
人老能如花更春
惟有青山常對峙
年年花落路傍塵
小鳥欲答忽飛去
宛轉如歌昔時句
但使衰年無病侵
歲歲花前常小憩

130　Although there are a number of temples with this name, this may refer to the one lo-
cated in Suzhou. Built nearly 1,500 years ago, it has been rebuilt many times over the
centuries and is still active today.

Passing by Yongqing Monastery, I Came upon Its Peonies and Wrote This[130]

The east wind blows quite gently
    as spring eases into summer.
Expensive steeds and fancy carriages,
    as if it were a festival day,
Are lined on both sides with pines and firs,
    casting the paths in shade.
All the while yellow orioles chatter away
    in the springtime breeze.
Swaying gracefully, the peonies
    show off their charming faces.
I stroll around the entire day
    with no thought of returning home.
It's like a "king of flowers" palace,
    commissioned by the King of the East,[131]
With beautiful birds in the treetops,
    competing like flutes and drums.
Don't say that withering flowers
    cannot be compared to people,
Or that people, when they age,
    can spring up like flowers again.
It is only the blue mountains
    that always stay facing each other,
Whereas every year the flowers fall
    into the dust by the roadside.
A little bird was about to answer me,
    before it suddenly took flight,
With a sweet and melodious song
    having lines from olden times.
I only hope that when I grow old,
    I will not find myself so ill
That I can't come here every year
    to rest in front of these blooms!

131 The peony is often called the king of flowers. The King of the East is the name of a Daoist deity who is regarded as being a manifestation of yang energy, that is, the active energy of the sun that allows for the growth of plants and other living things.

贈楊夫人

一種高風迥絕塵
何緣邂逅覺生春
青蓮堪證無生法
紫誥仍輝現在身
性潔自甘泉石操
談玄喜與法王親
金陵風物稱殊絕
道左流連話轉深

For Lady Yang

Yours is a lofty style
  that utterly transcends the worldly dust.
How have I chanced upon a springtime
  that awakens living beings?
The blue lotus can serve as a testimony
  of the Deathless Way,
Even as the vermilion imperial edict adds
  luster to your current incarnation.
A pure nature is perfectly content among
  mountain rocks and stones,
Discussing life's mysteries and delighting
  in being close to the Dharma King.
The sights and scenes of Jinling[132]
  are famous for their special beauty,
So we linger by the roadside, reluctant to leave,
  as our conversation deepens.

詠秋蘭

長林衆草入秋荒
獨有幽姿逗晚香
每向風前堪寄傲
幾因霜後欲留芳
名流賞鑑還堪佩
空谷知音品自揚
一種孤懷千古在
湘江詞賦奏清商

133   A reference to the poems and rhapsodies attributed to Qu Yuan (c. 340–278 bce), a slan-
      dered minister of the state of Chu who then lived in exile along a tributary of the Xiang
      River and allegedly eventually committed suicide by drowning himself in its waters.
      The *shang* mode is one of the five major modes of ancient Chinese music, described as
      having as particularly pure and melancholy sound. For this reason, it is sometimes also
      used to refer to the sound made by the autumn wind.

A Celebration in Verse of the Autumn Orchid

The dense trees and the wild grasses
   have all withered from autumn,
Leaving only this hidden beauty
   with its late evening fragrance.
Even buffeted by the wind,
   it manages to hold itself upright,
And even after repeated frosts,
   it can retain its scent!
Famous men may appreciate it
   and pluck it to adorn themselves,
But this empty valley knows its worth
   and there awaits a true friend.
Such a unique sentiment
   has persisted through the ages,
As the songs and rhapsodies of the Xiang River
   are performed in the pure *shang* mode.[133]

超衍密印

自贊

吳山頂上月輪孤
冷淡清貧一物無
來問頭陀何所事
蒲團坐久自歡娛

---

134 See Wang Duanshu 1667, 26:3b. Interestingly, Chaoyan's name and a few lines from one of her dharma talks also appears in Chaoyong 1697, 502c12–15, where she is listed as a dharma successor of Benchong Xingsheng, but with no indication that she was a nun and not a monk. Chaoyin Miyin's recorded sayings was titled *Recorded Sayings of Chan Master Miyin Yan of Mount Wu* (*Wushan Miyin Yan chanshi yulu* 吳山密印衍禪師語錄).

Chaoyan Miyin

Chaoyan Miyin was born in Hangzhou to the Qiu 丘 family. She appears to have been placed in a convent as a very young girl and became a nun at the age of eleven. She later became a disciple and dharma successor of Linji Chan Master Benchong Xingsheng 本充行盛 (d. 1671/1672), and eventually received dharma transmission. Chaoyan's convent was located on Mount Wu on the southern side of Hangzhou's West Lake. She was known for her literary gifts, and her poems may well have been included in the now lost collection of her recorded sayings.[134]

Encomium to Myself

Above the highest peak of Mount Wu
    is a solitary round moon.
Cold and dim, pure and poor,
    it doesn't own a single thing.
If you should come and ask this nun
    about how she passes her time:
Know that sitting on the meditation mat
    brings her pleasure and joy!

一真

中秋

空齋寂寂語
高臥一床秋
苔色渾無跡
溪光淡欲流
塵隨紅葉落
心與白雲休
蕭瑟聞寒鴈
鳴空萬籟幽

135   See Wang Duanshu 1667, 26.11b; and Chaoyong 1697, 502a11–17. Her collection of poetry was titled *Clear and Cool Collection* (*Qingliang ji* 清涼集).

Yizhen

Yizhen was the religious name of Wang Jingshu 王靜淑 (style name, Yuyin 玉隱), from Shaoxing, Zhejiang province. She was the elder sister of Wang Duanshu. When her husband Chen Shurang 陳樹勳 died, likely while fighting against the invading Manchu armies, she was forced to flee to the mountains with her in-laws and her children, the youngest of whom was only three. When she finally made it back home, she appears to have taken up residence in a small hermitage. This may have been the Cloud Hermitage referred to in some of her poems. This hermitage was built close to the family tombs, where her beloved father Wang Siren 王思任 (1575–1646) had starved himself to death in protest against the new Qing dynasty. Like Chaoyan Miyin (see p. 105), she became a disciple and dharma successor of Linji Chan Master Benchong Xingsheng. Toward the end of her life, she appears to have lived at Taiping Convent in Wuhu, Anhui province. She left one collection of poetry.[135]

Mid-Autumn

Resting up high, a bed full of autumn;
In the empty study, quiet talk.
Moss colors about to disappear;
Shallow creek waters almost moving.
The dust falls with the red leaves;[136]
The heart rests with the white clouds.
In the gloom I can hear the winter geese
Calling in the sky. Then all grows still.

---

136   The dust here refers to the dust of worldly life.

九日約玉映妹不至

> 細雨凄風阻鴈行
> 竹籬茅舍薄羅裳
> 登樓懶看黃花瘦
> 山老林紅一夜霜

山居落葉

> 林疎半已出秋微
> 歷亂飄零繞竹扉
> 峰氣逼人寒薄骨
> 聊將落葉製禪衣

雲菴次韻

> 淡墨朦山吹易去
> 光飛藉水拂天來
> 花憐老衲香茅室
> 幽竹輕推扉自開

137   Her younger sister, Wang Duanshu.

Younger Sister Yuying and I Planned to Meet on the Ninth Day, but She Didn't Arrive[137]

Drizzling rain and chilly wind
   impede the goose's flight.[138]
A bamboo fence, a thatched hut,
   a thin lightweight robe.
Climbing the tower, I notice
   that the yellow mums are gaunt,
The mountains old, and the trees red,
   all after a night of frost.

Living in the Mountains among Falling Leaves

Forest trees already half bare,
   a sign of early autumn.
Leaves swirling in confusion
   around the bamboo gate.
The mountain weather
   chilly down to the bone.
For fun, I gather up the fallen leaves
   to make a meditation robe.

Matching the Rhymes of "Cloud Hermitage"

The pale ink wash darkening the hills
   is easily blown away.
The light flitting over the water
   gently brushes the sky.
The flowers pity this old nun,
   and perfume her grass hut.
The dark bamboo lightly nudges
   so that the doors swing open.

138 That is, bad weather impeded her sister's travels.

上信

冰

妄念成證見
無參便為禪
冰消原似水
日落忽離天

---

139   In other words, she used only poetic forms associated with religious verse and largely
      eschewed those traditionally associated with mainstream poetry, such as classical
      poems. See Wang Duanshu 1667, 26:11b.

Shangxin

We have very little biographical information about Shangxin, although
Wang Duanshu appears to have known her personally, as she was a dis-
ciple of Wang's sister, the nun Yizhen (see p. 107). We do know that her
secular name was Luo Jinghui 駱靜慧, and that she was from Zhuji 諸暨 in
Zhejiang province. Wang Duanshu tells us that she was a very serious and
self-contained person who did not write many classical poems, but filled
sheets of paper with hymns and gāthās.[139]

> *Ice*
>
> When delusions become right views,
> The unawakened then becomes Chan,
> Just as melted ice becomes water again,
> And the sunset suddenly departs the sky.

元端御符

書齋偶詠

榻寄閑窗下
相攜話昔遊
烹茶成雅集
開卷足清幽
宿雨花生潤
微風鳥自謳
留將殘照影
靜拂素絲幽

---

140 See Xu Shichang 1990, 9157; and Wang Yu 1821, 178:7b.

141 That is, the type of refined gathering that literati men often enjoyed, with tea, conver-
sation, poetry writing, and so on.

Yuanduan Yufu

Yuanduan Yufu, whose family name was Lu 盧, was born in Jiading, Jiangsu province. She took the tonsure with a female teacher at Mount Yaofeng in Changzhou when she was only eleven years old. Later she became a disciple and dharma successor of Linji Chan Master Shanxiao Benxi 山曉本晳 (1620–1686/87). She served as abbess of Mingyin Convent in Hangzhou and of Fushi Convent in Jiaxing (the same one associated with Qiyuan Xinggang, see p. 149). Her poems were highly regarded by her contemporaries, though few remain extant.[140]

My Study: An Impromptu Verse

Leisurely we sit on the couch by the window,
Hand in hand remembering past excursions.
We brew tea and our get-together becomes an elegant gathering.[141]
Unrolling scrolls lends itself to deep silence.
In the evening rain, the flowers glisten.
In the gentle breeze, the birds chatter.
Stay and lead the shadows of the fading sunlight
To quietly stroke the stillness of pure strings.[142]

---

142 The Chinese is ambiguous here, but there seems to be a reference to the zither, which would commonly be played during an elegant gathering.

妙惠

般若招提曉坐

夜雨洗山岩
朝來翠獨濕
趺坐學觀空
清風滿香積
正因字本無
而我好翰墨
心即等死灰
未了人間孽
窗竹皆虛心
庭松多勁節
體此長青樹
原不在虛實
何況鐘魚間
梵理更無得
坐久聞妙香
慈航如何接

143 See Wanyan Yun Zhu 1831, 1836, *fulu* 17b. Her collection of poetry is titled *Epiphyllum and Water Grasses* (*Tanhua xuanzao* 曇花軒草).
144 Hollow bamboo is a metaphor for a person who is empty of self; the pine tree is a traditional symbol for a high-minded and upstanding person.
145 In other words, one must look beyond the surface to see the deeper essential nature of bamboo and pine, and by extension, of oneself and others.

Miaohui

Miaohui, whose secular name was Fan Luoxian 范洛仙, was from Chang-zhou. When her husband Li Shiyan 李峙岩, a scholar from Shanxi, died shortly after their marriage, Miaohui's parents urged her to remarry, but she refused, determined to remain faithful to her husband's memory. After her parents died, she became a nun at Bore (Prajñā) Convent in her hometown. She attracted many followers, lived over eighty years, and left one collection of poetry.[143]

Dawn, Sitting at Bore Convent

The night rain washes the mountain cliffs.
At daybreak, the brilliant greens are damp.
Sitting, I learn to meditate on emptiness
As a pure breeze fills the convent kitchen.
Words are inherently without substance,
But still I remain fond of brush and ink.
My mind may be like cold dead ashes,
But I still have unfinished karma.
The bamboo by the window is hollow;
The pine in the courtyard upstanding.[144]
I understand that the essence of these evergreens
Is not just a matter of being hollow or solid.[145]
How much more with the fish-drum[146]
Can the principles of Buddhism be realized!
After a long sitting, I smell the fine incense.
How can I board the Ferry of Compassion![147]

146 The fish-drum is a hollow wooden percussion instrument that is struck with a mallet. It is used to accompany the chanting of Buddhist sutras, as well as to signal different events of the monastic day, such as mealtimes. Just as fish never close their eyes to sleep, so Buddhist practitioners should remain constantly awake, or mindful.
147 The Buddha is sometimes referred to as the Ship of Compassion, which rescues beings and transports them across the sea of suffering.

石巖

憶夢

> 蕉團穩坐好安禪
> 炯炯金鐙法座燃
> 慧鳥鳴來深樹裏
> 亂山飛入小窗前
> 雲鎔碧海摩晴日
> 露洗空天散曉煙
> 記得夢中參我佛
> 色空空色悟真詮

148 See Peng Yuncan 1909, 70:23b.
149 The wisdom birds may perhaps refer to the sweet-voiced *kalavinka* birds (depicted as having a human head and a bird's torso), said to dwell in the Western Pure Land, where they preach the dharma.

Shiyan

Shiyan, whose secular name was Jiang Shunying 蔣蕣英, was from Renhe, Zhejiang province. In addition to writing poetry, she was a gifted zither player, calligrapher, and painter of elegant bamboo and orchids. She served for a brief time as concubine of a high-ranking official, and was selected to enter the Inner Palace just as the Ming court fell into disarray. She was attracted to Buddhism at a young age and is said to have had an experience of "sudden enlightenment" while reading a Buddhist text. After the fall of the Ming, she took ordination and become a nun at Bizhi Convent in Hangzhou. Her dharma talks were well received, and she attracted many followers.[148]

Recalling a Dream

Sitting firmly on a plantain-leaf mat,
    I meditated in tranquility,
Surrounded by the golden lamps
    that flickered by the dharma seat.
The wisdom birds sang
    from deep within the trees,[149]
While randomly flying out and back
    in front of the little window.
The clouds fused with a blue sea
    to mold a glorious day.
The dew bathed the empty skies,
    scattering the morning mist.
I remember how in my dream,
    I met with my Buddha.
Form is emptiness, emptiness is form:[150]
    now I understand what that means!

150 These lines are from the Heart Sutra, a very popular short Buddhist text that encapsulates the Mahayana Buddhist teaching that says that all phenomena are empty, or lacking an unchanging essence, but that at the same time, this emptiness itself is also devoid of any sort of unchanging essence.

燕

滿院晴光好
穿簾小燕紛
數聲驚午夢
雙翦碎春雲
戲水香泥溼
衝煙夕照曛
參差頻上下
紅嘴掠青芹

曉起遣興

風掃雲殘霽色開
松根馴鶴舞蒼苔
蟻拖榆莢緣牆去
蜂抱花鬚撲檻來
一雨綠盈分竹院
四山青壓鼓琴臺
悠然獨立斜陽下
結陣烏鳶噪古槐

---

151 This appears to be the name of a small courtyard inside Shiyan's convent, where after
     a rain, the bamboo in the garden is bright green.

Swallows

The courtyard is filled with a fine clear light.
Little swallows fly through the hanging screen.
Their chirping wakes me from a noontime dream,
As their pairs of wings disperse the spring clouds.
They frolic in the water, damp with fragrant mud,
Then soar into the mist in the light of the setting sun.
They intermittently dart up and back down,
Their red beaks grazing on the green cress.

Rising at Dawn: An Expression of Feelings

The wind disperses the scattered clouds,
    and the sky turns a rosy hue.
The tame cranes beneath the pines
    dance on the dark green moss.
Ants drag seeds from the elm tree
    along the window ledge.
Bees laden with flower pollen
come bumbling to the railing.
The green of a single downpour
    floods the Split-Bamboo Garden,[151]
The blue of the surrounding mountains
    pressing against the Zither-Playing Terrace.
Feeling peaceful and calm, I stand alone
    beneath the setting sun
As rows of crows stir up a racket
    in the old scholar-trees.

答蕊仙六姊

巫峽行雲夢已遥
不須禪棒與詩瓢
白雲深處青山裏
一箇蒲團萬慮消

152 Ruixian 蕊仙 was the style name of Wu Qi, 吳琪 (d. 1672), who, like Shiyan, was known
    for her painterly and poetic skills, and who, like Shiyan, also became a nun (see Shangjian
    Huizong 上鑒輝宗, p. 69). The term "older sister" is used affectionately to address a
    close female friend.

A Reply to Sixth Elder Sister Ruixian[152]

The clouds drifting over Wu Gorge
    are now but a distant dream.[153]
There is no need for Chan blows
    or gourds for storing poems.[154]
In my hideaway in the blue mountains
    deep in white clouds,
On a single meditation mat,
    ten thousand worries melt away.

153 According to a popular legend, King Huai of Chu once visited Mount Wu, where he
    fell asleep and dreamed that he had a sexual encounter with the Yaoji, the goddess of
    Clouds and Rain. The image of clouds over Mount Wu is often used to suggest sexual
    desire, which in this line the poet suggests she has completely relinquished.
154 Literally, "poetry gourd." The late Tang dynasty poet and recluse Tang Qiu 唐求 (fl. c.
    880–907) used to toss his poems into a large dipper that he'd fashioned from a gourd.
    When he grew ill, he threw the gourd into the river, saying, "If these writings do not
    sink, then the one who finds them will understand the sorrows of my heart." In fact,
    some of his poems are included in the *Complete Tang Poems*.

宛仙

庵中寫懷

禪關晝掩絕塵蹤
前有修篁後有松
野鶴去時人少伴
曉雲起處壁添峰
當時自識塵緣淺
今日誰知道味濃
千里赤繩從此斷
超然何用講三從

---

155 See Wanyan Yun Zhu 1831, 1836, *fulu* 18b; and Shen Shanbao 1846, 12b. Wanxian's poetry
collection was titled *Wanxian's Poetry Drafts* (*Wanxian shichao* 宛仙詩鈔).

156 According to Chinese folk belief, the gods bind the feet of couples karmically destined
to be together with red silk cord. Here, the poet is referring to the fact that this bond
has been cut by the death of her husband.

Wanxian

Wanxian 宛仙, whose family name was Shi 石, was from Changzhou, Jiangsu province. She married, but, it appears, her husband died prematurely, and the family fell on difficult times. She became a nun and took up residence in a small hermitage on East Dongting Mountain on the southern end of Lake Tai in Jiangsu province. She left a collection of poetry, but the poem translated here appears to be the only one extant.[155]

Inside the Convent: Reflections

The Chan gates were closed the entire day,
    untouched by worldly affairs.
In front, groves of slender bamboo,
    and in back a forest of pine.
The wild cranes have gone away,
    and few companions remain.
When the clouds emerge at dawn
    the peaks beyond seem to multiply.
In times gone by, I came to realize
    the shallowness of worldly roots.
Today who is there who understands
    the profound flavor of the Way?
The red cord that stretched a thousand *li*
    has now been cut in two.[156]
In this sublime setting, it makes no sense
    to talk about the Three Followings.[157]

---

157   The Three Followings 三從 refers to the traditional Confucian assertion that as a daughter, a woman should follow, or submit to, her father; as a wife, to her husband; and as a mother, to her son.

蓮花可度

偈

脫體風流竟莫窮
堂堂獨露主人公
朝來換水焚香課
盡在尋常日用中

158   See Chaoyong 1697, 447b04–11.

Lianhua Kedu

Lianhua Kedu was the eldest child of the Tian 田 family of Huai'an, Jiangsu province. When she was young, her father, a court official, was executed, and after seeing his corpse, she set her heart on leaving the world. In her late thirties, she was finally able to pay a visit to Chan Master Sanyi Mingyu 三宜明盂 (1599–1665) and later to Chan Master Jie'an Wujin 介菴悟進 (1612–1673). She repeatedly asked to be allowed to take the tonsure, but apparently to no avail. Only when she coughed up blood did Jie'an Wujin, convinced of her determination, agree to give her tonsure and allow her to be his disciple. After many years of arduous practice under his guidance, she received dharma transmission and subsequently became the abbess of Lianhua Convent in Xiuzhou, Zhejiang province.[158]

Gāthā

Get naked, and the ease you feel
   will know no end,[159]
As you manifest most gloriously
   your original true self.
At daybreak, change the water
   and light the incense.
It's all about the ordinary things
   of the everyday world.

---

159 To cast off the body, or to "get naked," is to become enlightened. This verse was apparently composed after Lianhua Kedu's first experience of awakening.

印月行霖

山中偶

伏龍不會禪
問者只粗拳
高臥重岩下
都忘歲與年
堪嗟逐世客
勞勞天地間
愧予百不會
贏得一身閒

---

160 See Wang Duanshu 1667, 26:1b. The collection of Yinyue Xingling's recorded sayings
was titled *The Recorded Sayings of Chan Master Yinyue of Fulong* (*Fulong Yinyue chanshi
yulu* 伏龍印月禪師語錄).

Yinyue Xinglin

Yinyue Xinglin, family name Pan 潘, was from Yuyao, Zhejiang province. She was the niece of the well-known scholar, naturalist, and politician Huang Zongxi 黃宗羲 (1610–1695). Even as a young girl, she showed a distaste for worldly things and found pleasure in quiet sitting. Although she was married at the age of fifteen, she did not abandon her spiritual aspirations and began to dress in Daoist garb. It is unknown whether her husband died or she decided to leave him, but at the age of twenty-seven, she took the tonsure with Linji Chan Master Ruo'an Tongwen 箬庵通問 (1604–1655) and four years later received full ordination under Chan Master Feiyin Tongrong 費隱通容 (1593–1661). She lived for a time in a grass hut in the mountains, but left to study with the Linji Chan master Linye Tongqi 林野通奇 (1595–1652), who named her as one of his dharma successors just before he died. Wang Duanshu, who apparently carefully read Yinyue's (now lost) collection of recorded sayings, remarks that Yinyue's religious poetry provides evidence for those who need it that "the ability to realize the Great Way has nothing to do with whether one is a man or a woman."[160]

In the Mountains

This hidden dragon knows nothing of Chan.[161]
Anyone who asks will get but a fist in reply!
Living in seclusion beneath the rows of cliffs,
I completely forget the passing of the years.
Pitiable are those who chase after the world,
Toiling wearily between heaven and earth.
Although ashamed that I don't know a thing,
I've succeeded in realizing a life of leisure!

161 People of insight and integrity who retreated to the mountains during times of political corruption were often referred to as hidden dragons.

三頓棒

> 臨濟枉遭三頓棒
> 令人千古恨難休
> 而今冷地思量起
> 悔不當初打睦州

頌古

> 纔有纖毫即是塵
> 何須啐啄辨疎親
> 太平本是將軍定
> 不許將軍見太平

---

162 According to the version of Linji's enlightenment found in the *Blue Cliff Record* (Cleary 1998, 72), when the young monk who would one day become the great master Linji Yixuan went to study at the monastery of Huangbo Xiyun 黃蘗希運, he spent the first three years doing menial labor before coming to the attention of Muzhou, the head monk. Recognizing Linji's potential, Muzhou advised him to seek out Huangbo and ask him the question "What is the fundamental principle of Buddhism." Linji took his advice but instead of answering his question, Huangbo Xiyun hit him three times. Bewildered, Linji left the monastery and embarked on a genuine spiritual search. Yinyue appears to be playing with this story. Clearly, Muzhou's role turned out to be pivotal, even though at the time it may have seemed unhelpful to Linji. See also CBETA T48, no. 2003, 151c27–a13.

The Three Blows

Linji had to endure
    three unfair blows,[162]
Making people through the ages
    feel resentful!
But today considering
    the situation objectively,
They'd probably regret
    not striking Muzhou at the start!

A Verse Commentary

Even if just a tiny particle remains,
    it is still considered dust.[163]
So why peck from inside and out,
    and distinguish distant and near?[164]
Although in the end the great peace[165]
    is decided by generals,
The generals are never allowed
    to witness that great peace.[166]

163 In Buddhist terminology, dust (which is stirred up by the busy traffic of carts and horses on the road) is a symbol for the secular world.

164 Pecking from inside and outside refers to the relationship between teacher and student, the one "pecking" at the egg from outside, the other from inside, with the ultimate goal of having the student emerge from the "egg" as an awakened person. Here the poet seems to be saying that even this sort of gradual training is ultimately unnecessary, as there is ultimately no distinction between teacher and student.

165 The great peace refers to an utopian era of social order and tranquility. Here it clearly refers to a state of awakening.

166 This popular adage is used to lament a situation in which someone who has achieved something meritorious is often forgotten or ignored afterward. Chinese Chan masters, however, often used this expression to convey the notion that once worldly delusions are exhausted, all of this becomes irrelevant.

三聖逢人即出興化逢人不出

一唱無生曲
一撫沒絃琴
一曲兩曲無人會
雨過夜塘秋水深

---

167 The Tang dynasty Linji Chan master Sansheng Huiran 三聖慧然 once told his congregation that when he saw people coming, he would go out right away to meet them, but then do nothing for them. When he heard about this, Chan Master Xinghua Cunjiang 興化存奬 told his own congregation that he did not go out when he saw people coming, but he did immediately do something for them. The question posed by the poet is whether there is any difference between these two approaches. CBETA X68, no. 1315, 34b20–21; translated in Luk 1974 (189). See Wang Duanshu 1667, 26:2b.

When Sansheng Saw People, He Went Out; When Xinghua Saw People, He Did Not[167]

One sings the tune of the Birthless,
And one strokes the stringless zither.
There are one or two tunes neither one knows.
After a night of rain, the well is full of autumn water.

安生

詠蠶

甕繭空傳異
人衣豈誑天
只應方老病
未合喻參禪
死去悲絲盡
甦來羨翼全
本無鱗角勢
雪覆亦徒然

168 See *Wuxian zhi* 1642, 74:39. This source also notes that originally there was a painted
     portrait of her in the convent.
169 There may be an allusion here to a famous line from a poem by the Song poet Lu You
     陸游 (1125–1209) in which he compares a human life to a spring silkworm spinning a
     cocoon in which it binds itself.
170 This line may refer to a passage in the *Jingde Era Transmission of the Lamp* arguing that
     when one is overly attached to method and form, then sitting in meditation is to be
     like a silkworm spitting out silk and wrapping itself in it. If so, Ansheng seems not to
     agree with the analogy.

Ansheng

There is very little biographical information about Ansheng, apart from the fact that she was from Wuxian, Jiangsu province, and lived at Shanshuiyue Convent located on Dongting Mountain at the southern end of Lake Tai. Apparently, she was known for her zither playing, as well as for her poems. According to one source, Ansheng died when she was in her late teens, so she may well have entered the convent at a very young age.[168]

Ode to the Silkworm

The emptiness of the silk cocoon produces marvels
Like clothing. How can one fault Heaven?
This may work as an analogy for illness and aging,[169]
But not for sitting in meditation.[170]
When it dies, one is sad the silkworm's threads have finished;
When it's reborn, one marvels at its butterfly wings.
It lacks the power of scales or horns,[171]
And if covered by snow, all will be lost.[172]

---

171 The silkworm lacks scales or horns to protect itself, yet can still achieve transformation.
172 The meaning of this line is not entirely clear. The poet may be referring to the fact that a practitioner needs the supportive environment of a convent, or perhaps a meditation practice, to make spiritual progress, just as silkworms need warmth to survive.

輓旃那

玉容從此謝空華
小閣游絲護碧紗
宛轉曾遮松下扇
清幽誰供佛前花
蒲團初撤憐春月
貝葉空遺映晚霞
幾處香温悲手澤
青鞋倚壁冷袈裟

173　See Xu Shichang 1990, 9146.

Mourning Zhanna[173]

Her jade-like face is now
  but an illusory flower.
The cabinet in the little pavilion
  is draped in gossamer.[174]
Who now will use the pleated fan
  beneath the pine trees?
Who will place delicate flowers
  before the Buddha?
Her meditation mat, now unused,
  is pitied by the spring moon.
Her sutra book left abandoned,
  is lit up by the sunset clouds.
In a few places lingers a sweet warmth—
  the sadness of things left behind.
Her blue shoes against the wall,
  her cassock grown cold.

---

174 Zhanna appears to be the name of a fellow nun who died young. The reference here is
to her funerary portrait, which would be placed in a small memorial cabinet or shelf
within the convent, along with various objects that once belonged to her.

傳正

辭世偈

　五十餘年似夢中
　今朝四大各西東
　了明性海無生法
　更有何言説苦空

Zhuanzheng

Zhuanzheng, whose family name was Miao 繆, was from Renhe, Zhejiang province. She was married off as a concubine to Ni Shaosu 倪昭素 after the death of both his children by his first wife, Madame Wang. After Zhuanzheng gave birth to a son, she left to become a nun at Wanshan Convent in Hangzhou. Eight years later, however, Ni Shaosu died and Zhuanzheng took over the care of both Madame Wang and her own son, who himself eventually took ordination, assuming the religious name of Zhaodeng 超燈. By this time, Zhuanzheng had become quite well known for her religious teaching, especially among the local gentry women.

Deathbed Gāthā

A little over fifty years,
  appear as if in a dream.
Today the four elements
  scatter east and west.
I've seen reality as it is,
  birth and death both illusions.
What need is there to say any more
  of suffering and emptiness.

智生

詠雪

霏霏玉屑點窗紗
碎碎瓊珂響翠華
乍可庭前吟柳絮
不知何處認梅花

菊花

簾幕暗生香
奇葩勝艷妝
不隨秋草萎
獨立傲繁霜

175   See Wanyan Yun Zhu 1831, 1836, *fulu* 17a–b; and Shen Shanbao 1846, 5b.

Zhisheng

Zhisheng (1635–1653) was from Qiantang (present-day Hangzhou), Zhejiang province. Her secular name was Huang Ling 黄埈, and she was the granddaughter of the famous female scholar Gu Hezhi 顧若璞 (1592–1681). She started to compose poetry very early, it is said, and she gave up eating meat and devoted herself to Buddhist practice as a child. In her early teens, she took the tonsure with her uncle, the Buddhist monk Shigong Dabin 石公大璸 (1593–1661). Having long suffered from ill health, she died not long afterward. It is said that when she died, the room filled with a marvelous fragrance, and over twenty relics were found in her ashes after her cremation. Apart from her poetry, she may also have written a commentary, unfortunately no longer extant, on the Diamond Sutra.[175]

Ode to the Snow

Thick and fast the powdered jade
　　dots the window screen,
Gently tinkling like the ornaments
　　on a royal headdress.
Here in the courtyard, I can only
　　recite the willow catkin poem,
Having no idea where I might
　　glimpse the plum blossoms.[176]

The Chrysanthemum

The hanging screen secretly exudes the fragrance
Of a flower more exotic than any adorned beauty.
It does not wilt along with the autumn grasses,
But stands alone defying the heavy frost.

176　The fourth-century woman poet Xie Daoyun 謝道韞 is best remembered for a few lines she composed as a girl in which she compares the swirling flakes of snow to willow catkins.

德日

初秋

蕭然一葉下梧桐
初覺涼生小閣風
暑氣潛消人意爽
臥看新月到簾櫳

涼夜西風枕簟清
鐘聲送月傍柴荊
寒蛩也識秋光到
砌下窗前處處鳴

輕煙冷露染衣寒
無數流螢繞畫欄
睡起悄然時悵望
秋聲一片在林端

177   See Wanyan Yun Zhu 1831, 1836, *fulu* 8b. Deri's most well-known collection was titled
The *Brushing Away Melancholy Collection* (*Fuchou ji* 拂愁集).

Deri

Deri, whose secular name was Jiang Kui 蔣葵 (style name Bingxin 冰心)
was from Jiashan, Zhejiang province. She became known at a young age for
her poetry writing, precocious intelligence, and good memory. It would
appear that even after her marriage, she continued her studies at night. Her
marriage, however, was an unhappy one, and she left to take up residence
at Qinglian Convent. Deri left several collections of poetry, most of which
were written before she became a nun.[177]

Early Autumn

A single sad and sorry leaf
    falls from the paulownia tree.
For the first time I feel a chill
    in the breeze by the small pavilion.
As the summer heat abates,
    people begin to feel refreshed.
I lie and watch the new moon
    approach the curtained window.

A cool night, a western breeze,
    pillow and mat both fresh.
The sound of bells sends the moon
    to accompany the brushwood gate.
The autumn crickets also know
    that the autumn glow has come.
On the steps in front of the window,
    everywhere, they chirp away.

A light mist and cold dew
    render my robe damp and chilly
While countless flitting fireflies
    circle the painted railing.
Waking, I quietly rise from bed
    and gaze into the distance,
Toward the sounds of autumn
    at the far end of the woods.

雨窗有感

梨花零落事堪悲
訴與孤窗夜雨知
靜坐幾回憐命薄
顰蛾正是斷腸時

Feelings by a Rainy Window

Pear blossoms bedraggled and worn
    make things even sadder.
I complain with the lonely window;
    the night rains understand.
How many times have I sat quietly
    grieving over my sad fate?
Brow furrowed over what is truly
    a time of heartbreak.

德月

秋夜聞蛩

　蛩音唧唧最關情
　無限秋光映畫屏
　銀燭高燒更漏永
　不堪聽處總成吟

178　See Wanyan Yun Zhu 1831, 1836, *fulu* 13b.

Deyue

Deyue, whose secular name was Jiang Hui 蔣蕙 (style names Yujie 玉潔 and Xueluan 雪巒), was from Taizhou, Jiangsu province. Some unknown misfortune led her to join her elder sister, Jiang Kui 蔣葵, at Qinglian Convent. There she took the religious name "Virtuous Moon" to complement her sister's religious name "Virtuous Sun" (Deri 德日).[178]

On an Autumn Night, Listening to the Crickets

The sound of crickets chirping away
    is the one that most stirs the heart.
An autumn moon that has no bounds
    shines on the patterned screen.
The silver candle burns on high;
    the sand clock drips without end.
When I can no longer bear to listen,
    I decide to pen a verse.

智圓

弔彭娥

匹婦得成名
寒門志甚貞
乳雛憐燕羽
逐婦惡鳩聲
智以窮愁短
身因激烈輕
寸膚如可鬻
涇渭不分明

---

179 See Wanyan Yun Zhu 1831, 1836, *fulu* 13b.

180 Destitute, Peng E was urged by her husband to sell her services as a wet nurse. She appears to have considered this to be akin to prostitution, and she hung herself rather than comply with his demands. Her story can be seen as a refutation of the assumption that women not fortunate enough to be born into the gentry class were incapable of adhering to the Confucian ideals of female chastity. In her comment on this poem, the nineteenth-century female critic Shen Shanbao wrote, "This story and this poem are both worthy of being remembered through the ages" (see Shen Shanbao 1846, 12:16a).

Zhiyuan

Zhiyuan was from Changshu (present-day Suzhou), Jiangsu province. Little is known about her, except that she was lauded for her poetry writing skills, and that her family name was Yin 殷.[179]

A Lament for Peng E

An ordinary woman who attained fame—
Though poor, she kept her chaste ideals.[180]
Suckling her chicks, caring for the swallow wings,
A pressured woman, she resented the cooing dove.[181]
Poverty makes short shrift of wisdom;
Drastic action makes light of the body.
To think that an inch of skin can be sold
Is to fail to distinguish the Jing and Wei.[182]

181 The female dove, often used in Chinese literature as a symbol of simplicity, if not stupidity, is sometimes seen as a virtue in a woman. Here, however, the cooing dove appears to refer to the husband rather than to the wife. The poet may have been thinking of the poem "The Cooing Dove" (*Mingjiu* 鳴鳩), by the great Song dynasty poet Ouyang Xiu 歐陽修 (1007–1072), about a husband who chases his wife away during times of adversity and is surprised when she does not come running back when he tells her to return. See Fu Xuancong, ed., *Quan Songshi* 全宋詩 (*Complete Song Dynasty Poems*), p. 3648.
182 When the waters of the Jing River flow into those of the Wei, it becomes impossible to distinguish between the clear waters of the one and the turbid waters of the other. In other words, her husband has confused the good and the bad.

祇園行剛

孟夏關中閒詠

諸老門庭家業盛
自知疏拙隱為安
玄機棒喝都休歇
萬法虛融莫問禪

183   For more on Qiyuan Xinggang, see Grant 2008, 37–76. The collection of Qiyuan Xing-
gang's recorded sayings is titled *Recorded Sayings of Chan Master Qiyuan of Fushi* (*Fushi
Qiyuan chanshi yulu* 伏獅祇園禪師語錄).

Qiyuan Xinggang

Qiyuan Xinggang (1597–1654), born in Jiaxing, Jiangsu province, was the only child of the scholar Hu Rihua 胡日華 and his wife, Madam Tao 陶. Even as a young girl, she was known for her intelligence and talent for writing poetry. Attracted to the religious life, she expressed a desire to remain unmarried, but her parents betrothed her to a young scholar who died before the wedding could take place. She subsequently devoted herself to the care of her fiancé's parents and her own. In her early thirties and after the death of her parents, she finally entered the religious life. She became a disciple of the Linji Chan master Miyun Yuanwu and then later of Shiche Tongsheng 石車通乘 (1593–1638), who before his death named her as one of his dharma successors. Eventually, she was invited by Madame Dong 董, a Buddhist laywoman of means, to live in her private nunnery, then called simply the Dong Nunnery, in nearby Meili 梅里 not far from Jiaxing. Several years later, the nunnery was renamed Fushi Chan Hall (Fushi Chanyuan 伏獅禪院), and with Qiyuan as abbess, it began to attract followers. Qiyuan was a charismatic and eloquent teacher, and people came from all over to listen to her sermons and dharma talks. When she died, she left behind numerous lay disciples, both male and female. Most significantly, she named seven female dharma successors at a time when women—if they received dharma transmission at all—did so from male teachers. The collection of her recorded sayings is one of the few of such collections by women Chan masters extant today.[183]

The First Month of Summer Retreat: A Song of Leisure

Behind the old gates of the convent,
    the household is flourishing.[184]
Aware of my failings and inadequacies,
    I seek some peace in seclusion.
Esoteric methods, blows, and shouts—
    I set them all aside.
All phenomena merge in emptiness,
    so quit asking about Chan!

---

184 Here Qiyuan Xinggang is referring to the work of maintaining the convent of which she
     is abbess.

百結鶉衣倒掛肩
饑來吃飯倦時眠
蒲團穩坐渾忘世
一任窗前日月遷

高臥雲嶒寄幻軀
白雲翠竹兩依依
眼前幻境隨遷變
深掩柴扉樂有餘

茅舍風高孰敢親
棒風喝月走煙雲
儼然寶鉢虛空托
淡飯黃齏自現成

A tattered patchwork robe
   hangs on my shoulders.
I eat when I'm hungry;
   when I'm tired, I sleep.
Sitting firmly on the meditation mat,
   I completely forget the world
As in front of my window
   the days and months go by.

Resting up in these cloudy peaks,
   all illusions are swept away.
White clouds and green bamboo
   lean against each other.
Before my eyes this magical scene
   performs its transformations.
Shutting my brushwood gate,
   my happiness spills over.

A thatched hut buffeted by winds—
   who would dare come near?
The blows of the wind and shouts of the moon
   keep away the mist and clouds.
Solemnly, I raise my alms bowl
   up to the empty heavens.
Plain rice and minced yellow pickle
   will soon be ready.

示徐道人超古

> 修行須忍耐
> 煩惱自然輕
> 真實為生死
> 念佛貴精勤

> 一心無間斷
> 有何不解脫
> 念念不離佛
> 從此生死歇

> 平等自性中
> 蕩然了無物
> 拍手任逍遙
> 不負余饒舌

示明元

> 在家學道人
> 不用別追尋
> 貪嗔憎愛斷
> 步步證無生

---

185 "Person of the Way" 道人 is a term used by both Daoists and Buddhists that refers to someone who has embarked on the religious path, whether a monastic or a lay practitioner.

Dharma Instructions for Person of the Way Xu Chaogu[185]

Practice demands patience and forbearance,
But then your anxieties will naturally ease.
Ultimate Reality is a matter of life and death.
You must diligently recite Buddha's name.[186]

If you are single-minded and undistracted,
How can you not achieve liberation?
Once every single thought is on the Buddha,
The cycle of life and death will cease!

In the midst of equanimity and essential nature,
You will understand that things do not exist.[187]
You will clap your hands in untrammeled joy,
All without needing to blather about it!

Dharma Instructions for Mingyuan

Someone who studies the Way at home
Has no need to search for it elsewhere.
Cut off greed, anger, and attachment,
And step by step realize the Unborn.

---

186 Note that although Qiyuan Xinggang is a Chan master, here she is recommending the
     Pure Land practice of reciting the name of Amitabha Buddha to this lay practitioner.
187 That is, that all things are empty of a fixed and unchanging essence.

誕日示眾

　　衲僧不與世人同
　　無滅無生任運中
　　若是慶生應有死
　　箇中窺破壽無窮

和鄭雲渡秋亭吟

　　大地渾然一草亭
　　煙雲晨夕繞為櫺
　　松龕石壁無餘響
　　秋色空清誰解聽

詠梅花

　　梅開雪裏倍精神
　　清徹馨香遍界聞
　　透出一枝天外動
　　園林獨占自芳芬

188　Jiang Yundu 鄭雲渡 was a layman who often visited Qiyuan Xinggang.

Addressing the Congregation on My Birthday

A robed monastic is not the same
    as a worldly person:
No extinction and no arising,
    just going with the flow.
If one is attached to birth
    then there will be death;
But when one sees into one's true self,
    one will live forever!

Matching Jiang Yundu's "Autumn Pavilion Song"[188]

The great earth completely merged
    into a single thatched pavilion:
Mist and clouds at dawn and dusk
    encircle the carved windowsills.
A shrine of pines and walls of stone:
    there are no lingering echoes.
Autumn colors and a clear sky—
    who knows how to hear them?

Ode to the Plum Blossom

The plum tree blossoms in the snow,
    with their especially fecund spirit,
Fill the air with a pure fragrance
    that one can smell from afar.
Just a single blossoming branch
    wafts beyond the heavens,
And in every garden its scent
    is the most aromatic of all.

義公超珂

Yigong Chaoke

Yigong Chaoke (1615–1661) was a native of Meili, Zhejiang province. Little is known of her life, apart from the fact that she was placed in a convent at the age of seven. It is not known where she lived or with whom she studied over the next several decades. Sometime around 1646, right in the middle of the violent upheavals of the Ming-Qing transition, Yigong and a fellow nun, Yiquan 義全 (d. 1660), moved to Nanxun, not far from Meili, where the pious laywoman Madame Dong (see p. 149) arranged for them to take up residence at a small convent that she had established there. Over the next several years, she studied with several eminent male Chan masters, including Caodong Chan Master Shiyu Mingfang 石雨明方 (1593–1648), who was then living in Hangzhou, and Linji Chan Master Jiqi Hongchu, who was living on Mount Lingyan, outside of Suzhou. It was during this time that Yigong met Zukui Xuanfu 祖揆玄符, one of Jiqi Hongchu's female dharma successors (see p. 183). Around 1650 Yigong and Yiquan both became disciples of Qiyuan Xinggang at Fushi Convent. For the next few years, Yigong studied intensively with Qiyuan, serving also as her personal attendant. She appears not to have taken much pleasure in her many administrative duties, however, and requested permission to return to her old convent in Nanxun to do a solitary closed retreat. In the spring of 1654, Qiyuan Xinggang fell ill and summoned Yigong to her bedside, giving Yigong dharma transmission and entrusting her with the leadership of Fushi Convent, with Yiquan serving as her assistant. In 1660 Yiquan suddenly fell ill and passed away, leaving Yigong with the sole responsibility not only of maintaining the convent but of keeping Qiyuan Xinggang's lineage alive. Soon Yigong herself fell gravely ill. A year later, after entrusting the leadership of the convent to another of Qiyuan Xinggang's disciples, Yikui Chaochen, Yigong died at the age of forty-six. Fortunately, the collection of Yigong's recorded sayings remains extant today.[189]

哭本師和尚

> 月落西沉三度秋
> 床頭麈尾不曾收
> 簷前祇樹分枝淚
> 風起禪堂雨潺愁
> 二十年來海內師
> 縱橫拄杖絕支離
> 爐煙丈室何曾滅
> 慚愧兒孫似舊時

登靈隱茅蓬望飛來峰偶占

> 靈隱峰巒瑞氣騰
> 英賢到此盡沾恩
> 飛來踏破無痕跡
> 大地山河一掌平

190 The fly whisk is the symbol of a Chan master's spiritual authority.
191 Qishu or Jetavana (Jeta's Grove) was the name of one of the most famous monasteries
     in India where the Buddha often spent time. Here it refers to Qiyuan as well as all of
     her grieving disciples, who are compared to the branches of a mighty tree.

Grieving for My Master

The moon sinks in the west
   and autumn comes to an end.
The fly whisk at the head of her couch
   has not been put away.[190]
In front of the eaves of the Jetavana,
   all the branches weep.[191]
A breeze rises in the meditation hall
   as the rain mournfully falls.
For the past twenty years
   she was everyone's teacher,
Freely wielding her walking staff,
   putting an end to dissent.
The smoke from her quarters
   never once faded away.[192]
I'd be ashamed if her descendants
   are as they were before.[193]

*Climbing Up to a Thatched Hut on Lingyin and Gazing at
Feilai Peak: An Impromptu Poem*[194]

From the peaks and cliffs of Lingyin,
   the auspicious vapors rise.
The heroic and wise have come here
   and been bathed in compassion.
Clambering over Feilai Peak
   without leaving a single trace,
While the world's mountains and rivers
   lie flat in the palm of one's hand.

192 In other words, the stove in her abbess quarters was constantly lit, as she was always
     meeting with students.
193 Yigong felt a deep responsibility to carry on the rare female lineage established by Qi-
     yuan Xinggang. Her fears appear to have been justified, as after her death it essentially
     disappeared, largely due to a lack of support by the male monastic community.
194 Feilai Peak 飛來峰 faces Hangzhou's Lingyin temple. Its name means "Flying-Over
     Peak" and refers to the traditional legend that it flew over from India to its present spot.
     It has long been an important scenic site and is covered with numerous odd-shaped
     boulders, as well as hundreds of Buddhist statues dating from the tenth to the fourteenth
     centuries.

一揆 超琛

和禪坐偈五首（步原韻）

　打破重關隨處安
　無心于物更瀟狀
　閒來危坐松陰下
　漸看蟾蜍東上懸

195　For more on Yikui Chaochen, see Grant 2008, 77–106. The collection of her recorded
　　sayings is titled *Recorded Sayings of Chan Master Cantong Yikui* (*Cantong Yikui chanshi
　　yulu* 參同一揆禪師語錄).

Yikui Chaochen

Yikui Chaochen was one of the seven dharma successors of Chan Master Qiyuan Xinggang. Born to a family of scholar-officials, she quickly acquired a reputation for artistic and poetic talent. She married a young scholar, who died suddenly in 1648. The young widow turned to Buddhism, and after spending some years living in seclusion at home, she sought out the guidance of Qiyuan Xinggang at Fushi Convent, where she eventually took ordination. After Qiyuan Xinggang's death in 1654, Yikui became the abbess of Cantong Convent, which her younger brother had built for her. Over time, Yikui attracted many disciples, and the convent began to grow. In 1661 Yigong Chaochen, the abbess of Fushi Convent, asked Yikui to take over her position. Yikui spent six years as the abbess of Fushi Convent before returning to Cantong Convent, where she died in 1679 at the age of fifty-three. The collection of her recorded sayings was included in *The Jiaxing Chinese Buddhist Canon* (CBETA J), which ensured its survival.[195]

Five Gāthās: Sitting in Meditation (To a Previous Tune)

The layered gates having been smashed open
    everywhere is peaceful.
When the mind is unattached,
    everything becomes pure.
In these moments of leisure,
    I sit in the shade of the pines,
Watching the toad in the moon
    slowly rise to hover in the east.[196]

---

196 According to Chinese legends, Chang'e, later known as the Moon Goddess, stole the elixir of immortality from her husband, Houyi the archer, after which she fled to the moon and hid from him in the form of a toad.

假饒說法墜天花
擬議尋思被物遮
觸境遇緣無不是
敲空取髓作生涯

浩浩談玄疊似雲
相逢難得箇知音
紅爐突出超凡志
宿有天機轉法輪

197 Before leaving China, Bodhidharma posed a question to his students to determine who
would receive his dharma transmission. When the monk Huike answered not with
words but with silence, Bodhidharma declared that Huike had "grasped his marrow"
and he declared Huike his dharma successor (see the Introduction).

When one freely speaks of the dharma,
    heavenly flowers fall,
But when one deliberates and debates,
    one just ends up confused.
Given opportunity and good fortune,
    there is nothing that can't be done.
Knocking and extracting the marrow
    will become a way of life.[197]

How wonderful it is to discuss
    mysteries layered like clouds.
It is truly rare to meet someone
    one can call a kindred soul,
Who burns like a red-hot furnace
    with extraordinary resolve,
And has the natural capacity
    to turn the dharma wheel.[198]

198 A metaphor for spreading the Buddha's teachings.

勞生汩汩姿貪嗔
頓發心花大地春
烹雪煮茶消白晝
胸懷廓徹若永輪

輕舟帶月水生花
菡萏花開暗度香
聞見覺知無別法
頭陀嬾散髮垂長

步原韻

沒絃琴不落
宮商調轉新
二十餘年空裏覓
瞻風撥草少知音

破茅菴兩扇
柴扉不用關
翠竹老梅真我友
白雲堆裏露青山

199 These refer to the functions of the six sorts of consciousness: seeing, the function of
visual consciousness; hearing, a function of auditory consciousness; recognizing, the
function of the senses of smell, taste, and touch; and knowing, the function of the
intellect.

This hard life is chaotic and confusing:
    lust, greed, and anger.
But when suddenly the flower of the mind opens,
    it is spring everywhere in the world.
Melting snow to make the tea,
    I while away the entire day.
My mind wide-open and far-reaching,
    like the round bright moon.

My little boat, bathed in moonlight,
    stirs up flowers of foam.
Water lilies that have blossomed
    send over their fragrance.
Seeing, hearing, recognizing, knowing[199]
    are all a single dharma.
Lazy when it comes to asceticism,
    I let my hair grow long.

To a Previous Tune

The stringless zither has not been laid down,
But the tune has changed to something new.
For over twenty years I've sought the Void,
Uprooting weeds and hoping for a breeze, but true friends are rare.[200]

A tumbledown hermitage with a shuttered door.
A brushwood gate that never needs to be shut.
Jade bamboo and old plum trees are truly my friends.
Blue mountains peek out from within the white clouds.

200 The weeds being uprooted are those of delusion, and the anticipated compassionate
    breeze is that of the Buddha and his teachings.

朽木舟把定
風帆泛逆流
野塘謾唱無生曲
且向清波再下鈎

破衲襖零零
落落無人要
脫下方知棒底恩
夜半日輪當午照

諸兄臨別

蓬門常掩勝居山
為惜浮光未敢閒
今夕共君談不二
黎明分袂荻蘆間

---

201 "Rotten" or "dead wood" is often used to refer to something or someone useless, and certainly not something with which to construct a boat. Here it probably refers to the body, which in the Buddhist worldview is only of limited and temporary use.

My boat of rotten wood is now controlled
And set to sail against the stream of *samsara*.[201]
By a country pond, I unabashedly sing melodies of the Unborn,
And again lower my hook and line into the crystal-clear waves.[202]

My ragged robe and coat are worse for wear,
So tattered and torn that no one would want them.
Only when it's put back down do you know the stick's compassion:
In the middle of the night it shines like the sun shines as if it were
    noon.[203]

Just Before Parting from My Elder Brothers[204]

A bramblewood gate often closed,
    making mountain life the best.
But I regret the quickly fading light
    that leaves us little time for leisure.
This evening, you and I will talk
    about the undivided.[205]
Then at daybreak, we'll part ways
    alongside the river reeds.

202 A golden-scaled fish is a metaphor for an enlightened person not caught by either net
     or hook.
203 The reference here is to the stick with which the compassionate master may strike stu-
     dents to bring them out of their mental ruts and precipitate an experience of awakening.
204 "Elder brothers" probably refers to fellow nuns who have come to visit, although it
     might also refer to her own biological brothers, one of whom Yikui was particularly
     close with.
205 That is, the one undivided reality or Buddha nature.

辭梅溪諸護法

自脫巾瓶隱碧溪
埋名誓不出幽居
禪宗說法如雲疊
祖印高懸別請提
入理深談君自會
涉言形筆眼中翳
當陽一句無私語
千古昭然豈再移

206 Meixi is another name for Meili, where the poet's convent was located.

Bidding Farewell to the Lay Dharma Protectors of Meixi[206]

Having liberated myself, I dip my flask
    in the secluded green brook,
And so retiring to obscurity, I vow to never
    leave my life of seclusion.
In the Chan lineage, dharma preachers
    repeat themselves like clouds,
But the patriarchs' seals hang up high,
    and no one is asked to raise them up.
Penetrating principal with profound talk,
    you will naturally understand
That wading through words and tracing the brush
    is to cover the eyes with a film.
If someone comes up with a single phrase
    that does not stem from ego,
There will be an eternal radiance
    that will never be removed.

參謁雄聖惟極和尚不值有懷

三度參求不見師
聆音未卜在何時
幾回燕語添惆悵
數轉鶯啼動所思
彼亦道豐留錫早
我因德歉遇緣遲
傀無一法堪憑據
幸有東風獨自知

207 In other words, Weiji has found what she was looking for and no longer needs to take
up her staff and travel in search of spiritual enlightenment.

*My Feelings after Visiting Nun Weiji from Xiongsheng and
Not Finding Her In*

I have come seeking counsel three times,
   but have never seen the Master.
I have not yet heard your voice
   and am wondering when I will.
The bursts of swallow chatter
   add to my disappointment,
And the rounds of oriole cries
   stir the reflections in my mind.
The Way flourishes in you,
   and you've already hung up your staff.[207]
Because my virtue is lacking,
   I'm late in finding my destined path.
I'm ashamed that I don't have a single dharma
   that can serve as evidence.
Thankfully, there's an east wind
   that instinctively understands me.

蜂房頌

（其狀甚異有尺餘闊五臺層絡）

行遍青山萬木圍
披雲吸露啟風規
層層樓閣空中建
密密幽居向下垂
活計水邊漚影寂
生涯花底謾徘徊
奔流度刃遭人忌
窠臼掀翻春正回

208 A *chi* is aproximately one-third of a meter.

Hymn: The Honeycomb*

* Author's Note: Its shape was quite unusual: over one chi wide and five tiers high.[208]

Traveling around the blue hills,
 circling ten thousand trees;
Parting the clouds, sipping the dew,
 showing off their high style.
Tier after tier of a tower pavilion,
 built up into the heavens,
This secluded and hidden home
 hangs toward the ground.
Eking out a livelihood by the riverbank
 among the bubbles and shadows;[209]
Spending their lives among the flowers.
 wildly rushing back and forth.
Swarming and rushing with their stingers,
 the bees provoke people's rage;
But even when their nest is knocked over,
 in the spring they'll return again!

209 My translation here is tentative. Water bubbles and shadows are traditional images of
 transience.

頌竹尊者（步原韻）

四時積翠沒榮枯
脫體心空不老臞
歲歲添條留晚節
山山獨坐笑村夫

吟風愒月誰為伴
頑石蒼松可作徒
昔日擊聲空所有
今將眼聽實難無

---

210 "The venerable bamboo" refers to the tallest and largest bamboo in a particular bamboo grove.
211 The bamboo is hollow at its core, and, of course, an empty heart or mind is also key to Chan practice.

In Praise of the Venerable Bamboo (To a Previous Tune)[210]

In all four seasons, a lush emerald green
    that neither flourishes nor fades.
Because its heart is completely empty,[211]
    the bamboo neither ages nor grows weary.
Year after year, it sends out new shoots,
    though it is no longer young.
On mountain after mountain, it sits alone,
    smiling at the village folk.

It sings of the breeze and moon.[212]
    Who will keep it company?
None but silent stones and hoary pines
    to serve as its disciples!
In the past, the sound of its booming
    would empty everything out.
Nowadays, listening with the eyes
    is truly a difficult thing to do.[213]

212 To sing of the moon and the wind is to write verse. In other words, the poem asks, Who
    can keep the bamboo company, as a good friend, by writing an occasional verse.
213 The meaning of this last couplet is unclear, and my translation is tentative. The cou-
    plet may be saying that in the past just the sound of cracking bamboo (or perhaps the
    crack of the master's bamboo warning stick on the student's back) could precipitate an
    enlightenment experience, whereas nowadays, few have the spiritual acuity to "listen
    with the eyes."

臘月十五雪後歸棹口占

西風吹散玉花飛
湖面連坡去路迷
凍鎖蓬窗寒入骨
水晶宮裏作安居

贈竹影禪師

同條天性志超群
五葉流芳互古今
千里盡從初步起
到家不必問途程

214   The five petals refer to the five major sublineages of Chan Buddhism.

On the Fifteenth of the Twelfth Lunar Month, after the Snow,
While Returning Home by Boat, I Improvised This Poem

The gusting west wind sends
    the jade flowers flying.
Rippling waves on the lake surface
    obscure the way ahead.
Ice locks shut the boat's window
    as cold seeps into one's bones.
It's like sitting in a meditation retreat
    inside the crystal moon palace!

Presented to Chan Master Zhuying

The two of us share a similar disposition,
    and an uncommon aspiration.
The five petals send out their fragrance
    over past and present.[214]
The journey of a thousand miles
    begins with the first step.
Once you get home, there's no need
    to inquire about the Way.

洞庭歸舟中偶占

七十二峰雲溫溫
縹緲高頂露華曉
太湖三萬六千頃
閱盡古今人未了

洞庭船子浪滔天
范蠡湖船亦有年
人在此中休問渡
地分南北驗當賢

要知一貫悟先賢
吾道當思痛自鞭
駒隙光陰空過了
百年搔首亦徒然

---

215 East Dongting Mountain is one of two large islands—the other is known as West Dong-
ting Mountain—located on the southern end of Lake Tai in Jiangsu province. Lake Tai
is China's largest freshwater lake, known for its many islets well as the seventy-two
mountain peaks located on the islands and around the lake.

Inside the Boat on My Return Home to Dongting:
An Impromptu Poem

Above the seventy-two mountain peaks
    are clouds of purest white.[215]
From behind the dimly visible summits,
    a glorious dawn breaks.
The waters of Lake Tai extend
    for thirty-six thousand *qing*.[216]
It has seen things past and present
    that humans cannot know.

The boatman from Dongting
    stirs up sky-high waves,
Like Fan Li, who sailed this lake
    so many years ago.[217]
When you are at its center,
    don't ask how to cross over.
You would have to be a sage
    to know north from south!

Understand the one unifying principle
    and be awake, like sages of old.
One should reflect on what I say,
    to avoid causing oneself pain.
Like a colt passing by a crack in the door,
    time passes by in vain.
Pondering on this for an entire lifetime
    will also be of no avail!

216 One *qing* is equivalent to approximately 6.67 hectares. The surface area of Lake Tai is
    quite large, approximately 935 square miles.
217 Fan Li 范蠡 is the name of a fifth-century military strategist best known for having
    helped King Goujian 勾踐 of Yue (present-day northern Zhejiang province) destroy
    the state of Wu in 493 BCE, after which he retired to Lake Tai and spent his days on a
    fishing boat.

辭世偈

這漢一生骨硬如釘
一處轉腳最難移根
二十四上知有此事
十年克苦忘形
四十九上憫絕娑婆世界
覷得世態如冰
實求早離如願
業緣又使七春
目今鐵釘如灰
四大風火分散
葉落知秋
正是歸根時候
啊呵呵
逍遙惟我

218 The term *xiaoyao*, meaning to wander freely, originally comes from *Zhuangzi* and is
     used in Chan literature to describe the unfettered way of life of one who has attained
     enlightenment. "I am the only Honored One" is said to have been uttered by the newly
     born Prince Siddhartha, destined to become the Buddha. More generally, it refers to
     attaining enlightenment.

Deathbed Gāthā

This one has always been as tough as nails.
Once she dug her heels in, she would not budge.
At twenty-four, she first found out about this matter,
Then for ten years struggled to forget the bodily form.
At forty-nine, she cut loose from this suffering world,
Having seen through mundane affairs as if through water.
Having grasped the truth of things, she did as she pleased.
Yet karma kept her going through seven more springs.
Right at this moment, the iron nails will turn to dust,
And the four great elements will disperse like wind and fire.
When the leaves fall, one knows that autumn has come,
And that is the time to return to the root.
Ha! Ha! Ha!
Free and unfettered—"I am the Only Honored One"[218]

祖揆玄符

蜜蜂頌

勘遍諸方得意時
競將同調喚來歸
無餘聲色呈君也
花藥欄邊自在飛

219 In previous publications, I have referred to this nun as Zukui Jifu 祖揆濟符, which
    is the name ascribed to her by the twentieth-century monk-scholar Zhenhua (1988).
    However, Zhenhua appears to have been mistaken.

220 For more on this nun, see Grant 2008, 146–164. Baochi Xuanzong's collections are
    titled *Baochi Zong chanshi yulu* 寶持總禪師語錄 [*The Discourse Records of Chan Master
    Baochi Zong*] and *Lingrui chanshi Yanhuaji* 靈瑞禪師嵒華集 [*Chan Master of Lingrui's
    Cliffside Flower Collection*].

Zukui Xuanfu

Zukui Xuanfu was born in Huzhou, Zhejiang province.[219] We have very little biographical information about her early life, apart from the fact that her family name was Li 李. At some point, she became a disciple of the Linji Chan master Hongchu Jiqi while he was abbot of Lingyan Monastery in Hangzhou. After receiving dharma transmission, Zukui Xuanfu was abbess first of Miaozhan Convent in Xiushui, Zhejiang province, and then of Lingrui Convent, which appears to have been located on East Dongting Mountain. Despite the lack of information about her life, Zukui Xuanfu was one of the most prolific nun-poets of the seventeenth century. She left two collections of writings, both of which are extant and each of which has five chapters. The first is her recorded sayings, compiled during her time as abbess of Miaozhan Convent, and the second is a collection comprised largely of poetry. She also collaborated with her fellow nun Baochi Xuanzong on a collection of over forty poetic responses to poems written by the Song dynasty nun Wuzhuo Miaozong (see the Introduction, p. xvi).[220]

Ode to Honeybees[221]

After exploring in all directions
    and finding what they want,
All of them to the same tune
    are summoned back home.
"There are no other sounds or colors
    that I can give to you:"[222]
By the balustrade around the peonies,
    they freely fly.

221 Zukui Xuanfu notes that she wrote this series of verses using the rhymes of a series of the same title by Linji Chan Master Tianfeng Foci 天封佛慈 of the Song dynasty (see the Introduction, p. xxviii).

222 This may be an allusion to the well-known *gāthā* attributed to Chan Master Sanping Yizhong 三平義忠 (781–872) that reads, "Just this seeing and hearing is not 'seeing' and 'hearing' / and there are no other sounds or forms I can offer you. / If you realize this right here, then nothing will be the matter / and what need will be there to distinguish between theory and practice" (see Chaoyong 1697, 494c18–20.)

逢人便劄遶天涯
苦屈無從一叩銜
莫怪巡官偏杜撰
針鋒要驗當行家

工夫及盡蜜成時
萬別千差永棄離
金網縵縵猶是難
漫云無事即寬脾

同門出入各風光
為眾忙如為己忙
不立一塵家國盛
從前勳業悔承當

---

223 There would appear to be a reference here to the methods of the Chan master, who,
      like a patrolling official, often used rather harsh-seeming methods that were, however,
      regarded as necessary for helping students overcome their delusions.

Chancing upon a human, they sting
   wherever they are in the world.
Regardless of your pain, there's nowhere
   to appeal for justice!
Don't blame the patrolling official
   for willfully fabricating lies.
The needle's point must be sharp
   if one wants to be an expert.[223]

When all their work is finished
   and the honey is made,
All distinctions and differences
   are tossed away forever.[224]
The golden net spreads out like silk,
   but difficulties remain.
Don't say there is no more to be done
   and just let things slide!

From a common gate, they come and go,
   each one in its own style.
They work more for the community
   than they do for themselves.
Without establishing one speck of dust,
   the nation flourishes.[225]
I am ashamed to take any credit
   for achievements from the past.

224 In other words, delusion has been replaced by awakening.
225 The allusion here may be to the words of Chan Master Fengxue Yanzhao 風穴延沼
   (896–973), which became the title of case 61 of *The Blue Cliff Record*: "If you set up
   a single atom of dust, the nation flourishes; if you don't set up a single atom of dust,
   the nation perishes." The general idea seems to be that there are always unintended
   consequences to seemingly good actions. CBETA T48, no. 2003, 193b10–12; translated
   in Cleary 1998, 285–286.

不貪寶惜戀枯桐
個個臨機善變通
堪笑眼中添翳者
忙忙空裏覓花紅

爆竹頌（和靈嵒僧首師原韻）

怪得名喧宇宙中
慣將一喝振玄風
果知響逐聲來也
不必窮年費苦工

收放同時放較危
要通一線蘉頭錐
奮然爆著虛空碎
閃電光中霹靂追

<hr>

226 People who do not understand the nature of suffering are like those with an eyelash in
   the palm of the hand, whereas the wise, who do understand, are like those who know
   the pain of an eyelash in the eye. Here the poet seems to be saying that the foolish have
   an eyelash in the eye, but do not realize the larger implications.

I have no desire for precious baubles,
    but am quite fond of the zither.
Whenever I'm faced with a challenge,
    I can skillfully adjust.
I can't but laugh at all those
    Who have an eyelash in an eye,[226]
As they hustle and bustle in the void,
    always seeking out profit.[227]

*Ode to Fireworks**

* Author's Note: Written using the rhymes of the head monk of Lingyan[228]
I marvel at the famous great clamor
    at the heart of the universe.
I am more used to the single shout
    that stirs the Mysterious Wind.[229]
Once you understand how the echo
    follows upon the sound,
There will be no need to struggle
    to the end of your days.

When grasping and releasing simultaneously,
    releasing is the riskier![230]
The fireworks must be threaded with a single cord
    and drilled straight through.
Then vigorously they go off,
    exploding in the empty void,
As from the gleaming lightning's flash
    comes the thunder's peal.

227   My translation is tentative.
228   This may refer to Zukui Xuanfu's teacher, who was living on Mount Lingyan when she
     studied with him. However, I have found no poem on fireworks among his writings.
229   The mysterious wind is a term used to refer to the profound teachings of the Way, be
     they Buddhist or Daoist.
230   In Chan Buddhism, the ideal is to be able to hold on or let go freely, as required by the
     circumstances and without being attached to one or the other.

金圈拋出自音王
儘有其人瞌睡忙
誰是見煙須辨火
色聲頭上立承當

大小隨緣任去留
正當轟烈得心休
買來輸與他人放
本色金錢肯浪酬

嚇人嚇鬼有多方
拍手呵呵笑一場
勘破恁般關捩子
裝聾作啞又何妨

This may be an allusion to the ancient Buddha by the name of Cloud Thunder Sound, whose name appears in the Flower Garland Sutra.

Flung out of his golden prison
    is the King of Spontaneous Sound,[231]
Sending all the dozing men
    into a sudden flurry.
The one who witnesses the smoke
    and makes out the fire,
Ahead of all the colors and sounds,
    he will quickly take charge.

Large or small, one adapts to things,
    allowing them to come or go.
Then amidst all the *sturm und drang*,
    one's mind will find rest.
As for getting or giving things away,
    leave that to other people.
The gold coins of one's true nature
    will be ample reward!

They frighten people and scare ghosts
    from so many sides.
I clap my hands with a *ha!*
    and a burst of laughter.
Thus have I seen through
    to the heart of the matter.[232]
If I pretend to be deaf and dumb,
    what harm is there in that?

232 In other words, to the heart of Buddhist teachings.

折梅供佛

> 玉顏鉼骨老冰霜
> 眾壑無人獨自芳
> 折得寒香隨手至
> 真堪供養法中王

自贈

> 住山歲月總不記
> 但見四山青又黃
> 博飯栽田爭如我
> 說禪浩浩讓諸方

233　Chan texts abound with criticism of those who talk about Chan, presumably instead of
practicing it. For example, in case 11 of *The Blue Cliff Record*, we find the ninth-century
Chan master Huangbo Xiyun 黃蘗希運 complaining about Chan followers who travel
around endlessly speaking of Chan. He goes so far as to call them "gobblers of dregs!"
See CBETA T48 no. 2003, 151b12–14; translated in Cleary 1998, 73.

Breaking Off a Plum Branch to Offer to the Buddha

With its jade complexion and iron bones,
    the plum branch is older than the ice and frost.
There is no one in the ravines and valleys;
    in solitude it gives off its scent.
Breaking it off, I have its chill fragrance
    conveniently at hand.
It is indeed worthy of offering
    to the King of the Dharma.

To Myself

Living in the mountains for years on end,
    I've long stopped keeping count.
All I notice are the surrounding mountains,
    first green, then yellow.
I barter for rice and plant a garden.
    Who can compete with me?
To go on and on talking about Chan,
    I leave that for others![233]

閒遊古寺

> 古廟香爐冷不禁
> 落花芳草伴啼鶯
> 象王鼻孔無尋處
> 迦葉低頭問世尊
> 翠竹蒼松夾路生
> 得閒領鶴自經行
> 夕陽西下水東去
> 獨立不聞人語聲

還山渡湖

> 舞棹呈橈泛水雲
> 鷺鶿飛入蓼花汀
> 天然一色難分別
> 孤負身心百不靈

---

234   The Lord of the Elephants is another epithet for the Buddha.
235   An epithet for the Buddha.
236   My translation here is tentative.

A Leisurely Visit to an Ancient Temple

The incense burner in the ancient temple
　　has been left to grow cold.
The fallen flowers and fragrant grasses
　　keep chattering orioles company.
In the nostrils of the Elephant Lord's trunk
　　there is no discursive thought.[234]
Yet Mahakasyapa lowers his head
　　to ask the World-Honored One.[235]
Verdant bamboo and hoary pines
　　grow alongside the road.
I am guided at leisure by a crane
　　on a contemplative stroll.
The evening sun sets in the west,
　　while the river flows east.
Standing alone, I cannot hear
　　a single human voice.

Returning to the Mountain, I Cross the Lake

Dancing oars and lifting paddles,
　　I drift with the water's mist.
Ducks and geese wing their way
　　to the lush flowery isle.
Everything is naturally a single hue
　　and hard to tell apart.
Dropping away body and mind,
　　everything is useless![236]

萬頃湖光接遠空
片帆搖曳破秋風
漁歌一曲無人會
蘆葉紛紛對蓼紅

亂雲堆裏數峰高
曳履經行不憚勞
記得去年當此際
石床趺坐聽松濤

歸山自嘲

妙峰孤頂無行路
到者全心當下灰
堪笑白雲無定止
被風吹去又吹來

237 Lake Tai.

The shimmering of this vast lake[237]
   merges with the distant sky.
The little boat rocks and sways
   through the autumn wind.
The song that the fishermen sing
   is one nobody knows.
All the while, the leaves of reeds swirl around
   the pink-hued knotweed.

From a mass of billowing clouds,
   a few peaks rise up high.
There I will wander at ease,
   with no worries or cares.
I recall how in years gone by,
   at this time of the year,
I sat meditating on a stone bed,
   listening to the pine winds.

Returning to the Mountains, I Laugh at Myself

On the lonely summit of Mystic Peak,
   there is no walking path.[238]
The mind of the one who reaches it
   should be reduced to ashes.
It is laughable how the white clouds
   have no resting place.
They are blown away by the wind,
   then blown back again.

---

238 Mystic Peak is the Chinese name for Mount Sumeru, the five-peaked mountain at the center of the universe in Buddhist cosmology. Here the name is being used metaphorically, perhaps to refer to a state of high realization.

月夜閒行

門外峰巒列翠鬟
昏鴉隊隊帶聲還
微風吹落浮雲片
月色如銀萬境閑

秋江如練浸長天
萬籟無聲月正圓
好景不須他處覓
清光只在指頭邊

夢中曾說悟圓通
剔起雙眉月正濃
長嘯一聲驚宇宙
有誰同上最高峰

---

239 There may be an allusion here to the verse by the famous Song dynasty monk painter
and calligrapher Wuzhun Shifan 無準師範 (1178–1249) that reads, "Heavy as a mountain
/ Peaceful as a river / Touch it lightly, a pair of eyebrows have been raised." See CBETA
X70, no. 1382, 271a10.

A Leisurely Stroll on a Moonlit Night

Beyond the gate, rows of peaks
  like coils of a lady's dark hair.
Flock after flock of evening crows
  return with raucous cries.
A gentle breeze blows down
  bits of floating clouds.
The moon the color of silver,
  and the entire world at ease.

The autumn river, like pale silk,
  seeps into the heavens.
Ten thousand soundless flutes,
  and a moon perfectly round.
No need to seek elsewhere
  for a beautiful view
When pure radiance is found
  at your fingertips.

In a dream I heard it said:
  once awakened one sees all.
Raising up my eyebrows,[239]
  the moon, I see, is at its brightest.
Letting out a piercing whistle,
  I startle the universe.
Who will join me in ascending
  to the highest peak?

靈光獨耀迥無鄰
大地山河絕點塵
若謂南泉超物外
馬師賺殺幾多人

芒鞋竹杖破蒼苔
瀟灑胸襟向月開
萬里無雲天一色
好山如畫疊成堆

冬日舟行

雪覆蘆花欲暮天
一江風色正堪憐
螭文萬派難區別
重鼓蘭橈泛鈺船

240 There is a Chan story that also takes place on a moonlit night: "One evening, the monks
Xitang, Baizhang, and Nanquan were viewing the moon with Master Mazu. The master
asked them, 'At just this moment, what is it?' Xitang said, 'Perfect support.' Baizhang
said, 'Perfect practice.' Nanquan shook his sleeves and walked away. Mazu said, 'A sutra
enters the Buddhist canon. Zen returns to the sea. Only Nanquan has gone beyond
things.'" See Ferguson 2000, 68–69.

The numinous light shines alone,
    distant from any neighbor.
On earth's mountains and rivers,
    not a single speck of dust.
If you say that Nanchuan
    has transcended all things,
Then Teacher Ma has deceived
    who knows how many![240]

With straw sandals and bamboo staff,
    I tread the dark green moss.
Feeling free and easy, with my heart
    bared open to the moon.
Ten thousand cloudless miles,
    the skies a single hue.
Fine mountains, as in a painting,
    are piled up against each other.

Traveling by Boat on a Winter Day

Snow blankets the reed flowers
    as the sun begins to set.
A river full of wind colors
    is truly worth treasuring![241]
The myriad lines of dragon script
    are difficult to decipher.[242]
To the steady beat of magnolia oars,
    this iron boat sails along.[243]

241 The term "wind color" is often used in Chan writings to refer to what is nonexistent, such as rabbit's horns or tortoise hair. Here it could also indicate the river scene in general.

242 Here the poet appears to be comparing the ripples of the waves to the so-called dragon script, an old-style calligraphic form with twisty shapes resembling a hornless dragon.

243 Iron boats, like stone maidens and holeless flutes, are paradoxical symbols of a truth that is beyond ordinary mental conceptualization.

探梅

山前一片白雲橫
七十峰頭次第登
看到色空香不住
故宜相對坐禪僧
數點梅花冷結愁
芒鞋踏遍小溪幽
坌人不辨香來處
風起山中雪滿頭

可仁道者住庵示之

小小茆菴含法界
善財何必向南參
拈香擇火真三昧
瞥爾情生便不堪

244　My translation here is tentative.

245　The last and longest chapter of the Flower Garland Sutra, which circulated independently and was very popular, recounts how the youth Sudhana, in his quest for enlightenment, embarks on a pilgrimage that involves visiting fifty-three different spiritual teachers. His journey culminates with a meeting with the Maitreya, the future Buddha, who affords him with a vision of a fundamentally unified reality in which everything is interrelated and interpenetrating.

In Search of Plum Blossoms

Extending in front of the mountains
    is a ribbon of white clouds.
I clamber up the seventy peaks,
    first one and then another.
I see that their coloring is empty
    and their fragrance doesn't last,
Which is why facing them is so fitting
    for a meditating Chan monastic.
I count the plum blossoms,
    the cold linked with sorrow.[244]
In grass sandals, I went everywhere
    along the secluded streams.
Still, this recluse couldn't figure out
    the source of their scent,
As the winds rose from the mountains
    and snow covered their peaks.

*Dharma Instructions for Practitioner Keren Taking Up
Residence in a Hermitage*

A small thatched hermitage
    can contain the dharma realm!
What need is there for Sudhana
    to go south on pilgrimage?[245]
Burning incense, making offerings,
    this is the true *samādhi*.[246]
If emotions should suddenly arise,
    don't allow them to stay.

---

246 *Samādhi* is a Sanskrit term that refers basically to a high state of mental absorption or meditative concentration, leading to perfect mental equanimity. Buddhist texts describe many different methods by which to attain such a state.

山居即事

> 松花香飯剛個飽
> 荷葉碎衣勞再拴
> 斗大茆庵傍溪住
> 不知是馬是驢年

讀龐居士語錄

> 靈炤人貧智短
> 龐公年老心孤
> 蕩盡家私無賴
> 百草頭邊亂屙

247 There is no "year of the donkey" in the Chinese zodiac. Rather, this term is used in Chan writings to refer to the sort of time that cannot be counted or calculated, i.e., timelessness.

248 A merchant by trade, Layman Pang, or Pangyun 龐蘊 (740–808), and his family were dedicated Chan practitioners. The use of the term "recorded sayings," normally only used for eminent Chan masters, indicates the high regard in which he has been held in Chan circles.

249 Pang's daughter Lingzhao 靈炤 appears to be have been more spiritually advanced than her father. Here Zukui Xuanfu seems to be having some Chan fun with both of them.

Living in the Mountains: An Impromptu Poem

Pine flowers and fragrant rice:
  I just barely eat my fill.
Lotus leaves and tattered robes,
  I struggle to fasten them.
Living in an ample thatched hut
  by the side of a stream;
Not knowing if it's the year of the horse
  or the year of the donkey.[247]

Reading "The Recorded Sayings of Layman Pang"[248]

Lingzhao was destitute and dumb;
Master Pang was old and faint of heart.[249]
Their money gone, they lived like bums,[250]
Pissing on the tips of the hundred grasses.[251]

250 Layman Pang, worried about the obstacles posed by material possessions, put all of his
     money into a boat and then sank it in the river. After this, the family led an itinerant
     life, making bamboo utensils to support themselves.
251 A famous episode in the *Recorded Sayings* reads, "The Layman was sitting in his thatched
     cottage one day. 'Difficult, difficult, difficult,' he suddenly exclaimed, '[like trying] to
     scatter ten measures of sesame seed all over a tree!' 'Easy, easy, easy,' replied Mrs. Pang,
     'just like touching your feet to the ground when you get out of bed.' 'Neither difficult nor
     easy,' said Lingzhao." See "On the tips of the hundred grasses, the Patriarchs' meaning,"
     CBETA X69, no. 1336, 134a18–20; translated in Sasaki 1971, 74.

別洞庭舊隱

自攜瓢笠下雲岑
彼此無言意甚深
分付洞庭峰頂月
清光留取照同心

水月頌

山僧口裏無舌
解道虛空是橛
可憐伎死禪和
秖管水中撈月

述志

佛祖之道淵且微
淺深悟入隨群機
後人碌碌昧此意
持刀追逐爭傳衣

252 The reference here appears to be the many peaks around Lake Tai.
253 Here the poet seems to be referring to her old friends, the mountains.
254 To speak without a tongue is to convey the truth of what is beyond words.

Leaving My Old Retreat on Dongting

Ladle and bamboo hat in hand,
  I descend the cloudy mountains.[252]
Nothing to say to each other,[253]
  but with thoughts that run deep.
I send instructions to the moon
  above the peaks of Dongting;
Put aside some of your bright glow
  to shine on a kindred soul.

The Moon in the Water: A Gāthā

In this mountain nun's mouth, there is no tongue;[254]
She knows that even to speak of Emptiness is a mistake.
She feels sorry for those followers of dead Chan,
Intent only on scooping up the moon in the water.[255]

My Aspirations

The Way of the Buddhas and Patriarchs
  is both profound and subtle.
It can be realized at all different levels,[256]
  according to different people's needs.
People of these later times are second-rate
  and do not understand what this means.
Brandishing swords, they chase in pursuit
  of the transmission of the robes![257]

255 That is, those who latch on to appearances (the reflection of the moon in the water), rather than enlightenment (the moon) itself. There may also be an allusion here to Li Bai, the great Tang poet and lover of the moon and wine, who is said to have drowned trying to grasp the moon reflected in the river.

256 It is often said that the teachings of the Buddha all have one taste, the taste of liberation. Thus, the teachings can help all people, whether they are expressed in easy or more complex ways.

257 In other words, they are more interested in acquiring formal transmission, or certification from a famous master, than they are in actually becoming awakened.

阿誰能達禪河底
蠡測管窺欺爾汝
縱然奪得舊袈裟
心印雕鐫不相似

莫怪今朝太穿鑿
當初已見源頭濁
瞿曇偶爾自拈花
迦葉無端便輕薄

東土西天兩脫空
敲骨取髓情難容
慣傷物義絕回互
驅雷策電難尋蹤

---

258 Meditation is sometimes compared to a river whose waters extinguish the fires of the mind.

259 This line may refer to the fact that Mahakasyapa just smiled when the Buddha held up the white flower.

Which one enables one to reach
  the riverbed of meditation?[258]
Shortsighted and narrow-minded,
  they just deceive you all!
Even if they've managed to filch
  some old monastic robes,
Their carved transmission seals
  are nothing but imitations!

Don't blame just the present times
  for these skewed interpretations,
For from the start, one can see
  the fountainhead being muddied.
Gautama would from time to time
  take a flower and raise it up;
Kashyapa would for no reason
  just take it all very lightly![259]

Whether from China or India,
  both are empty and ineffective.
Breaking the bone and extracting the marrow
  is not so easily accomplished![260]
Habitually damaging people's thoughts
  without answering for a thing;
Then escaping without a trace
  like thunder and lightning.[261]

260 In other words, one has to undergo suffering, including physical suffering, to achieve
     one's spiritual goals.
261 My translation of this couplet is tentative.

山僧秖個莫妄想
要與古今呈榜樣
善財童子向南參
歷盡門庭無背向

百千三昧空納空
了無隻字填心胸
渾如金翅劈溟渤
恣情快口皆神龍

塵說剎說熾然說
何必豐干重饒舌
把茆自立好生涯
銕鑄飯鐺一腳折

---

262 The reference here is to Suparṇa, a mythical golden-winged bird that serves as the
      vehicle for the Hindu god Vishnu. It is often used to refer to either to the companion
      of the Buddha or to the Buddha himself.

263 My translation of this couplet is tentative. In the Chinese mythical tradition, the divine
      dragons govern the weather, and especially the rain that is so essential in an agricultural
      society.

This rustic monastic merely practices
    not having deluded thoughts,
Striving to model herself on exemplars
    from the past and the present.
The young lad Sudhana traveled south
    to meet with teachers;
He visited each of their dwellings,
    without ever turning back.

The thousands of states of *samādhi*
    is but Emptiness taking in Emptiness;
I inscribe the characters "Realize Emptiness"
    upon my heart and chest.
I will be like the golden-winged bird
    slicing through the ocean waves,[262]
Giving rein to joy and speaking as one pleases,
    just as the divine dragons do.[263]

Words as numerous as grains of sand,
    words heated and feverish.
Why would one be like Fenggan,
    who just couldn't stop talking?[264]
I can make a living bundling thatch;
    I'll get by just fine,
As with a single kick I break
    my fetters and rice pot.

---

264 Fenggan 豐干 was a Tang dynasty monk known for his poetry. Along with Hanshan 寒
    山 and Shide 拾得, he was one of the three recluses of the Guoqing Monastery in the
    Tiantai Mountains. It is said that one day some officials came to the temple looking for
    Hanshan and Shide, and Fenggan showed them to where the two were sitting, talking
    and laughing together. Seeing the officials, they completely ignored them, and then,
    saying "Fenggan talks too much," they left the monastery, never to be seen there again.

示迅機道者

　迢迢歷劫秖如今
　須信凡心即佛心
　莫鎖自家無盡藏
　苦拈黃葉當真金

贈趙封初居士（第三、四首）

　塵中不染古君子
　林下自高閒道人
　倦即投床飢便食
　從來雕偽不如真

　龐公未了婚姻事
　陶令偏多兒女纏
　獨有南村趙居士
　比他二老更超然

265　The family treasure here refers to the truth of the Buddha nature.

Dharma Instructions for Person of the Way Xunji

So many successions of kalpas up to this day.
You must trust that the ordinary mind is the Buddha mind.
Do not put locks on your own family's bottomless treasure,
Carefully gathering yellow leaves as though they were gold.[265]

To Layman Zhao Fengchu [Verses two and four]

Untainted by the dust of the world,
    an old-fashioned man of integrity.
Living a lofty life among the forest trees,
    a man of the Way at leisure.
When he is weary, he takes to his bed,
    and when he is hungry, he dines.
A fake façade has never been
    as good as what is true.

Master Pang never did fully grasp
    the business of being married;
Magistrate Tao was led astray
    by the bonds of sons and daughters.[266]
There is no one like Layman Zhao
    from the Southern Village,
Who, compared to those other two,
    is far more detached!

---

266 Tao Yuanming, a fourth-century poet who quit his official post and retired to the country-
    side with his family, where he lived as a farmer-recluse.

行路難（臨江仙）

貴賤形骸隨業轉
世人顛倒堪悲
初生便有死追隨
纔分你我相
骨肉已參差

未入娘胎何處也
好教猛省深思
刹那不住苦凄其
炎炎三界內
跳出是男兒（生苦）

記得少年多意氣
轉頭萬事皆空
雞皮鶴髮漸成翁
眼昏常帶霧
齒漏不關風

老健春寒秋後熱
謾誇心尚孩童
急須學佛悟真宗
遷延如有待
日暮怨途窮（老苦）

267 Originally the title of a popular anonymous ballad (*yuefu*), and later used by poets such
     as Li Bai, this phrase was more often than not used to describe the trials and tribulations
     suffered on a long journey. Here, of course, the poet is describing the sufferings on the
     journey of life, including birth, illness, aging, and death. What is interesting, however,
     is that she is making use not of the ballad form, but rather that of the song lyric (*ci*), in
     this case to the tune "Immortals by the River."

The Road Is Hard (To the Tune "Immortals by the River")[267]

The suffering of birth

Every single person's body changes according to karma.
The deluded thinking of people is to be pitied!
As soon as we are born, death follows us in pursuit.
No sooner is one divided into "you" and "me"
Than one's flesh and blood grow unruly.[268]

Before entering the mother's womb, where can we be found?
One should ponder this deeply to achieve realization.
For a moment, one can't help being miserable and sad
As from the scorching triple realm[269]
There springs a male child.

The suffering of aging

You recall the energy of youth
Then turn your head and everything is empty.
Wrinkled skin, brittle hair, you become old.
Eyes blurry and often misting over,
Teeth rotten, you wheeze away.

Aged, you feel the cold in spring and the heat in fall,
Even if you claim the alertness of a child.
Study Buddhism, awaken to the truth.
If you delay, thinking there's still time,
Nightfall will find you lamenting at the journey's end.

---

268 My translation here is tentative.
269 The triple realm is a Buddhist term referring to the three realms of *saṃsāra*, even the
      highest of which is still ablaze with the fires of suffering.

石火電光能幾幾
終朝 美酒肥羊
莫言災退遇良方
兒孫雖得力
痛苦自支當

病後始知身是累
健時多為人忙
爭名奪利走風霜
生平無片善
前路黑茫茫（病苦）

百年信是無根蒂
心驚陌上飛塵
全憑一氣作天鈞
不知渾似夢
卻認夢為真

呼吸不來長逝矣
休論我富他貧
田園妻子與家珍
萬般將莫去
惟有業隨身（死苦）

休夏東山

白雲影裏種空花
捩轉風頭景色賒
堪笑閒身無著處
卻來煙島臥寒沙

The suffering of illness

Flint sparks and lightning flashes don't last,
Nor do days of fine wine and fattened calf.
Don't say that disasters end and life goes on.
Even with sons and grandsons to help,
You still must endure the suffering alone.

Ill, you begin to see your body as a burden;
Healthy, you are busy with your career.
Striving for fame and profit, you endured it all,
But never did any good in your life.
The road ahead is dark indeed.

The suffering of death

A human life is a rootless thing,
Fearful like dust drifting on the road.[270]
Everything hangs in the balance of a breath.
Unaware that all is a dream,
One takes the dream to be the truth.

When the breathing stops, the dream will be over.
So stop going on about I'm rich and he's poor.
Your land, wife, children, and wealth—
None of them can you take along.
Only your karma will go with you!

Summer Rest on the East Mountain

In shadows cast by the white clouds,
    I plant flowers of emptiness;
The winds twist this way and that
    over the distant scenery.
Laughable is this idle self
    unattached to any place;
And yet I come to this misty island
    to sleep on its cooling sands.

---

270 There is an allusion here to lines from the first poem in a series of eight miscellaneous
verses by Tao Yuanming in which he notes that human life is rootless, drifting along
like dust on the road.

十二時歌

夜半子
夢裏紛紛不知止
踏破東山西嶺青
翻身原在被窩裏

雞鳴丑
日用頭頭自諧偶
那邊水洗面皮光
這裡啜茶濕卻口

平旦寅
萬象之中獨露身
佛祖到來難著力
惟人自肯乃方親

271 Traditionally, the Chinese divided the day into twelve units, each equivalent to two
modern hours. From the Song dynasty, the first of these dual hours referred roughly
to the time between midnight and 2:00 a.m., the second to the time between 2:00
and 4:00 a.m., and so on. Each of these twelve units carried the name of one of the
twelve sequential earthly branches, beginning with *zi*. As noted in the introduction,
the "Song of the Twelve Hours" was a popular vernacular song title adopted early on
by Chan Buddhist monastics, one of the first and most well-known examples of which
is attributed to the Tang dynasty master Zhaozhou Congshen.

Song of the Twelve Hours of the Day[271]

i   The middle of the night, the zi *hour*
In my dreams, I dash here and there,
    not knowing how to stop,
Traipsing over the eastern hills
    and the western peaks so blue,
Then turning to find myself
    still inside my bedroll!

ii   Cockcrow, the chou *hour*
All the things used daily
    are naturally harmonious.
Over there, washing with water
    until the skin gleams;
Over here, taking a swig of tea
    to rinse out the mouth.

iii   Daybreak, the yin *hour*
Amid the ten thousand forms,
    the solitary body is revealed.[272]
The Buddha and patriarchs come,
    and one must try one's best.
Only if a person is willing
    can she become their intimate.

272 These lines may have been borrowed from a *gāthā* by the Tang dynasty monk Changqing
     Huiling 長慶慧稜 (854–932) that reads, "Amid the myriad realms the solitary body is
     revealed. / Only persons self-allowing are intimate with it. / Before, I wrongly searched
     among the paths, / But today I see, and it's like ice in fire." (See CBETA T51, no. 2076,
     347b27–28, translated in Ferguson 2000, 279.)

日出卯
珊瑚樹林色杲杲
不須別處覓瞿曇
丈六金身一莖草

食時辰
別甑炊香玉粒新
喫粥了洗缽盂去
便道宗師指示人

禺中巳
莫向太虛分彼此
風中鈴鐸善宣揚
歷歷分明無一字

日南午
愛聞不打禾山鼓
無事上山走一遭
倦來又上蒲團坐

273 The coral or night-flowering jasmine is known in Indian mythology as the king of heavenly trees and thought to have wish-fulfilling properties.

iv   Sunrise, the mao hour

In the coral jasmine groves,[273]
   the colors are brilliant.
No need to go elsewhere
   in search of Gautama.
His enormous golden body
   in a single blade of grass.

v   Mealtime, the chen hour

From the steamer comes the smell
   of freshly cooked rice.
After we finish our porridge,
   we go and wash our bowls.
Then a chance for the dharma master
   to provide us with instruction.

vi   Late morning, the si hour

Don't break up the Great Void
   into this and that.
The chimes ringing in the breeze
   are expert preachers,
Explaining everything in detail
   without a single word!

vii   Midday, the wu hour

Lovers of leisure do not beat
   on Heshan's drum.[274]
When free, we climb the mountains
   and wander everywhere.
Growing tired of that,
   we return to the meditation mat.

274 The Tang master Heshan (890–960) was known for replying to questions, including
those having to do with such things as "What is the real truth?" with the phrase, "Know-
ing how to beat the drum."

日昳未
十二部經可知禮
稽首南無上大人
試問何為丘乙己

晡時申
會得依然猶隔津
自怪脩行不得力
順成歡喜逆成瞋

日入酉
一彎月掛窗前柳
吹火柴生滿灶煙
頭上青灰三五斗

黃昏戌
老鼠便來偷白蜜
床頭打絮到三更
連累山僧不得息

275   The Mahayana Buddhist canon is traditionally divided into twelve sections, according
      to genre, such as sutras, parables, and *gāthās*.
276   A short primer used to teach children to write began with the simplest characters:
      shang 上, *da* 大, and *ren* 人. This became the title by which the text was known, roughly
      translated as "the great man of old," otherwise known as Confucius.

viii   Sunset, the wei *hour*
From the twelve divisions of the canon,[275]
   one will understand proper decorum.
We bow our heads and pay obeisance
   to the "great man of old."[276]
One may well ask why
   it refers only to Confucius.

ix   Late afternoon, the shen *hour*
My understanding hasn't changed;
   I still haven't crossed the ford.[277]
I chide myself that in my practice,
   I've not made more progress.
When all goes well, I'm happy,
   and when it doesn't, I'm angry!

x   Sunset, the you *hour*
A crescent moon hangs over
   the willow by the window.
My blowing the flame to ignite the kindling
   fills the furnace with smoke;
On my head, several flecks
   of dark-colored ashes.

xi   Nightfall, the xu *hour*
Time for the mice to venture out
   to steal the white honey.
At the foot of my bed, they make a racket
   late into the night,
Disturbing this mountain monk
   so that she cannot sleep.

---

277 In other words, I have not yet crossed the stream of *samsara* and attained awakening.
    The image of knowing where to cross the ford, that is, knowing the truth, comes from
    the *Analects* of Confucius.

人定亥

芥子吸乾香水海

衣內摩尼忽放光

露柱燈籠齊喝采

山居

一舍三楹翠岫圍

離離橘柚晚香飛

石床昨夜生秋夢

似向松門跨虎歸

山居雜偈

白雲夜半正明

青山天曉不露

但秪閒坐困眠

管甚有過無過

雲過松濤瀉碧

雨餘柳帶垂青

好景無人顧著

飛來獨許幽禽

---

278 A mustard seed is used as a metaphor for that which is extremely small. According to
Buddhist mythology, the axis mundi is surrounded by eight mountain ranges and by
eight seas, all but one of which is filled with fragrant waters. This line refers to something
tiny absorbing that which is huge, much like the notion of a world in a grain of sand.

xii   Late night, the hai *hour*
The mustard seed drinks dry
   the fragrant seas.[278]
Beneath my robes, the *mani* jewel
   suddenly gives off a light.[279]
The bare pillars and the lanterns
   all cry out bravo![280]

Living in the Mountains

A single dwelling with three rooms,
   encircled by verdant peaks.
Luxuriant pomelo trees,
   their evening scent wafting by.
On my stone couch last night
   I had an autumn dream:
I was headed back to my pine doors
   riding astride a tiger!

Living in the Mountains: Miscellaneous Gāthās

The white clouds at midnight are bright;
The green mountains at dawn are hidden.
All I do is sit in leisure and nap when sleepy.
Who cares whether I'm breaking the rules or not?

Clouds drift by, pines sigh, the sea is overflowing.
After the rain, the willow droops green strands.
A fine landscape with no one else to see it;
I've come here just to find a hidden place to nest.

279   The *mani* jewel, like the mirror, reflects all the colors of the world without itself having
   any color. Like the mirror, it is also symbolic of complete and perfect liberation, or of
   the Buddha within.
280   The poet appears to be describing an insight that is applauded even by the lanterns and
   pillars of the temple.

有感

禪到今朝不耐看
神頭鬼面幾何般
憑君轉日迴瀾手
扶起靈山舊刹竿

蜂起禪門日已非
魔風滾滾盡緇衣
不如插腳蓮華會
一任諸方笑鈍機

281　Literally, with the head of a god and the face of a ghost.
282　Flagpoles stand in front of the gates of many monasteries. The historical Buddha often
　　 met with his disciples on Vulture Peak, where he wordlessly held up a flower, signaling
　　 the beginning of the Chan tradition of transmission.

Thoughts

I can barely stand to look
    at the Chan of today.
Grotesque and strange,[281]
    what has it become?
Why don't you do something
    about the corruption,
And help to raise again
    the flagpole at Vulture Peak?[282]

The flourishing school of Chan
    is disappearing by the day
As an evil wind sweeps over
    the black-robed monks.
It would be better to join up
    with a Lotus Society,[283]
Than to allow everyone to
    mock the Sudden Teaching.[284]

283 That is, the practitioners of Pure Land Buddhism.
284 The Sudden Teaching refers to the school of Southern Chan Buddhism, to which Zukui
     Xuanfu belonged, which taught the possibility of a sudden and unmediated awakening
     in this lifetime.

寶持玄總

Baochi Xuanzong

Baochi Xuanzong was from Xiushui, Zhejiang province.[285] Her secular name was Jin Shuxiu 金淑脩. She came from an established gentry family and later married the scion of another such family, Xu Zhaosen 徐肇森. She had several children, among whom Jin Jiayan 金嘉炎 (1631–1703) would become a well-known official. During the upheavals of the Ming-Qing transition, her father-in-law and numerous other members of the Xu family died in the anti-Qing resistance. Xu Zhaosen fell ill and died not long after that. Even before her husband's death, Baochi had often visited Miaozhan Convent in Xiushui, where she had come to know the Abbess Zukui Xuanfu. When her son was grown, she took the tonsure and then ordination with Zukui Xuanfu's teacher, Jiqi Hongchu. Eventually, she too was named one of his dharma successors, and was named the abbess of Miaozhan Convent after Zukui left. She lived there until retiring at the end of her life to Nanxun Convent in nearby Yanguan. As a young woman, Baochi had acquired a reputation primarily as a painter, although she also wrote poetry. She was less prolific than Zukui Xuanfu, her primary claim to literary fame being the collection of verse commentaries written in collaboration with Zukui Xuanfu on forty-three verses selected by Wuzhuo Miaozong (see p. xvi).[286]

285 Baochi Xuanzong is referred to as Baochi Jizong 寶持繼總 in Zhenhua 1988, as well as in some of my previous publications. However, this appears to have been an error.
286 For more on Baochi Xuanzong, see Grant 2008, 130–145. Her extant collection is titled *Recorded Sayings of Chan Master Baochi Zong* (*Baochi Zong chanshi yulu* 寶持總禪師語錄).

和宋慈受深禪師披雲臺十頌

行盡千山又萬山
那知人世有餘閒
杖頭點出金剛眼
脫落皮膚指顧間

仰天長嘯遏行雲
流出桃花賺世人
踏破芒鞋呈舊面
森羅萬象現全身

杜鵑聲裏覓殘紅
南北東西路莫窮
短笛有聲催午夢
鐵鎚無孔舞春風

287 The adamantine (diamond) eye, originally a Tantric Buddhist term, is used in Chan texts to refer to the eye of wisdom, which "illumines and sees everywhere without obstruction. It can not only make out clearly a tiny hair a thousand miles away, but also determine what is false and decide what is true, distinguish gain and loss, discern what's appropriate to the occasion, and recognize right and wrong." CBETA T48, no. 2003, 150a9–11; translated in Cleary 1998, 62.

Matching the Ten Verses of Chan Master Cishou Huaiyin's "Cloud Dispelling Terrace"

I

Walking through a thousand mountains
  and then ten thousand more.
Who'd have imagined there'd be so much leisure
  in this human world!
The tip of my walking staff points out
  the adamantine eye,[287]
And with a snap of the fingers,
  the skin drops away.[288]

II

I look up to heaven and give a long cry
  that stops the floating cloud.
The peach blossoms drifting downstream
  deceive the people of the world.[289]
My straw sandals are completely worn out,
  and my face is showing its age,
But the myriad forms of the universe
  manifest truth's whole body.

III

In the sound of the cuckoo's call,
  I seek the fallen flowers.[290]
North and south, east and west,
  the roads never end.
The sound of the bamboo flute
  brings on a noontime dream.
The hammer without a hammer-hold
  dances in the springtime breeze.[291]

288 In other words, to let go and be free of delusion.
289 An allusion to the story, made famous by Tao Yuanming, of the Peach Blossom Stream that, when traced back to its source, led to a utopian realm.
290 The cuckoo, whose cry is said to be one of sadness, is also said to have wept tears of blood, which later became the red azalea flower.
291 Literally, a hammerhead without a hold in which to insert a handle. This can be used to indicate a state of mind that cannot be grasped, but still serves a function.

鳴條破塊撲窗櫺
石火光中閃電明
臺上野花零落盡
空山寂寂鳥無聲

衰病難將藥石攻
扶筇巖畔強從容
湖水盡翻青白眼
七十二峰返照中

昨日少年今白頭
滿腔熱血付東流
日長無事倚松立
笑指嶺頭雲未休

292 A popular saying used to describe times of peace and stability is "The winds do not
cause new willow branches to whistle; the rainstorms do not damage the farm fields."

293 The images of sparks produced from striking a flintstone and the sudden flash of light-
ning are used as metaphors for the spontaneous nature of the awakened mind. Here
they can also be read literally, as part of the description of the violent weather.

IV

Wind-blown branches; field-damaging rains
    pound against the windows.[292]
In the gleam of sparks from the flintstone,
    the lightning flashes bright.[293]
The wildflowers growing on the terrace
    are completely tattered and torn.
The empty mountain is quiet and still
    and does not utter a sound.

V

Old age and illness are hard to treat
    with medicinal herbs.
A walking stick on the cliff-side paths
    makes the going easier.
The lake waters completely reverse
    thoughts of acclaim or disdain.
Seventy-two mountain peaks[294]
    in the returning light of dusk.

VI

Yesterday I was young,
    but today my hair is white.
A chest filled with righteous ardor
    yields to the easterly flowing river.[295]
My days are long, and I have nothing to do
    but to lean against the pines.
Smiling, I point to the mountaintops,
    where clouds keep drifting by.

294 Probably a reference to the mountains around Lake Tai.
295 A human life is compared to a river that flows easterly and empties into the sea, in
    contrast to plants that reappear each spring. The term translated here as "righteous
    ardor" is often used to reflect patriotic ardor, and may well refer to the anger and grief
    experienced by the those who lost family members in the violent political upheavals
    of the time, including the poet herself.

不問吳山越水前
平生活計钁頭邊
收來放去渾閒事
撒出珍珠顆顆圓

嘯月披雲足比鄰
閒花野艸總成真
琴臺響屧渾無恙
人面于今花更新

淡飯黃虀飽便休
鶉衣百結任悠悠
倦來收足蒲團坐
客至從教不舉頭

296 Wu-Yue is an old name for the area that comprises much of southern China. Here the
     poet may be expressing a desire to set aside her sorrows.
297 The mattock symbolizes the work of everyday life, especially pulling weeds from both
     the ground and the mind.
298 The Moon-Whistling Terrace was likely a scenic spot near the Cloud-Dispelling Terrace
     where Cishou Huaishen penned his famous verses.

VII

Don't ask about what came before
    the hills of Wu and the rivers of Yue.[296]
All my life I've managed to get along
    with just a mattock by my side.[297]
Grabbing hold and letting go
    are both ordinary matters.
Scattering pearls all around,
    each of them complete.

VIII

The Moon-Whistling and Cloud-Dispelling Terraces
    make the best of neighbors.[298]
The wildflowers and rustic bamboo
    fully embody reality.[299]
Zither Terrace and the Promenade of Musical Shoes
    remain safe and sound,[300]
As today the sentiments of the past
    are made new again by the flowers.[301]

IX

At a simple meal of yellow leeks,
    when full, I stop.
Wearing tattered robes,
    I'm footloose and free.
When tired, I tuck in my feet
    on the meditation mat.
Even should a visitor arrive,
    I would not lift my head!

299 My translation here is tentative.
300 Zither Terrace refers to a site on Mount Lingyan. The Promenade of Musical Shoes was
     built by the King of Wu in the fifth century BCE for his concubine, Xi Shi 西施. Under
     its marble floors were thousands of earthenware jars that rang out like chimes when
     she walked across them.
301 My translation here is tentative.

莫怪平生用力麤
掀翻大地一耕夫
了了了時無可了
何妨淹殺赤梢魚

絨牡丹

魏紫姚黃各不同
同根一體自相通
天姿不假陽和力
一段風光爍太空

和劭監院師贏得楊岐第一籌四首

一道平懷萬事休
青蛙白笲度春秋
十年勳業高叢席
贏得楊岐第一籌

---

302 There is a legend that a red-tailed fish (or red-tailed carp) had its tail fin burned by
lightning, which gave it the ability to shape-shift. The reference is to someone who
manifests superior spiritual abilities after overcoming adversity. Here the poet seems to
be indicating a stage that transcends even the religious achievement of perfect clarity.

X

It's no wonder that all my life
    has been spent doing rough labor.
Tilling and turning the earth
    no different from that of a farmer.
When everything is perfectly clear,
    nothing can be clarified.
One might as well drown
    the red-tailed fish.[302]

Peonies Embroidered on Silk

Wei purples and Yao yellows[303]
    are each unique,
But in sharing roots and stems,
    they are still connected.
Their charm does not rely
    on the summer's heat.
They present us with a view
    that shimmers there in space.

Harmonizing with Temple Manager Teacher Shao's "Mastering Yangqi's Primary Strategy": Four Verses

With a tranquil everyday mind,
    ten thousand affairs cease.
Green frogs and white bamboo,
    as the seasons pass by.
With ten years of meritorious service
    in your high position,
You have mastered the primary
    strategy of Master Yangqi.[304]

303 These are the names of two of the famous so-called four kinds of peonies.

304 Yangqi Fanghui 楊岐方會 (992–1049) was the founder of one of the two major branches of the Linji school of Chan Buddhism. In the Yangqi branch, everyday activities (such as serving as the manager of a monastery) were the best kind of religious practice. This would appear to be the strategy, or principle, being referred to here.

贏得楊岐第一籌
亂峰雲靄鳥聲幽
庭前柏子青無盡
到處香風滿钁頭

贏得楊岐第一籌
東山西嶺恣優游
玄關踏破無塵跡
截斷千谿水逆流

贏得楊岐第一籌
卉枯石冷雪埋丘
知君自有天然概
活計些些孰敢儔

---

305 Literally, the pickax used to break up the soil for farming.

You have mastered the primary
  strategy of Master Yangqi.
Amid jumbled peaks and floating clouds
  and the sound of hidden birds,
The cypresses in the front courtyard
  are always a bright green,
And fragrant breezes everywhere
  envelop the farming tools.[305]

You have mastered the primary
  strategy of Master Yangqi.
On the Eastern Mountain and Western Peak,
  one can wander at will.
The mysterious gate is shattered
  without a trace of dust,
Cutting off the thousand rivers
  as the water flows upstream.[306]

You have mastered the primary
  strategy of Master Yangqi.
Grasses wither, rocks grow cold,
  and snow buries the hills.
I know that you, sir, possess
  a nature endowed by heaven.
So when it comes to your life's labors,
  is anyone your equal?

---

306 The mysterious gate is the gate that leads into the profound way of the Buddha. To
    embark on the Buddhist path is to travel against the stream of *samsara*, the river of
    birth and death.

南洲鳳舉樓望雪

> 截流一棹骨毛寒
> 六出花飛宇宙漫
> 奮起玉龍金鎖斷
> 劈開華嶽劍光殘
> 奚囊有句從教覓
> 少室無心不用安
> 試問五湖參學者
> 盛歸銀碗若為看

307 The jade dragon may refer to the frozen Yellow River.
308 According to an ancient legend, the great river god Juling Shen is said to have split
     Mount Hua (a major mountain range located in Shaanxi province, east of Xian) into
     two halves so that the Yellow River could flow eastwards. Here the notion of cleaving
     through Mount Hua appears to refer to cutting through ignorance with the sword of
     discerning and achieving awakening, after which there is no need for the sword.
309 The Tang poet Li He 李賀 (790/91–816/17) is said to have spent his time wandering
     around riding a mule, followed by a servant boy with a tattered tapestry bag. Whenever
     he would come up with a line of poetry, he'd scribble it down on a piece of paper and
     toss it into the bag.

Watching the Snow from Nanzhou's Rising Phoenix Tower

A single craft blocking the river
    in marrow-piercing cold,
As six-petaled snowflakes flutter down
    and blanket the world.
When the jade dragon surges up
    the golden lock will shatter.[307]
When Mount Hua splits apart,
    the shining sword will break.[308]
A sack filled with scribbled lines[309]
    for students to seek out.
Bodhidharma and his "no mind,"
    which have no need of settling.[310]
I ask all of you scholars
    in the Five Lakes area:[311]
When I return with a silver bowl full of snow,
    how will you see it?[312]

---

310 In the original, the term used to refer to Bodhidharma is "Mount Shaoshi," the name of
the mountain where the Buddha is said to have sat in a cave meditating for nine years.
The traditional story is that when Huike once asked Bodhidharma to settle his mind
for him, Bodhidharma replied by asking Huike to show him the mind that needed to
be settled. When Huike was unable to produce that mind, Bodhidharma declared it
settled (see the Introduction).

311 The Five Lakes area refers generally to eastern and central China, which boasts five
large freshwater lakes.

312 The image of a silver bowl piled up with white snow can be found in a popular Chan
text titled *Song of the Precious Mirror Samādhi* (*Baojing sanmei ge* 宝鏡三昧歌), attrib-
uted to Dongshan Liangjie 洞山良价 (807–869). The lines read, "A silver bowl filled
with snow; a heron hidden in the moon. / Taken as similar, they are not the same; not
distinguished, their places are known. / The meaning does not reside in the words,
but a pivotal moment brings it forth." CBETA X79, no. 1560, 492b19–20; translated in
Leighton and Wu 2000, 76.

示力嚴道人

抛卻珍奇錦繡緣
卻從枯淡樂餘年
祖師皮骨休分析
閒即加餐困即眠

313 When Bodhidharma was about to go back to India, he asked his four major disciples
(including the nun Zongchi) to express their understanding of what they had learned
from him. After listening to their responses, he declared who had acquired his skin,
who his flesh, who his bones, and who his marrow. Zongchi was said to have acquired
his flesh, and Huike his marrow, the deepest understanding of all, and it was to Huike
that he passed on his dharma transmission. Here Baochi Xuanzong seems to be urging
her disciple not to worry about these levels of understanding, and perhaps implying
that gender is not a consideration.

Dharma Instructions for Person of the Way Liyan

Get rid of your ties to precious things
    and your beautiful brocades.
Follow instead the ancient and plain
    and be happy from now on.
As for the Patriarch's "skin" and "bones"
    stop trying to analyze it all.[313]
When you're at ease, have a meal,
    and when you're tired, sleep.

繼總行徹

---

314 For more on Jizong Xingche, see Grant 2008, 107–109. For a close reading of an important autobiographical text, see Grant 2014. The collection of her recorded sayings is titled *Recorded Sayings of Chan Master Jizong Che* (*Jizong Che chanshi yulu* 繼總徹禪師語錄).

Jizong Xingche

Jizong Xingche was born in 1606 in Hengzhou, Hunan province. In an autobiographical account, she relates that on the night she was conceived, her father had a dream that a Buddhist monk came to his door asking for food and shelter, and that he gladly acquiesced. She also notes that even as a child she felt an aversion to meat and was strongly attracted to the Buddhist teachings—hagiographic details found in many stories of holy men and women in the Buddhist tradition. She married and bore several children but was left a widow when her husband suddenly died. Jizong began to study Chan with the Linji Chan master Shanci Tongji 山茨通際 (1608–1645), who was then living in the nearby Nanyue Mountains. She eventually took ordination and moved into a small hermitage in the mountains, not far from where her teacher lived. In 1646 Shanci died after eating a meal of poisonous weeds, all other food having been destroyed by the invading Manchus. Jizong then traveled to southeast China to visit other teachers in her lineage. She ended up receiving dharma transmission from Master Wanru Tongwei 萬如通微 (1594–1657). She subsequently served as abbess in several convents, including Huideng Chan Convent in Suzhou, and attracted many disciples, both monastic and lay. Little is known about Jizong Xingche's later life, but it would appear from her poems that she returned to her beloved Nanyue Mountains to pass her final years. Her collection of recorded sayings is one of the few by women Chan masters preserved in *The Jiaxing Chinese Buddhist Canon* (CBETA J).[314]

南嶽山居雜詠

澗底風來蕭
情空物物幽
不聞車馬鬧
遠卻世塵憂
葉落知秋老
林疏露瀑流
忘機鷗與鷺
相狎若相投

門倩閒雲護
清幽丈室臨
塾猿探果熱
巢鳥入林深
撇卻浮名網
超然樂道心
空空四句外
得意芥投鍼

靜看秋光好
楓紅滿耳聲
松濤聯鶴唳
谷響荅蟬鳴
遊客衣冠古
憨僧風度清
舉頭空際望
楚澤有餘英

315   *Qing* in Chan texts refers not just to feelings or emotions, but more generally to the deluded thoughts or mental tendencies that rise in response to sensory contact.

316   This is an allusion to a poem by Tao Yuanming.

Living in the Nanyue Mountains: Miscellaneous Verses

I

From the valley depths a cleansing wind rises.
Thoughts are empty, and everything is secluded.[315]
One can't hear the clatter of carts and horses,
So distant is one from the dusty cares of the world.[316]
When the leaves fall, we know it is autumn;
When the trees are bare, the waterfall appears.
Lacking all guile, the seagulls and egrets[317]
Become the most intimate of friends.

II

The gate asks the idle clouds to watch over it
And the small secluded hut nearby.
Wild gibbons go in search of ripe fruit.
Roosting birds enter the deep woods.
Liberated from the snare of empty fame,
Detached, my mind delights in the Way.
Emptiness of emptiness, beyond the four alternatives.[318]
Grasping this is like finding a needle in a haystack.

III

At peace, I gaze out at the fine autumn scene:
Red maples fill my ears with their rustling.
The pine's soughing joins in with the cries of the crane.
The valley's echo answers the chirps of the cicada.
The traveler's clothes and cap are old-fashioned.[319]
The foolish monastic's demeanor is pure-hearted.
Looking up, we gaze out at the distant horizon:
There are still heroes left in the marshes of Chu.[320]

---

317   There is a famous story in the ancient Daoist text titled *Master Lie* (*Liezi* 列子) about a
       boy who so lacked any guile that seagulls would play with him without fear. Once his
       father ordered him to come to the shore to catch one of the birds, however, they no
       longer would approach him.

318   Ultimately, the notion of emptiness must also be emptied out or destroyed. The tradi-
       tional Buddhist tetralemma (or lemma of four alternatives) is all things are empty, not
       empty, both empty and not empty, and neither empty nor not empty.

319   The implication may be that this visitor is still loyal to the fallen Ming dynasty, as is the
       poet herself.

320   Chu is an old name that included the province of Hunan, where the Nanyue Mountains
       are located. It was known for its seven fertile marshes, the most famous of which was
       the Great Marsh of the Cloud Dream.

日出通身暖
風來大地涼
人心多障礙
聖道獨揮揚
白玉生成白
黃金不煉黃
古今無改變
在在露真常

坐對西窗下
碧峰蒼翠排
白雲峰頂去
清風竹塢迴
山閣餘清夢
溪松覆碧苔
荒林無異味
果熱鳥啣來

拶到忘人處
人忘法亦空
兩忘俱寂滅
萬有絕羅籠
正入真三昧
如斯號大雄
含靈雖異象
定慧理玄同

321 In other words, one's essential Buddha nature is already enlightened and needs only to
     be realized through insight rather than refined through practice.
322 Literally, what is undifferentiated or unchanged.

IV

When the sun comes out, it warms the body,
And when the wind rises, it cools the great earth.
The human heart is filled with so many difficulties
That only the Way of the sages can scatter and dispel them.
White jade is white from the moment it is formed;
Yellow gold needs no refining to become yellow.[321]
Ancient or new, they never undergo any change,
And in each and every place, they reveal the eternally real.

V

I sit by the window that faces west:
Jade peaks line up in rows of kingfisher green.
White clouds depart for the mountain peaks.
Clear breezes encircle the low bamboo hedge.
Lucid dreams linger in the mountain pavilion.
Creek-side pines are covered in jade-green moss.
The deserted woods have the flavor of thusness.[322]
When the fruits ripen, the birds come for them.

VI

After much probing, one reaches the point of forgetting the person;
Forgetting the person, one realizes the emptiness of the *dharmas*.[323]
When both person and *dharmas* are forgotten, all is at peace:
The ten thousand things are like birds freed from their cages.[324]
The one who properly enters the true *samādhi*
Is the one who may be called a great hero.
Though sentient beings may all differ in appearance,
In meditative wisdom and profound mystery, they are one.

323 The "person" can be said to refer to the body, and the *dharmas* to the "mind." For an example of how this is used in a dharma talk, see Broughton and Watanabe 2014, 113.
324 To catch a bird and cage it often alludes to how we entrap ourselves in delusion.

亂石千峰裏
危廬倚碧岑
黃鶯鳴翠柳
白鷺點芳林
曲徑穿雲細
荊扉落葉深
幾番移住處
山色亦沉吟

世路風塵老
歸休咬菜虀
儉勤貧亦足
戒懼禍終輕
學自不欺始
智依無事清
書紳及銘座
黽勉盡餘生

幽鳥緡蠻處
煙華映嶽容
樹深偏見鹿
寺遠不聞鐘
竹勁分青靄
泉飛挂碧峰
無人知此況
獨對萬年松

325   My translation of this couplet is tentative.

VII

A jumble of boulders amid thousands of mountaintops;
A thatched hut leaning precariously against a jade peak.
Yellow orioles singing in the deep green willows;
White egrets dotting the sweet-smelling woodlands.
A winding path slices narrowly through the clouds;
A bramble gate nestles deep in the fallen leaves.
The several times I have moved my dwelling
The mountain scenes too seemed perplexed.[325]

VIII

In the wind and dust of worldly roads, I've grown old.
Time to return home now to eat wild greens.
If you are frugal, even in poverty you will have enough;
If you are watchful, in the end even disaster will be light.
Learning begins with not deceiving oneself or others;[326]
Wisdom depends on pure freedom from worldly affairs.
I write on my sash and inscribe on my seat:
"Exert yourself for what remains of your life!"

IX

Secluded birds hover around their hibernation spot.
Cloud-like flowers shine brightly from the cliff face.
The trees so deep that one can just glimpse the deer;
The temple so distant that one cannot hear its bell.
The bamboo forcefully parts the blue-gray clouds;
The waterfall hangs from the jade peaks.
There is no one else here to appreciate these sights.
I alone face the ten-thousand-year-old pines.

---

326 This phrase comes from a chapter titled "On Learning" from *Words of the Cheng Brothers* (*Er Cheng cuiyan* 二程粹言), a collection of works by the Neo-Confucian philosophers Cheng Hao 程顥 (1032–1085) and Cheng Yi 程頤 (1033–1107).

拭目疏林望
風煙節候殊
秋聲千葉墜
遠影一巢孤
不避秋霜鴈
驚飛夜月鳥
庭前來又去
幾度遣榮枯

高隱平生志
今來住此山
幻塵都覷破
浮世漫相關
石乳隨時汲
藤花任意攀
乾坤空浩大
誰識此中閒

林壑晴雲鎖
亭亭幾樹梅
汲泉吟詠去
採藥帶香回
葉上寒山偈
雲中般若臺
杖藜隨所至
石几布蒼苔

327　This is a fragrant tea that grows in dense bushes on the rocky faces of cliffs.
328　Wisteria flowers can be cooked and eaten, or used as a tea substitute.

X

Attentive and alert, I observe the woodland scene
Where wind and mist alter according to the season.
Autumn sounds: a thousand leaves falling to earth.
Distant shadow: a single bird's nest left abandoned.
Geese that cannot escape from the frost of autumn;
Crows that are startled by the night moon's gleam.
They come and go from the courtyard.
How many times has it seen flowering and fading!

XI

Dwelling in lofty solitude has been the dream of a lifetime:
From now on, I'll spend my days here on this mountain.
I have seen through all the illusions of this dusty world;
I've nothing to do anymore with this floating existence.
There is tea from the cliff sides to sip when one wishes,[327]
And wisteria flowers to pluck when one feels inclined.[328]
The emptiness of heaven and earth, so great and so vast:
Who can fully fathom the leisure to be found within it all?

XII

Wooded ravines locked in by fair-weather clouds,
And several plum trees standing tall and graceful.
Humming and singing, I go to fetch spring waters;
Wrapped in fragrance, I return from gathering herbs.
On the leaves, the *gāthās* of Cold Mountain;[329]
In the clouds, the Terrace of Enlightened Wisdom.[330]
I follow my walking stick wherever it takes me:
A stone bench covered with deep green moss.

329 The Tang Buddhist poet-recluse Hanshan (Cold Mountain) is said to have inscribed
his poems on trees and stones, after which they were copied and collected by others.
See Rouzer 2017, 42.
330 Bore (*prajñā* or enlightened wisdom) Terrace was one of the original names of a temple
in the Nanyue Mountains built by the Tiantai master Huisi 慧思 (515–577) sometime
around 567. In 713 it was converted into a Chan monastery by the eminent Chan master
Huairang 懷讓 (677–744). During the Northern Song dynasty, its name was changed
to Fuyan Temple.

古刹清虛境
停機問老翁
山高月漸小
源遠脈微通
虎嘯千峰肅
龍吟萬壑雄
丹青為佇望
繪入畫圖中

古樹蟠奇石
清谿遶碧苔
飯餘山鳥靜
雲破缽龍回
壁老形如畫
人間冷似灰
三生如半日
何處得愁來

紅葉都零落
山泉覺有聲
應知秋月朗
不及夜燈明
竹影埽階靜
花閒映塢清
松間拈埜句
長嘯萬峰鳴

---

331   This may well be a comment on the state of Chan Buddhism, which by the seventeenth
      century was regarded by many as being in a state of decline.

XIII

The ancient monastery is a pure and empty realm.
Having ceased all scheming, I visit the old master.
The mountains are so high that the moon grows small;
The source is so distant that the bloodline grows faint.[331]
Tigers howl in the thousand awe-inspiring peaks;
Dragons chant in the ten thousand mighty ravines.
I gaze long and hard at the reds and greens
And endeavor to capture them all in my painting.

XIV

Ancient trees coil around odd-shaped stones;
Clear streams circle around jade-green moss.
Bellies full, the mountain birds settle down;
Clouds burst: the alms-bowl dragon returns.[332]
The ancient cliffs are like those in a painting,
While the human world is as cold as ashes.
Three lifetimes are like a mere half a day.
From where can sorrow and grief emerge?

XV

The red leaves have all withered and fallen.
The mountain spring seems to be speaking.
It must know that the clearest of autumn moons
Does not shine as brightly as the nighttime lamp.
Shadows of bamboo brush silently cover the stairs.
The light shines on the flowers along the low wall.
Here among the pines, I play with rustic phrases,
While lingering sighs sound in the ten thousand peaks.

332 This may be an allusion to a story about the Indian monk Sengshe 僧涉, also known
   as Master Sha, of the Northern Wei dynasty (386–534). He would recite a spell every
   morning, and a hungry dragon would descend into his alms bowl, bringing a downpour
   of rain in its wake. Dragons in Chinese culture are regarded as bringers of rain, and
   Buddhist monks were often celebrated for their rainmaking powers.

巖老山房瘦
閒僧許暫棲
雲深天墜地
影淡日沉西
勞我烏藤杖
看人白壁題
悠悠清興永
說偈對潺谿

疏狂難入世
甘老白雲巔
實際原無地
清虛賴有天
棲心空劫外
拭目古崖前
蘭若傍谿結
隨時了幻緣

藤華飛石徑
流水遶東津
久與世人隔
時來垫鹿親
縈縈深壑路
杳杳大江濱
嘯傲忘情處
風和樹又春

333　Perhaps a poem left by someone who had traveled through.
334　Ultimate truth or reality is limitless, undefined by territorial or earthly boundaries.

XVI

The cliffs are ancient, the mountain hut ramshackle.
Perhaps this idle monastic can lodge here for a while.
The clouds are thick where the heavens birth the earth;
The shadows are faint where the sun sinks in the west.
Relying on the efforts of my dark rattan walking stick,
I catch sight of someone's inscription on a white wall.[333]
Carefree and content, with endless pure delight,
I recite these gāthās while facing a gurgling brook.

XVII

By nature I am unrestrained and not fit for society,
Content to grow old on these white cloudy peaks.
Ultimate reality has no earthly location;[334]
The pure void is dependent on the sky.[335]
Settling my mind beyond the eons of nothingness,[336]
Cleansing my eyes, I stand before the ancient cliffs.
My forest hermitage sits next to a crook in the river,
A constant reminder of how illusion arises.

XVIII

Wisteria blossoms flutter over the stone path;
Flowing waters circle round the eastern ford.
For a long while I've lived apart from the world,
And over time I have befriended the wild deer.
The road twists and turns through the deep ravines,
Dark and secluded along the shore of the great river.
Whistling, I wander in the realm of dispassion.
The breezes gentle, the trees again bloom in spring.

335 My translation here is tentative.
336 "Eons of nothingness" is a Buddhist term referring to long periods of time during which
    there are no buddhas in the world.

苔砌谿邊路
茆簷覆百花
年來何甲子
節至幾春華
策杖臨高石
傾缾步淺沙
猿聲歸洞晚
和月弄煙霞

窗碧映清輝
開門納翠微
離霞孤鶴迴
繞石亂雲飛
矮榻苔為席
疏簾葉作衣
斜陽西去遠
倦鳥自知歸

獨向山居老
松門露兩乂
書經集貝葉
挂錫落藤華
種竹開青徑
穿林摘紫茶
相逢塵外客
秋信寄誰家

337 That is, in the traditional sixty-year cycle.
338 This line comes from the famous poem "Let's Return Home!" by the fourth-century
     poet Tao Qian upon retiring from official life to live in the countryside as a semi-recluse.

XIX

Mossy stone steps line the path along the stream;
Thatched eaves are covered with white blossoms.
The years pass: where are we now in the cycle?[337]
The seasons arrive: how many springs have bloomed?
Aided by my walking stick, I wander among tall boulders;
Emptying out my water flask, I tread the shallow sands.
Gibbons cry as they return to their caves at dusk;
A tender moon flirts with the rosy evening clouds.

XX

The green screen shines with a clear bright light;
The open door takes in the blue-green of the hills.
Leaving the rosy clouds, the lone crane returns;
Circling the boulders, the nimbus clouds drift by.
On a low couch, moss is my meditation mat;
Behind thin bamboo blinds, leaves serve as my robe.
When the setting sun disappears far into the west,
The weary birds instinctively know the way home.[338]

XXI

Facing the hills, I will live out my days alone,
My door of pine exposed on both sides.
I gather leaves on which to copy out the sutras;[339]
Hanging up my staff, I lower the rattan flowers.[340]
Planting bamboo, I open up a verdant pathway;
Wending through the woods, I gather purple tea.
I meet someone coming from the dusty world,
But to whom would I send an autumn letter?[341]

339 My translation of this couplet is tentative. Early Indian Buddhist texts were written on
     patra leaves.
340 My translation here is tentative.
341 In other words, though there is an opportunity to send a letter by way of the fellow
     traveling monastic, the poet has no family to write to.

瀑響決長河
藤芽挂綠蘿
推雲出岫杳
埽徑落華多
簷柳拖金線
谿藤亂碧波
晴明天氣暖
凍解沒前坡

葉落滿山黃
茫茫匝地霜
搜林番潤柳
穿隙入山房
池凍梅花吐
空清鴈字狂
埜燒增烈燄
風送晚煙香

秋至梧先老
涼生鴈早歸
蛩聲依戶切
水潦出途稀
明月舒光皎
孤雲抱雨飛
夜來風過樹
紅葉滿荊扉

342 A style of calligraphy writing.

XXII

Echoes of the waterfall spill into the long river.
Buds of wisteria hang from the green vines.
Clouds are nudged from the mountain depths.
On the swept path, fallen blossoms pile up high.
The willows by the eaves dangle golden threads,
And the wisteria by the river tangles in the green ripples.
The day is clear and sunlit, the weather is warm,
The melting ice disappears from the hillsides.

XXIII

Leaves fall, flooding the mountains with yellow,
And over a great distance, frost covers the ground.
Searching the woods for the willow by the stream,
I negotiate a crevice to enter my mountain hut.
The pond is frozen, but plum blossoms poke out;
The clear sky is etched by a line of geese in mad cursive.[342]
The fire I build in the wild burns ever more brightly;
The breeze sees off the evening with incense smoke.

XXIV

Autumn arrives and the paulownia is the first to shed;
A chill arises and the geese have long ago returned.
The chirping of crickets fills the stairs by the doorway;
The rivers flooded, few now venture onto the roads.
The luminous moon unrolls its glow and shines bright;
A solitary cloud embraces the rain and drifts away.
As night falls, the wind blows through the trees,
And the red leaves cover up the brushwood gate.

桂輪偏照垺
嵐氣滿幽林
愛見澂清景
恒持虛白心
苔平趺坐穩
風勁入林深
老衲來相問
焚香一鼓琴

煙霞峰

策杖遙登最上山
真風須向翠巖攀
世間濁質難相許
雲外清游信自閒
怪石欲飛形躍躍
驚流直下響潺潺
行來不覺幽玄處
蹋碎煙霞信步還

XXV

The moon illuminates particularly the wilds;
The mountain mist fills the secluded woods.
I love to look at this crystalline landscape,
Which lends itself to a clear and empty mind.
On the flat moss, I sit quietly in meditation
As gusty winds blow deep into the forest.
When an elderly monastic stops by to see me,
We light some incense and strum on the zither.

Mist and Clouds Peak

With my walking stick, I climb far
    into the highest mountains;
A rippling wind also clambers up
    these emerald-green cliffs.
The turbid muddiness of the world
    finds it hard to enter here;
Beyond the clouds, I roam in purity,
    completely free and at ease.
Strange boulders look as if about to fly
    or leap up into the sky;
Rushing streams flow straight down
    burbling and gurgling away.
I've wandered without realizing
    into this hidden place of mystery.
Treading on the mist and clouds,
    I leisurely make my way home.

神僊洞

萬疊蒼黃鎖翠嵬
山峰寂歷絕塵埃
半谿影出清泉竹
幾陬香飄碧澗梅
暮雨濕侵藤下路
斜陽光襯洞中苔
從來不學長生術
到此還思一溯洄

---

343 The Gods and Immortals Grotto is another scenic site in the Nanyue Mountains. Grottos
are traditionally believed to be the place where Daoist immortals reside.

Gods and Immortals Grotto[343]

Ten thousand layers of pale yellow
  envelop its green rugged rocks.
The mountain peak, solitary and silent,
  does away with all dust and dirt.
The valley is half filled with shadows
  of the bamboo by the clear spring.
Sporadic whiffs of wind-carried scent
  come from the plum by the green brook.
The late-afternoon rain drenches
  the road beneath the reeds.
The glow of the setting sun sets off
  the moss inside the grotto.
Although I've never studied
  the arts of immortality,
Coming here makes me think again
  of swimming against the stream.[344]

344 This grotto has also been sometimes associated with Tao Yuanming's Peach Blossom
   Stream, and the idea of going against the stream may be related to that. Aware of the
   Daoist associations of this spot, the poet is perhaps noting that as a Buddhist, her main
   aspiration is not immortality, but rather going against the stream of *samsara* to realize
   enlightenment or nirvana.

天台寺

> 蹋破浮雲望彼蒼
> 松濤深處石為梁
> 千山月色侵人夢
> 一樹梅花透塢香
> 幽谷豈妨春信早
> 懶雲寧解客情忙
> 我從鳥道行將遍
> 黃葉鳴爐欲沸湯

中山大明寺

> 芒鞋拄杖腳頭寬
> 信步行來路不艱
> 明敞高懸連褐淨
> 清光返照逼窗塞
> 兩廊素壁真堪畫
> 一帶青山色可餐
> 春去巳知花柳瘦
> 大家列坐是團欒

---

345 Tiantai (Heavenly Terrace) Monastery on Mount Heng should be distinguished from
the better known Tiantai Monastery located in Zhejiang province and associated with
the eminent monk Zhiyi 智顗 (538–597), traditionally regarded as the First Patriarch
of the Tiantai school of Buddhism.

Heavenly Terrace Monastery[345]

My feet break up the drifting clouds
    as I gaze at the azure skies.
The wind sings deep in the pines,
    and boulders bridge the streams.
Over a thousand mountains, the moon
    invades people's dreams
While a single tree of flowering plum
    perfumes the embankments.
How can this hidden valley
    resist the early signs of spring?
The leisurely clouds help relieve
    the traveler's harried mind.
We have come along the bird path
    and will very soon arrive.
Yellow leaves crackle in the fire;
    the soup is about to boil.

Mount Zhong's Great Illumination Temple[346]

With straw sandals and walking stick,
    I've traveled far and wide.
Taking my time, I have come here;
    the road was not difficult.
I hang up my tattered belongings
    and clean my inner robes[347]
As a limpid light reflects back
    and strikes the windows.
Two corridors and a white wall
    are worthy of a painting.
A ribbon of dark-blue mountains
    is a feast for the eyes.
I know that spring has departed,
    for flowers and willows are slender.
The rows of seated meditators
    are in complete bliss.

---

346 This temple, built in 764, was located near Yanxia Peak, where Jizong Xingche had her
    hermitage.
347 My translation here is tentative.

太陽泉

引出峰頭噴未休
太陽何處不隨流
穿林渡海離塵網
傲雪經霜得自由
勢湧沖開千嶂碧
津流吞卻一輪秋
斗牛不動真常處
宇宙無雙第一幽

仲秋留別

煙水無停枻
年來如自然
林花邀副墨
池草倩書玄
有句非平仄
無心任折旋
吾今非孟浪
作息信前緣

---

348 This is the name of another scenic site on Mount Nanyue. The term "Great Yang" (*tai-yang* 太陽) is used in Daoism to refer to the point when yang energy is at its greatest. It is also used to refer to the sun. Nanyue has long been considered a sacred mountain by Daoists, as well as Buddhists.

The Great Yang Spring[348]

The spring emerges from the peak's summit,
  and gushes without cease.
Where do the rays of the sun
  not follow in its flow?
Threading through forests and seas,
  it escapes the dusty net;
Overcoming both snow and frost,
  it finds its freedom.
Surging out, it smashes open
  the green of a thousand cliffs,
And its flowing waters swallow up
  the circle of the autumn moon.
The Dipper and the Ox don't budge
  from their true constancy.[349]
The first among mysteries,
  There is nothing like it in the world!

The Second Month of Autumn: A Parting Poem

Endlessly rowing along the misty waters,
Over the years it has become second nature.
Woodland flowers invite duplicates in ink.
Pond grasses ask for calligraphic mystery.[350]
Lines with neither oblique nor level tones
That mindlessly can shift and turn at will.[351]
I am not just being impulsive,
But am living according to my karma.

---

349 The Dipper and the Ox are the names of two of the twenty-eight so-called "lodges" into which the sky was divided in traditional Chinese astronomy. As a compound, the Dipper-Ox is used to refer to the heavens in general or the entire sky.

350 My translation of this couplet is tentative.

351 In Chinese regulated verse, the words in each poetic line must adhere to a prescribed pattern of oblique and level tones. Here the poet seems to be referring to a kind of poetry that is not subject to these norms.

自分非高遁
行蹤任卷舒
無心棲虎市
有志悏鶉居
暑氣消衣袂
秋聲散牧漁
雌黃隨眾口
端不掩瑕瑜

元旦玩雪

極目平沉大地通
孤燈照映草堂中
梅花一樹誰知白
玉壁千峰我幸逢
禪室飄來風說法
香臺飛去鳥談空
年年好景原無別
眼界于今更不同

---

352 In *Zhuangzi*, the true sage is described as "a quail at rest, a little fledgling at its meal, a
bird in flight that leaves no trail behind" (Watson, trans., 2013, 88).

It is not my lot in life to be a lofty recluse,
At times found living in seclusion, and at times not.
When one is mindless, one can settle down with tigers.
Full of resolve, one can live content among quails.[352]
The summer heat dissipates in the sleeves of my robe
With the autumn sounds of scattered shepherds and fishermen.
Even when maligned in the court of public opinion,
The upright do not conceal their strengths and flaws.

Enjoying the Snow on New Year's Day

Extending as far as the eye can see
    is this enormous world.
A solitary lamp puts forth its light
    inside this grass hut.
A single blossoming plum tree—
    who appreciates its whiteness?
A thousand peaks with cliffs of jade,
    I've been lucky to find them!
Gusting its way into the meditation hall,
    the wind expounds the Dharma.
Flitting away above the incense tray,[353]
    the birds discourse on Emptiness.
Year after year this beautiful scene
    has always been the same,
But today the way I look at the world
    could not be more different!

353 This is a wooden or bamboo tray with a small censer used to burn incense in order to
     time a seated meditation period.

志感

> 勞勞車馬走風塵
> 幸是當年埋炤身
> 壁立不行屠狗客
> 懸巖豈坐釣魚人
> 溪山瀟散心加靜
> 雲月開明意自真
> 萬事如棋何足問
> 道緣心境幾番新

次韻酬愧菴居士

> 解脫場中共一家
> 如君立志巳堪誇
> 心田薙去無明草
> 覺樹開來智慧華
> 坐斷洞中猿鳥道
> 任從方外水雲賒
> 何時得遂幽巖隱
> 拍手谿頭笑落霞

---

354 People of low standing or character were often referred to as dog butchers.
355 The mind as the place where one plants and cultivates the seeds of Buddhahood.

My Aspirations

Toiling away, carriages and horses
    travel in the windblown dust.
Fortunately for me, this is the year
    I will hide myself away.
Here where the mountains rise steeply,
    no dog butchers ply their trade.[354]
And where among these precipitous cliffs
    would a fisherman drop his line?
Streams and mountains disperse the dust,
    and the mind becomes more still.
Clouds and moon make everything clear,
    and one's aims become sincere.
The myriad affairs are like a game of go
    and are not worth asking about.
When one feels an affinity with the Way,
    everything is always new.

Written to Rhymes by the Layman of Zhoukui Hermitage

Here on this site of liberation,
    we belong to one family.
The ends to which you've aspired
    are already worthy of praise!
The field of the mind is cleared[355]
    of the weeds of ignorance;
The tree of awareness is blooming
    with the flowers of wisdom.
Sitting in meditation inside the caves,
    traveling the arduous path.[356]
Moving at ease without constraint
    among the clouds and rivers.
When can I follow you
    to hide away in the cliff sides,
Clapping at the head of the stream,
    And smiling at the setting sun!

356 Literally, the path traversed by birds and gibbons, often used as an analogy for the
    difficulty of following the path of Chan practice.

次南嶽和尚臥病二首

空谷寥寥獨掩扉
為探心地卻忘機
病身一任同松老
瘦骨何妨與鶴肥
識破浮生真夢幻
好憑祖道逗光輝
縛茆已遂煙霞志
臥看閒雲自在飛

林間長日意閒閒
問疾無人日往還
有法利生猶未了
無心合道本非艱
不因疏漏幽藏壑
寧為清閒老臥山
魔佛兩頭俱坐斷
晴谿贏得步潺湲

357 Jizong Xingche's teacher, Shanci Tongji.
358 The crane symbolizes, among other things, wisdom and longevity. According to myth,
      once it reaches six hundred years old, the bird, with its elegantly long "skinny" legs, no
      longer needs to eat at all.

Visiting the Monk of Nanyue on His Sickbed: Two Poems[357]

The empty valley is sparse and bare
    and you stay alone with doors closed.
In your search for the basis of the mind,
    you've set aside all plans.
You allow your body, beset by illness,
    to grow old with the pines.
Just skin and bones, but why should you
    be any plumper than a crane?[358]
You've seen through this floating life,
    nothing but a dream or mirage.:
You rely on the way of the Patriarch[359]
    and rest in his radiance.
In your thatched hut, you achieved
    your transcendent ambitions.
Now you lie on your bed and watch
    the clouds drift idly by.

In the forest, the days are long,
    and one's thoughts are easy.
The ill man isn't here,
    but I can come another day.
The dharma benefits one's life
    even if not fully enlightened.
Casting off the mind to join the Way
    won't be difficult.
You haven't just slipped
    into this life of seclusion.
Rather, you wanted the pure leisure
    to grow old in the mountains.
Mara at one end, Buddha at the other:[360]
    you've meditated them both away.
The sun-lit stream has been reached,
    and you step into its flow.

359 That is, the way of Bodhidharma.
360 Mara is the name of the heavenly king who tried to tempt Prince Siddhartha away from
    his pursuit and attainment of Buddhahood, or ultimate awakening. Symbolically, he is
    associated with death, rebirth, and desire, or in other words, everything that does not
    lead to awakening.

壽再生禪兄五十

坐斷三吳百億川
神鋒凜凜耀當天
期同海宇恒沙數
獨露靈山面目全
滿袖清風施好手
半鉤明月接高禪
慶君能得無生樂
腦後圓明徹大千

361   This may well refer to the nun Zaisheng (see p. 55). As explained in the Introduction,
       p. xxxiv, Buddhist nuns traditionally used male forms of address when referring to nuns
       in their monastic family, as an indication that they have transcended gender.

To Chan Elder Dharma Brother Zaisheng on Her Fiftieth Birthday[361]

Meditating, you cut off the million streams
    that run through the Three Wus.[362]
The divine sword shimmers like ice
    as it shines toward the heavens.
Time is as vast as the sea and sky
    and as countless as the Ganges sands.
Independently, you've exposed
    the face of Vulture Peak.
Filling your sleeves with clear breezes,
    you demonstrate the skill of your hands.
The half-hook of a luminous moon
    joins the lofty meditation.[363]
I congratulate you on realizing
    the joy of the Unborn.
The radiance in the back of your mind
    penetrates the many worlds.[364]

---

362 Shaoxing in eastern Zhejiang province was once divided into three parts, the "three Wus": Wukui, Wubu, and Wuxing.

363 My translation here is tentative.

364 My translation here is tentative.

幽湖指息菴贈道明禪師

且喜高樓近水邊
眉開別是一壺天
帆從門外分南北
雲起村中遞後先
喋喋漁歌醒午夢
喃喃鳥語韻幽玄
箇中儘有真機現
到此何須更問禪

___

365 Literally, like being in a world of immortals. Legend has it that immortals have the
power to create an entire world within a single gourd.

At Zhixi Cloister on Hidden Lake, Presented to Chan Master Daoming

How delightful is this high tower
  right near the water's edge.
Worries lift, and we are
  in an entirely different world!³⁶⁵
The boats from beyond the gates
  divide into north and south.
The clouds rising from the village
  pass overhead in succession.
The words of the fisherman's song
  wake me from a noontime dream,
And the twittering of the birds
  resonates with subtle mystery.
In all this is completely manifested
  a most profound principle.
Here there is no longer any need
  to ask further about Chan!

贈敬可徐居士

稔識浮名似幻如
遠離人境結精廬
庭前修竹堪藏月
簷下環谿任走魚
明眼早知三要旨
忘心頓貫五車書
莫將世事空牢係
漢闕秦宮盡古墟

366 Xu Jingke 徐敬可 (also known as Xu Shan 徐善, 1631–1690) came from a well-known family of officials. He was only ten when his father was killed during the turmoil and violence that accompanied the fall of the Ming dynasty. He spent his life keeping the memory of his father alive, and became known for his studies of the *Classic of Changes* (*Yijing* 易經), as well as for his poetry. Jizong Xingche knew him personally.

Presented to Layman Xu Jingke[366]

When one knows ephemeral fame
    to be no more than an illusion,
One may distance oneself from the world
    and build oneself a hermitage.
In front of the courtyard, the slender bamboo
    allows the moon to hide;
Below the eaves, the winding brook
    allows the fish to freely swim.
Seeing clearly, you've long ago understood
    the three essential principles.[367]
Forgetting the mind, you right away mastered
    the five cartloads of books.[368]
Do not allow the affairs of the world
    to uselessly drag you along.
The Han pavilions and Qin palaces
    are now nothing but ruins.[369]

367 This refers generally to the three essentials of Buddhist cultivation: morality, meditation, and wisdom. Since Jizong Xingche belonged to the Linji school of Chan, it also refers to the three requisites for enlightenment according to the Tang dynasty master Linji Yixuan, namely, the great root of faith 大信根, the great ball of doubt 大疑團, and the great overpowering will 大憤志.

368 In *Zhuangzi*, his friend Master Hui Shi 惠施 is described as having many skills and five cartloads of books. Later this term came to refer to great breadth and depth of learning.

369 That is, the impressive monuments of the first two great Chinese dynasties, the Qin (221–206 BCE) and the Han (206 BCE–220 CE).

借靜室住冰禪人詩以贈之

借得三間近水傍
入門無件不荒涼
雲封瓦灶苔封壁
月滿蘿龕霜滿床
常憶古人穿紙襖
須知活計在空囊
相看別有安閒事
贈汝新篇話正長

370　In other words, over the simple mud cooking stove there is no roof, only clouds.

Having Borrowed a Meditation Hut from Chan Practitioner Zhubing,
I Wrote a Poem to Present to Her

I borrowed a three-room hut
  close to the riverside.
Though there's nothing inside,
  it does not feel bleak.
The clouds seal off the mud stove,[370]
  and moss seals off the walls.
The moon fills the mossy shrine,
  and frost covers up the bed.
I often think how people of old
  wore paper-lined jackets.[371]
They had to know how to survive
  with nothing in their pockets.
I've looked over this special place,
  and my mind feels at ease.
I present you with this new composition
  even though it's rather long!

371 In ancient times, Daoist hermits and the very poor would often line their clothes with
    paper to keep warm.

留別嚴嚴鞦道人

聖制相將期又終
何妨飛錫去凌空
濯盂就澗囊懸樹
舞棹橫波帆滿風
撩起便行無彼此
得緣方住任東西
一番法器難忘卻
明月天涯處處同

372　Yan Duoli (also known as Yan Dacan 嚴大參, 1590–1671) was a well-known Buddhist layman who was largely the one responsible for ensuring the publication of the collection of Jizong Xingche's recorded sayings, which includes the poems translated here.

A Farewell Poem for Person of the Way Yan Duoli[372]

The time of sagely rule and of being together
    eventually must end.
Why then should this wandering nun[373]
    not set out across the sky?
I rinse my bowl in the mountain stream,
    and hang my bag from a tree.
The dancing oars slant across the waves;
    the sails fill up with wind.
Then I haul the boat ashore and go by foot:
    there is neither here nor there.[374]
I will reside where karma takes me,
    be it in the east or west.
If one is a vessel of the dharma,
    it is hard to ever completely forget.
The bright moon illuminates all of heaven
    in each and every place the same.

---

373 Literally, "flying walking stick," used to refer to monastics who travel far and wide on
     pilgrimages or to visit other eminent masters.
374 This may be an allusion to the well-known comparison of the teachings of the Buddha
     to a raft that can ferry one across the river of *samsara*, after which it can be left behind.

戊戌元旦

又見東風度藥闌
可盤桓處且盤桓
金爐火在香初遠
石磬敲來聲未殘
躑遍吳山何地好
漫思楚水對春寒
老梅不減先年韻
把茗吮豪試詠看

顧孟調居士六十賦贈

會爾初年五十餘
算來甲子近何如
光陰有限頻頻惜
妄想無邊漸漸除
淨土覺華禪水灌
識田愛艸慧刀鋤
百千萬劫都空過
莫使今生又涉虛

375   The east wind is a harbinger of spring.

New Year's Day, 1658

Once again, the winds from the east[375]
    blow across the flowering hedge.
Wherever one can stay and linger,
    one should certainly do so!
In the gold censer, incense burns,
    its aroma beginning to spread.
The sounds of the stone chimes
    have yet to fade away.
I've traveled all the mountains of Wu
    and know not which spot is the finest.
But still I think of the rivers of Chu
    as I face the spring chill.
The old plum tree has not changed
    its tune of seasons past.
So, taking a sip of some good tea,
    I try to compose a poem.

Composed for Layman Gu Mengdiao on His Sixtieth Birthday

The year we first met,
    you were a little over fifty.
What is it like to find yourself
    nearing the sixty-year mark?
The flow of time has its limits
    as it hastens and hurries by.
Deluded thoughts have no end
    and are gradually uprooted.
Pure Land flowers of realization
    are irrigated by Chan waters,
While fields of knowledge and bamboo of attachment
    are felled by wisdom's sword.
Thousands and thousands of kalpas
    all pass away into emptiness.
So do make sure that this present life
    is not crossed over in vain!

秋日懷母

> 斫額萱堂秋信來
> 籬邊黃菊帶霜開
> 為憐消息無人寄
> 一日峰前望幾回

示眾居士四偈

> 大千劫火洞然
> 此箇原來不壞
> 誰知滿目青山
> 盡是法身三昧

> 指上豈能見月
> 鏡中何用尋頭
> 不道即心即佛
> 便去騎牛覓牛

> 假和地水火風
> 未免生老病死
> 寶藏人人現成
> 何必遺金孫子

> 幻影任歸露電
> 寂心俱付寒灰
> 直須休去歇去
> 那管魔來佛來

---

376 According to traditional Buddhist cosmology, during what is known as the kalpa of
destruction, the entire physical universe will be annihilated by fire.

On an Autumn Day, Thinking of My Mother

Gazing in the direction where my mother lived,
   where autumn has surely arrived,
The yellow chrysanthemums by the fence
   will have been touched by frost.
What I most lament is that there is no one
   to whom I can send my news.
All day in front of the mountain peak,
   I cannot keep from gazing out.

Dharma Instructions to the Lay Assembly: Four Gāthās

When the great universe burns in a blazing fire,[376]
Its origin will never be destroyed.
Who knew that to gaze at the blue mountains
Is to contemplate Absolute Reality?[377]

How can you see the moon on the tip of your finger?
What is the point of seeking your head in the mirror?[378]
Don't say that the mind is none other than the Buddha,
And then go looking for the ox while riding on its back.[379]

As long as you identify with earth, water, fire, and wind,
You won't avoid birth, aging, sickness, and death.
The precious treasure can be manifested by one and all.
What need to leave gold behind for your grandchildren?

Let transient things go like dew and lightning.
The tranquil mind will reduce them all to cold ashes.
All you need to do is to take a break from always going.
Who cares then if Mara or the Buddha comes?[380]

377 Literally, "is in every way a *samādhi* of the Dharmakaya." The Dharmakaya, or body of
    the dharma, refers generally to absolute reality, or Emptiness.
378 This is an allusion to the story found in the Heroic March Sutra of Yajñadatta, who
    glimpsed his head in a mirror and was convinced that he had lost it from above his
    shoulders.
379 In other words, don't go seeking enlightenment when you are already enlightened.
380 See n. 360.

子雍成如

---

381   For more on Ziyong Chengru, see Grant 2008, 165–184. The collection of her recorded sayings is titled *Recorded Sayings of Chan Master Ziyong Ru* (*Ziyong Ru chanshi yulu* 子雍如禪師語錄).

Ziyong Chengru

Ziyong Chengru was born sometime around 1648 to a family surnamed Zhou 周. Her father appears to have won honors for military service rendered to the Qing court, which is perhaps why he moved the family from Jingmen in central Hubei province to the capital city Beijing. Ziyong was an only child born to older parents. Perhaps in fulfillment of a vow, she was allowed to become a nun rather than being pressed to marry. After taking the tonsure, she went in search of Chan training, and during a visit to Mount Wutai she received dharma transmission from Linji Chan Master Gulu Yuanfan 古律元範, a second-generation disciple of the famous Linji Chan master Muchen Daomin 木陳道忞 (1596–1674). Ziyong Chengru went on to head two convents in the Beijing area, Yongan Convent and Hongen Convent. Her followers were no doubt primarily the wives of court officials and members of the royal family. As her reputation grew, she came to the attention of the Kangxi emperor (r. 1661–1722), who met with her at least twice and bestowed upon her the honorary title of Chan Master Compassionate Vehicle of Universal Salvation of Yanshan 燕山慈船普濟禪師. Around age fifty, Ziyong embarked on an extended pilgrimage to the southeast to visit temples, stupas, and other sites associated with her lineage. She was well received in the southeast, despite her loyalty to the Qing in a region that harbored many Ming loyalists. Her charisma and perhaps preaching skills won over many, and she was invited to give dharma talks at Tiantong Monastery in Ningbo, Zhejiang province, one of the most important centers of Chan Buddhism, as well as at Bixia Convent in Hangzhou. It is unclear where or when Ziyong passed away. Her recorded sayings have been preserved in the *Jiaxing Chinese Buddhist Canon*.[381]

鍾子擊碎於此有感隨作一偈

　忽聞鍾子落塵埃
　擊碎乾坤似震雷
　靜夜高歌欣自得
　引來明月上樓臺

聞斫木聲

　氣量含虛萬象沉
　水聲風樹應禪心
　能從百尺竿頭進
　枯木寒崖色更新

詠雪

　春風吹起晝生寒
　六出奇英舞玉欄
　須信一番寒徹骨
　老梅開遍好相看

山居二首

　蒼松帶雪寒
　曲折似龍蟠
　庭際春生草
　遊人仔細看

---

382 In other words, once you have reached the height of spiritual attainment, can you take
      yet another step into the unknown?

*A Bell Shattered after Being Struck, and I Was Moved to
Compose a Gāthā*

Suddenly I heard the bell
   plummet into the dust,
Smashing the world into bits
   like a crash of thunder.
In the still night, I sang out
   in joy and fulfillment,
Attracting the bright moon
   up to the tall tower.

Upon Hearing the Sound of Wood Being Chopped

When one's moral character is spacious,
   all things become settled.
The sounds of the river and the wind in the trees
   all echo the mind of Chan.
If you can step forward
   from the tip of a hundred-foot pole,[382]
The withered trees and cold cliffs
   will recover all their colors!

Ode to the Snow

The spring breezes rise up,
   and the day grows chilly.
Wondrous six-pointed flakes
   dance on the balustrade.
You must trust in this spell
   of bone-chilling cold.
The old plum tree will bloom,
   and then you'll see!

Living in the Mountains: Two Verses

Hoary pines, twisted and knotted like coiled dragons,
Are covered with cold snow.
The traveler closely examines
Spring grasses along the courtyard edge.

水抱孤村遠
山通一徑斜
不知深樹裏
還住幾人家

丙子述懷

韶華經幾度
四十九年春
處世雖無偶
問心只自親

炷香消白晝
闔戶遠紅塵
痴夢從今醒
如如閒道人

遊西山

西山佳景漫相尋
桃色紅分柳色金
滿目春光無限意
翠微古蹟到如今

上船偈

柳系含煙二月天
靈花異路白雲邊
花船已出清波上
一道神光萬景前

383   The Western Hills are located outside of Beijing.

The river encircles the solitary distant town,
And a single path slopes through the mountains.
One wouldn't know that deep within the trees
Are the homes of several families.

Thoughts in the Bingzi Year [1696]

How many days of youth have passed?
I've experienced the spring of forty-nine years.
Though in my life I've had no partner,
Looking within, I befriended myself.

The incense stick burns until dawn,
With doors closed, far from the dusty world.
From now on, no more deluded dreams
For this ever at-ease Person of the Way.

An Excursion to the Western Hills

Stretched out endlessly
    are the fine views of the Western Hills:[383]
The red of the peach trees,
    the gold of the willows.
The spring light that fills the eyes
    seems to go on forever,
With the green hills and old ruins
    both enduring to this day.

Gāthā: Boarding My Boat

Slender willow branches hold the mist
    on this early spring day.
Magical flowers and a different road
    sit at the edge of white clouds.
The painted boat has already set out,
    sailing on the clear waves.
A single road of spiritual radiance,[384]
    with ten thousand prospects ahead!

---

384 This could also be translated as "the spiritual radiance of the one path."

初秋感懷

> 香飄桂子憶南州
> 雨滴芙蓉露正稠
> 艷麗不知時節換
> 輪將衲被且蒙頭

贈如如法兄

> 知兄法柄異常流
> 暗去明來得自由
> 打破淨瓶全體現
> 他年拍掌笑無窮

省師四偈

> 訪師終日意寥寥
> 塵念何曾留一毫
> 喫飯著衣隨分度
> 一如木死未經燒

---

385 Nuns make use of male forms of address to refer to each other as well as to male monastics. In this case, Ruru is probably the name of a fellow nun.

386 To smash or kick over the water jug indicates transcending dualistic distinctions and awakening.

Early Autumn Sentiments

Fragrance wafts in the cassia trees
    as I think of the south.
Raindrops fall on the hibiscus flowers
    where the dew too is thick.
All this beauty is yet unaware
    of the season's changing.
Soon I'll need my patched quilt
    to pull up over my head!

To My Elder Dharma Brother Ruru[385]

I know my elder dharma brother's power
    is of an unusual kind.
The darkness is gone, the light has come,
    she has attained freedom!
She struck and smashed the water jug,
    and the totality was manifested.[386]
Then she clapped her hands
    and could not stop laughing!

Asking Questions of the Masters: Four Gāthās

After a day visiting with a master,
    all ideation is emptied out.
How could even a single iota
    of worldly thought remain!
Eat your food, don your clothes,
    and adjust to your lot,
Just be like that dead tree
    that has never burned.[387]

---

387 There are many allusions in *Zhuangzi* to the body being like a dead tree. For example,
    "'Can you be a baby?' The baby acts without knowing what it is doing, moves without
    knowing where it is going. Its body is like the limb of a withered tree, its mind like dead
    ashes. Since it is so, no bad fortune will ever touch it, and no good fortune will come
    to it, either. And if it is free from good and bad fortune, then what human suffering can
    it undergo?" See Watson 2013, 193.

一自無心萬事休
也無歡喜也無憂
無心莫謂便無事
尚有無心箇念頭

逆順未嘗忘此道
窮通一味信前緣
自從了卻虛空性
不動絲毫本自然

萬里長江一葉舟
風波歷遍志難酬
誰知水盡山窮處
覿面相逢話白頭

雜詠

中秋雖雨月還明
按指飛光道可成
霧濕紙衣原不透
虛空踏破好遊行

388   For all of its many methods and approaches, the dharma is said to have only "one taste."

389   A mudra is a symbolic or ritual gesture usually made with the hands and fingers. There would appear to be an allusion here to the following passage from the Heroic March Sutra: "When I arrange my fingers to form the ocean-mudra, the light of the ocean-

Once you cast off the mind,
  everything will end.
No longer any pleasure and joy;
  no longer any grief and sorrow.
Don't say that casting off the mind
  leaves nothing more to do.
For there may still remain
  the thought of having no mind!

Whether life goes smoothly or not,
  I have never forgotten the Way.
Having fully grasped the "one taste,"[388]
  I trust my karmic affinities.
As soon as one completely realizes
  the nature of Emptiness,
Without moving a single inch,
  you'll be just who you are!

Such a long distance along the Yangzi
  in a leaf of a boat,
Enduring the wind and the waves,
  I find my goals are hard to meet!
Who knows where the rivers end
  and the mountains stop.
Where can we meet face-to-face
  and discuss growing old?

A Miscellaneous Chant

Although it's raining this mid-autumn,
  the moon is still bright,
And under the radiance of the ocean mudra,
  the Way can be realized![389]
The mist may dampen the paper robes,
  but it can never penetrate them.
Once the empty void is stamped to pieces,
  walking on it is easy!

---

mudra *samādhi* shines forth. But the moment a thought arises in your mind, you must
endure the stress of involvement with perceived objects. It is simply because you have
not diligently pursued the path to supreme enlightenment." CBETA T19, no. 945,
p. 121b1–2; translated in Heng 2009, 158.

從稻地經過偶成一偈

渠流曲曲遶瓊墻
月落園林井墨粧
翠柳凝煙寒色淨
白蓮帶露吐青香
村名設舞臨高閣
鵲噪青山近草堂
風送春聲情未息
又添夏景引爐長

雜偈八首

一

老大年來無可得
只因皈佛出紅塵
出家傳法傳心要
藥病與他身有神

<hr/>

390 The meaning of this line is unclear. It may refer to the temporary stages erected in the countryside for the performance of plays during festivals.

Walking through the Rice Paddies, I Casually Composed This Gāthā

The water channels bend and twist
   around the glistening walls.
The moon sets in the fields and woods,
   and the village becomes a blot of ink.
Green willows congeal the mist,
   its cold color very pure,
And the white lotuses covered with dew
   emit a delicate scent.
In the village known for staging dances,
   I ascend the tall pavilion.[390]
As magpies cry in the dark mountains,
   I approach the thatched hall.
The breezes carry the sounds of spring,
   and the feeling doesn't end.
They add to the summer scene
   and draw out the oven smoke.[391]

Eight Miscellaneous Gāthās [a selection of three]

I

When old age comes around,
   there is nothing to be done
But to take refuge in the Buddha
   and leave the world of red dust!
I became a nun to transmit the Dharma,
   the essence of the mind.
Leave healing illness to others,
   for this body is spirit!

391 My translation here is tentative.

三

　　從來學道喜山居
　　靜夜彌陀意自餘
　　會取本來真面目
　　何須更要理鯨魚

七

　　鉏雲種月學山居
　　不盡山花道有餘
　　石做枕頭不是虎
　　一天明月半床書

付囑智西堂衣拂偈曰

　　燕山一派向南流
　　到處分明月映洲
　　打破機關全體現
　　自然瀟洒更何求

392 That is, the original nature of mind.

393 In popular tradition, the tiger is the king of beasts and thus very auspicious. Images
　　of tigers were painted on doorways to keep evil spirits away. Especially prized were
　　ceramic sleeping pillows made in the form of tigers, which were believed to ward off
　　demons and prevent nightmares.

III

Since becoming a student of the Way,
  I've been fond of mountain living.
In the quiet nights, Amitabha
  fills my mind to overflowing.
Once you come to realize
  your true original face,[392]
What need is there to go
  and subdue the whale!

VII

Cloud-hoeing and moon-planting,
  I learn about mountain living
With its endless mountain flowers
  and the Way in abundance.
A stone can serve as a pillow,
  even if it isn't a tiger,[393]
With a sky full of the bright moon
  and a bed half full of books!

Entrusting Head Student Zhi with Robes and Whisk,[394]
I Composed This Gāthā

The lineage stream from the Yan mountains
  flows toward the south.[395]
Everywhere, things are clear and plain,
  like the moon reflected between the isles.
All the stratagems having been smashed open,
  Everything manifests as it truly is.[396]
Now that all is natural and unrestrained,
  what more is there to look for!

394 It would appear that Ziyong Chengru wrote this on the occasion of bestowing dharma
     transmission on one of her senior students.
395 This is a reference to Ziyong Chengru bringing the teaching of her lineage down from
     her home in northern China (the mountains of Yan) to southern China.
396 In other words, the head student Zhi has passed all of the dharma tests put to her by
     her master, and has qualified to receive dharma transmission.

明修

397 See Yu Qian, *Xinxu gaoseng zhuan*, CBETA B27, no. 151, 466a5–20. Mingxiu's four collections were titled *Mirror Clouds Collection* (*Jianyun ji* 鑒雲集), *The Footprints Collection* (*Liuji ji* 留跡集), *Southern Recorded Sayings* (*Yulu nanzhi* 語錄南帙), and *Recorded Sayings of Chan Master Dongwu Ben* (*Dongwu Ben chanshi yulu* 東悟本禪師語錄).

Mingxiu

Mingxiu (style name Keshang 可尚), also known as Chan Master Dongwu 東悟 and as Mingben 明本, hailed from Changshu, Jiangsu province. According to her biography, just before her birth, her mother had a vision of a divinity who predicted that the child would become a worthy transmitter of the Buddhist teachings. Mingxiu was a precociously intelligent girl who showed a strong inclination toward Buddhist practice and kept to a vegetarian diet. She refused to marry and dedicated herself instead to caring for her elderly mother. She appears to have been ordained under Master Chaoyuan Lianfeng 超源蓮峰 (1691–1745) at Yixian Temple in Suzhou, but received dharma transmission from a third-generation successor of the famous Linji Chan master Feiyin Tongrong 費隱通容 (1593–1661) at the Weimo Temple on Mount Yu, just outside of Changshu. After her mother's death, she traveled extensively and visited all four sacred mountains of Chinese Buddhism: Putuo, Jiuhua, Emei, and Wutai. After completing her pilgrimage to Mount Wutai, she traveled to Beijing, where she appears to have been well received, including by many high-ranking members of the court. She is associated with two convents in the north: Zhilin Dharma Hall and Linguan Convent. Mingxiu was known not only for her poetry, but also for her paintings of Buddhist images, landscapes, and flowers. Many of her poems were written as inscriptions to paintings, presumably her own. She was a prolific writer, with four collections of writings, including one of recorded sayings; all appear to have been lost.[397]

送親禮師登戒

幻途無處不朝真
從此休言涉世塵
陟屺正堪慈月好
登堂又喜覺華新
三遷教子緣方得
六十耆英道正親
此去報恩兼利衆
坦然顯現法王身

<hr>

398 "Seeing off relatives" is a term used to refer to part of the traditional marriage ritual in
which the bride's family escorts the bride to the home of the groom. Here, of course,
the "bride" is being escorted to a Buddhist convent.

Seeing Off Relatives,[398] *Bowing to My Master, and Taking Vows*

On this illusory road, there is no place
    where one cannot sit in practice.
From now on, I will no longer speak
    of traveling through the dusty world.
As my mother crosses over the hills,
    the merciful moonlight is good.
As I ascend the hall, filled with joy,
    the flower of enlightenment is fresh.
Due to my mother's unstinting care[399]
    I have been able to fulfill this karma.
Thanks to my sixty-year-old hero,
    I've grown intimate with the Way.
Someday I will repay her endless love[400]
    by benefiting all sentient beings.
In calm tranquility, I will fully manifest
    the body of the Dharma King.

399 The original line reads "three times she moved house to educate her child," a description of the widowed mother of the great philosopher Mencius (372–289 BCE), who moved to try to find the best place for her son.
400 Here the poet voices the traditional Buddhist manner of fulfilling one's filial debt, which is to transfer any religious merit not only to one's family but to all sentient beings. Mingxiu's four arduous pilgrimages may have been a way of creating merit for her mother.

自題荊州寓庵求畫西湖

融融麗日洞天幽
一種清華近寶樓
香篆去從朝彩接
白雲來自曉風收
泉流竹葉將成筏
霞復桐枝欲化虯
瑞氣滿峰花滿麓
值教斗室作神州

---

401 Jingzhou is located in southern Hubei province on the banks of the Yangtze River. This
    inscription was probably composed for her own painting.

My Inscription for a Painting of West Lake Requested While Staying at
My Convent in Jingzhou[401]

Mild and gentle, a fine sun
   pierces the dark sky.
A kind of pure beauty
   grows near the jeweled tower.
Patterned incense smoke departs
   to meet the morning colors,
And pale clouds arrive, gathered
   by the breezes of the dawn.
The bamboo leaves floating
   on the stream become rafts,
And the paulownia branches
   will be dragons among rosy clouds.
Auspicious air fills the peaks;
   blossoms fill the foothills.
These suffice to transform this tiny cell
   into a realm of the immortals.

舒霞

深秋返里六叔父園亭對菊

此身自笑類寒蟬
衰病歸來亦偶然
一路詩篇殘夜月
到門樹色淡秋煙
漫將離別從頭數
且喜名花入座妍
茗椀爐香等閒事
追隨卻值淺涼天

臨江仙 舟中作

閒卻此身滄海外
帆輕不計途長
邨邨樹色染秋霜
波漂菰米熟
風送野花香

Shuxia

Shuxia was the religious name of He Yuanying 賀元瑛 (style name Chipu 赤浦). Born to a prominent family of Danyang, Jiangsu province, she was the granddaughter of the well-known lyric-poet He Shang 賀裳 (active 1662–1722). Two of He Shang's daughters, He Jie 賀潔 and He Lü 賀祿, were also highly regarded poets. It is not clear whether Shuxia also left a collection of poetry, but only a handful of her poems remain extant.[402]

Returning to My Hometown in Deep Autumn; Standing in Front of the Chrysanthemums in Sixth Uncle's Garden Pavilion

I can't help but laugh at this body,
    which is like a winter cicada,
Aging and unwell and returning here
    by fortuitous chance.
A few poems along the way,
    with the moon at night's end.
When I arrive at the gate,
    the trees are enveloped in light autumn mist.
I won't count from the start
    all of the partings.
I'm just delighted at the flowers
    enticing me to take a seat.
The tea leaves and scent of incense
    that are my everyday life
Have followed in my footsteps
    on this mild autumn day.

To the Tune "Immortal by the River," Composed While on a Boat

I've thrown myself into this journey on the deep blue sea,
Regardless of how far my little boat must travel.
In village after village, the trees are brushed with autumn frost,
And the rippling waves of wild rice ripen,
As the scent of wildflowers wafts in with the breeze.

蓼渚蘆灣何處宿
狎鷗一樣行藏
十年前事已相忘
只愁今夜夢
隨月到家鄉

菩薩蠻 留別

天涯芳草春歸路
無端風雨將花妒
相續古今愁
春江無盡頭

孤帆猶未動
先做思鄉夢
離恨盡今生
他生莫有情

Amid knotweed islets and river reed bends, where shall I pass the
    night?
Like river birds, I seek out a place to rest from my travels.
The events of ten years ago are already forgotten,
But sadness remains in tonight's dream
As I follow the moon back home.

To the Tune "Bodhisattva Barbarian": A Parting Poem

Everywhere, sweet grasses depart with the spring,
And the wind and rain grow jealous of the blossoms.
Unbroken sorrows of past and present
Are like the ceaseless flow of a river in spring.

Even before my solitary boat stirs,
I begin to dream of my old home.
May parting's sorrow end in this life,
And there be no such feelings in the next!

悟情

感懷

清淨而今遍六根
焚香幸作佛前人
已知性海須登岸
且向恆河試問津

口藏誰傳彌勒法
心鐙自照女兒身
癡情一點消難盡
吟到詩篇忘苦辛

Wuqing

Wuqing (style name Shilian 石蓮), whose family name was Weng 翁, was from Dantu, Jiangsu province. Her parents died when she was just a young girl, and she went to the capital Beijing to live with her elder sister Yunqing 雲卿, who had become the concubine of the Manchu high official Helin 和琳 (1753–1796). After Helin's death, her sister hanged herself, and the traumatized fifteen-year-old Wuqing turned toward the religious life. She went home to southeastern China, where she found a home with the woman scholar and poet Luo Qilan 駱綺蘭 (1755–1813?), who was also living a life of quiet Buddhist devotion. The scholar Qian He 錢泳 (1759–1844) described her as having "the appearance of a man and a heroic air. She played the flute well, was able to write lyrics, and was also quite expert at riding and shooting. She rode horseback as though flying." It was only after Luo Qilan's death that Wuqing actually became a nun.[403]

Feelings

Cleansed and purified
    are all of my six senses now.
Burning incense, I am fortunate
    to be a follower of the Buddha.
I already know one must reach
    the shores of the Ocean of Suchness,
And so, facing the Ganges,
    I ask where one can cross.
With the oral scripture, who transmits
    the Way of Maitreya Buddha?
The mind's lamp automatically
    illuminates this woman's body.
The last bit of attachment
    is hard to eradicate,
But reciting poems can help
    in forgetting all the bitterness.

蒼茫回首萬緣空
漫說平生塞與通
眼見公候興敗易
命憐姨妹死生同
只留此日袈裟在
不見當年錦繡叢
坐徹蒲團波浪息
心緣穩渡片帆風

404 The mind referred to here is the conditioned mind, which needs to be transcended, or
     as here, "crossed over."

When one looks around at the vast expanse,
   everything is inherently empty.
So do not speak about a lifetime
   of obstructions and opportunities.
I have seen dukes and lords
   rise and fall one after another,
And the pitiful fate of my sister,
   for whom life and death were one.
All that is left are these
   dark-colored nun's robes.
The embroidered brocades of yesterday
   are nowhere to be seen.
I will sit on my meditation mat
   till the waves grow still,
The mind making a steady crossing,[404]
   like a sail filled with wind.

慧機

答覺羅赫舍里夫人

　山雲歸自山
　水雲歸自水
　問雲雲無心
　還問看雲子

405 The Taiping Rebellion, one of the bloodiest civil wars in all of world history, was fought
     between the Qing court and a group of Han Chinese rebels known as the Taiping
     Heavenly Kingdom. The war lasted from 1850 to 1864.

Huiji

Huiji, whose family name was Tan 譚, was from Qiantang 錢塘 (Hangzhou). She first took refuge at Huixin Convent 慧心庵 and then took ordination at Chongfu Monastery 崇福寺 in Hangzhou. Between 1851 and 1852, Huiji got caught up in the Taiping Rebellion and fled into the mountains seeking safety.[405] In 1864 she returned to a devastated Hangzhou, where she took responsibility for restoring and greatly expanding Cixiao Convent 慈孝庵. She also worked with laywomen such as the Lady Gioro Hešeri 覺羅赫舍里, a devout Buddhist of the Manchu ruling class who was actively involved in the work of recovering and reprinting Buddhist texts that had been lost or destroyed during the rebellion.[406]

Reply to Lady Gioro Hešeri

Mountain clouds return from the mountains,
And river clouds return from the rivers.
You could ask the clouds, but the clouds are mindless.
So go back and ask the one who's looking at the clouds.

---

406 For more on Lady Gioro and her involvement in the Buddhist revival that took place after the suppression of the Taiping, see Grant 2021.

量海如德

無題

看他孤獨人
真為無事客
出入往來間
逍遙無杖策
既無兒女情
亦無妻子迫
偶然樹下坐
則見梅花白

---

407 See Zhiguan, n.d., 398c16–a7. Lianghai Rude's collection is titled *The Shadows and Echoes Collection* (*Yinxiang ji* 影響集).

Lianghai Rude

Almost nothing is known about the life of Lianghai Rude (pronounced Roo-duh) apart from the fact that she was the abbess of a large convent of as many as six thousand nuns on Mount Lingyan in Suzhou. By the eighteenth century, the convent had become an important center of Pure Land Buddhism, and it remains so today. To judge from her few extant sermons, it would appear that she was particularly concerned with reforming the discipline, spiritual practice, and reputation of Buddhist nuns at a time when Buddhism had fallen into considerable disrepute. Lianghai lived during the tumultuous years of the Taiping Rebellion and suffered the dislocation and destruction that followed in its wake. After her death, a hand-copied manuscript of her works was recovered in the home of a Buddhist layman from Suzhou and later included in the *Extended Chinese Buddhist Canon* (*Xu zangjing* 續藏經).[407]

Untitled Verses

I
Look at him, the solitary one,
Truly a wanderer with nothing to do!
Between coming in and going out,
He's free and easy, without even a walking stick.
He may lack the love of sons and daughters,
But he doesn't suffer the nagging of a wife.
On a whim, he sits himself beneath the trees,
Seeing only the white of the plum blossoms.

行到山盡頭
坐看雲起處
白雲天際飛
紅日空中住
滄海變桑田
邱陵夷無地
起滅水中漚
聚散小兒戲

堪嗟為僧者
未聞佛教音
但知噇飽飯
不悟本來人
終日心境鬪
拘牽利與名
能得幾時在
俄成一聚塵

今朝年初一
元旦是好日
鼕鼕鑼鼓響
个个衣冠飾
相逢咸打恭
茶話喜作揖
人人賀新年
我道是舊日

---

408 This is a traditional idiom referring to the momentous changes brought about by time, and more generally, to the instability and impermanence of all things.

II

He walks until he reaches the mountain top,
Where he sits and watches clouds rise.
The white clouds sail to the edge of heaven,
And the red sun rests in the center of the sky.
The blue sea turns into fields of mulberry.[408]
The hills are leveled flat, then disappear.
Rising and falling like foam on the water,
They gather and scatter like children at play.

III

Pitiable are those who call themselves monks,
But who've yet to hear the Buddha's teachings.
All they understand is how to fill their bellies,
And have not realized their original true self.
All day long they contend with mental states
And get themselves tied up in profit and fame.
Even if they do realize it for a moment,
In a split second it turns into a pile of dust!

IV

Today is the first day of the year.
New Year's Day is a good day!
Boom, the drums resound,
And everyone dresses to the nines.
Meeting, they exchange greetings,
And after tea and a chat, they cheerfully bow.
Everyone is celebrating New Year's,
But I say that it is just any old day.

石室寒巇客
不知晝與夜
坐來歲月忘
嬾把眾生化
真个自了漢
賊虎龍蛇怕
問他廬陵米
如今作麼價

但說世界空
時時行於有
空亦不自空
有亦不自有
空有本來無
無無何須守
論塵野犴鳴
談真獅子吼

今古往來客
奔波日夜忙
貪榮為底事
謀利作經商
富貴暫時樂
泥犁萬劫長
前程長遠在
何不早還鄉

409 There may be an allusion here to two well-known Buddhist hermit-poets, Hanshan
(Cold Mountain) of the Tang dynasty and Shiwu (石屋 Stone Hut) of the Yuan dynasty.

V

The guest of the stone hut and cold cliff[409]
Is unaware of the passing of days and nights.
He sits in meditation, all time forgotten.
Too lazy even to go out and convert others,
He just seems to think only of himself.[410]
He is feared by wily tigers, dragons, and snakes.[411]
Ask him about the price of Luling rice,
He replies, "How much do they want for it today?"[412]

VI

Although it is said the world is empty,
It repeatedly manifests as existence.
Emptiness does not inherently exist,
Nor is existence inherently empty.
Emptiness and existence are originally non-being.
But non-being is also empty, so why cling to it?
Ordinary discussion is the cry of the wild deer,
While authentic conversation is the roar of the lion.[413]

VII

Travelers from ancient times to now
Hustle and bustle day and night.
Lust for wealth their main concern,
They seek out profit from their trade.
Wealth and rank bring fleeting joy,
But the joyless hells go on for ages.
Think of the future lying ahead.
Why not return to your home right now?[414]

---

410 This behavior may seem to be lacking in compassion, but the poet appears to want to emphasize the complete lack of worldly concerns and personal religious ambitions.

411 Dragons and snakes are often used as metaphors for heroes and villains.

412 A monk once asked Master Qingyuan Xingsi 青原行思 (660–774), "What is the primary meaning of the Buddhadharma?" His reply was "What is the price of rice in Luling?"

413 The roar of the lion is often used as an analogy for the teachings of the Buddha himself. The Qing dynasty Linji Chan master Yufeng Zhi 與峰智 said in a dharma talk, "To preach the dharma without getting anything from it is the roar of the lion. To preach the dharma to get something from it is the cry of the wild deer." See Chaoyong 1697, 617c5–6.

414 The phrase "to return home" can also be used figuratively to refer to retirement from public life, or more existentially, to return to what is most important in life.

人壽不滿百
夭殤更可憐
況逢世路險
往復轉喬遷
恩愛終須別
冤親未了緣
無生極樂國
解脫自安然

業淨未曾乾
眾生處處著
回頭自反觀
旋轉皆旅泊
但覺本性空
諸緣自脫却
逍遙無事人
所在成安樂．

擬古為平湖陸孝女作

瞻彼鵡湖
維潔維清
厥有陸女
曰孝曰貞

415 My translation here is tentative. The line appears to suggest that although one has begun to engage in good behavior, there still remains much to be done.

416 That is, all the conditions or environmental causes that affect life.

417 Another name for East Lake in Pinghu, Zhejiang province.

VIII

A human life seldom reaches a hundred,
And dying young is sadder still.
What about all the dangers of the world,
As one comes and goes to better one's lot?
Favors and affection end up separated;
Enemies and friends are unresolved connections.
In the Land of the Unborn and Ultimate Bliss,
One will be liberated and completely at peace.

IX

With behavior cleansed but not yet firm[415]
Sentient beings cling to everything.
Look back and reflect on yourself;
Turn around and moor your boat.
Just realize that your original nature is empty,
And all conditions will naturally be freed.[416]
Unfettered, a person with nothing to do,
Wherever she is, at peace and full of joy.

Written in Imitation of an Ancient Style: The Filial Girl Lu of Pinghu

As I gaze at Egret Lake,[417]
How pure and clear it is!
Once there was a Miss Lu[418]
Said to be filial and chaste.

418　In the Pinghu gazetteer of 1886, there is a reference to a young girl by the name of Lu
　　Yinzhu 陸銀珠, who may be the filial girl referred to in these verses. According to the
　　gazetteer account, in 1863 bandits invaded the town where Lu lived. Her parents fell ill
　　trying to escape, and Lu desperately tried to find medicine for them. Before the year
　　was out, Lu's father committed suicide and her mother followed soon after. Lu herself
　　subsequently drowned herself in a river at the age of eighteen.

無父何怙
有母能慈
撫我育我
朝夕依依

俾我及笄
為我聯姻
夭桃未賦
孤雁沈淪

誓不再更
願終養母
裁雲縷月
不辭勞服

母沒女存
女淚濺濺
竟隨母逝
貞孝兩全

光明心地
一志允終
神其遠矣
名留淛東

---

419   In the original poem, the girl is referred to as a "soft and tender peach tree," an image
that comes from a famous poem in the *Classic of Poetry*, the first line of which reads,
"Peach tree, soft and tender, / how your blossoms glow! / The bride is going to her
home. / She suits this house well."

With no father to rely on,
But with a mother who loved her,
Comforted and taught her,
From morning till night.

When it came time to marry
A match was arranged.
But before the peach tree bore fruit,[419]
The lone goose passed away.[420]

She vowed to never remarry,
So as to care for her mother.
Cutting clouds and carving moons,[421]
She never rested from her toil.

The mother died, the daughter not,
And the daughter's tears fell like rain.
She followed her mother in death,
Still chaste and filial.

Of shining character,
She was single-minded up to the end.
Her spirit has gone far indeed,
But her fame has stayed in Zhejiang.

420 A reference to the young man she was engaged to marry.
421 A metaphor for skilled artistry, in this case probably sewing and embroidery, which
she then sold to support herself and her mother.

念佛詩

一句彌陀妙悟存
性空罪福不留痕
蓮花朵朵隨心現
聽法常依世所尊

一句彌陀信願真
東西土不離當人
箇中圓裹三千界
樹樹花開一樣春

一句彌陀體用真
當陽覿面露全身
無陰陽地翻觔斗
剎剎塵塵轉法輪

---

422 The Pure Land's ponds are described as being filled with lotuses, some in bud and others
     fully open, within which devotees are reborn.

Buddha Recitation [six selections from a series of forty-eight poems]

II

With a single "Amitabha Buddha"
　　comes a wondrous awakening.
Naturally empty of both sin and merit,
　　and not leaving a trace.
Lotus blossoms, stalk after stalk,
　　appear where one desires,[422]
Listening to the ever-reliable dharma
　　of the World-Honored One.

IV

With a single "Amitabha Buddha"
　　and a faith that is genuine,
There is no difference, east or west,
　　From what lies within.
Right here, completely contained,
　　are the three thousand worlds,
As on tree after tree, blossoms open,
　　their springtime all the same.

VIII

With a single "Amitabha Buddha,"
　　essence and function are true,[423]
And standing in the light,
　　the whole body is revealed.
Turn a somersault in the place
　　where there is no yin or yang,
And every single particle and mote
　　turns the dharma wheel.

423　In East Asian thought in general, the word pair "essence and function" is used to express
　　the relationship between concepts like internal and external, hidden and manifest, and
　　samsara and nirvana.

一句彌陀決定稱
別求向上更何能
聲聲遍滿處空界
落盡牽纏倚樹藤

一句彌陀辟惡氛
娑婆苦海頓超羣
風聲鳥語談真諦
淨穢何妨分不分

一句彌陀無古今
慈雲靄靄倍欽心
當觀落日如懸鼓
天樂盈空法韻深

---

424 The Buddha is said to extend great clouds of compassion over all suffering beings, the
   rain of the dharma falling upon each according to their needs and capacities.

X

With a single "Amitabha Buddha,"
    all anxieties are purified.
One is already among those
    born in the precious lotus flowers.
Why divide realms into two,
    the pure and the defiled?
Each and every person treads
    on the head of Vairocana.

XV

With a single "Amitabha Buddha,"
    all noxious influences are dispelled,
And the bitter sea of this world
    is suddenly left far behind.
The sound of wind, the chatter of birds,
    all speak of ultimate truth.
Why bother to make distinctions
    between the pure and impure?

XLII

With a single "Amitabha Buddha,"
    there is no past or present.
The gentle clouds of compassion
    are to be admired even more.[424]
When one contemplates the setting sun,
    that dangles like a drum,
A heavenly music fills the sky,
    with sweet dharma sounds.

淨土詩

能從忍界現西方
只要當人信願強
處處慈尊常接引
即時演出妙蓮香

廬山面目舊家風
嫡子親傳道自同
成佛以來今十劫
彌陀合在我心中

淨土昭昭在目前
不勞舉步問金仙
樂邦有路誰先到
咫尺家山落照邊

425 The term refers to the realm filled with beings who must undergo rebirth, that is, the
world we live in.

Poems of the Pure Land

I

One can, from this realm of endurance,[425]
    manifest the Western Paradise.
All that is required is that a person
    be strong in faith and resolve.
Everywhere the Compassionate One
    will receive and guide you,
And right then and there, send forth
    the scent of the divine lotus.

II

On the true face of Mount Lu[426]
    are the old breezes of home.
Whether a son or a disciple,
    the path is the same.
It has been ten eons
    since the attainment of Buddhahood.
Amitabha now exists with us
    here in our minds.

III

The Pure Land shines clear and bright
    in front of your eyes,
So don't bother to set out
    to seek the Golden Immortal.[427]
There is a path to the Land of Bliss.
    Who will be the first to arrive?
The mountains of home are as near
    as the glow of the setting sun.

426 A famous quatrain by the Song dynasty poet Su Shi describing the famous Mount Lu reads as follows: "Viewed horizontally, a mountain range. Viewed vertically, a peak. / Always different if seen from far or near, from high or low. / The reason why one cannot know the true face of Mount Lu / is simply because one is situated inside the mountain."

427 An epithet for the Buddha, in this case, the Amitabha Buddha.

瓦礫荊榛真淨土
見聞知覺古彌陀
但能當處忘分別
拍手呵呵唱哩囉

持戒嚴身福報真
金沙地上玉樓春
但觀自性彌陀佛
歷劫何嘗染一塵

要結西方淨土緣
是非人我盡傾蠲
脚頭脚底蓮花國
到岸何須更覓船

IV

Rubble and ruin, brambles and briars—
    this is the authentic Pure Land.
Seeing, hearing, knowing, feeling—
    these are the ancient Amitabha.
All you need to do is to be where you are
    and forget all distinctions,
Clapping your hands with a "Ha! Ha!"
    and singing with a "La! La!"

V

Keep the precepts, maintain discipline,
    and you will truly reap your karmic reward.
In the land of golden sands,
    it is spring in the jade towers.
Just contemplate the Amitabha Buddha
    that is your self-nature.
For eons it has been unsullied
    by even a speck of dust.

VI

If you want a karmic connection
    with the Western Pure Land,
Right and wrong, self and other,
    will all be washed away.
Wherever you plant your feet
    will be Lotus Blossom Land.
So why insist on looking for a raft
    after you've reached the shore?

佛語禪心兩不差
桃紅李白一般花
琉璃地上鋪金粟
瑪瑙堦前布玉沙

獨坐幽居萬慮忘
全身渾是法中王
休將迷悟遮心眼
正覺花開徧界香

VII

Buddha's words and the meditative mind—
    there's no difference between the two.
Peach blossoms are pink, pear blossoms white,
    but both are equally blossoms.
Across the floor of color-glazed tile
    are scattered nuggets of gold.
The agate stairwell
    is covered with bits of jade.

VIII

I sit alone in deep seclusion,
    ten thousand cares forgotten.
My whole body is absorbed
    into that of the Dharma King.
Don't use "delusion" and "awakening"
    to obscure the mind's eye.
When the flower of true awareness opens,
    its fragrance will encircle the world.

Abbreviations

J   *Jiaxingdazang jing* 嘉興大藏經 [The Jiaxing Chinese Buddhist Canon].
T   *Taishō shinshu Daizōkyō* 大正新脩大藏經 [The Taishō New Edition of the Buddhist Canon].
X   *Xuzang jing* 續藏經 [The Extended Chinese Buddhist Canon].
B   *Dazang jing bubian* 大藏經補編 [Supplement to the Chinese Buddhist Canon].

Digital Databases

CBETA   *Dianzi fodian jicheng* 電子佛典集成, Zhongguo dianzi fodian xiehui 中華電子佛典協會 [Chinese Buddhist Electronic Text Association]. http://www.cbeta.

MQWW   *Ming Qing Women's Writings*. http://digital.library.mcgill.ca/mingqing/.

ZJGK   *Zhongguo jiben guji ku* 中國基本古籍庫 [Database of Chinese Classic Ancient Books]. Beijing Airusheng shuzihua jishu yanjiu zhongxin 北京愛如生數字化技術研究中心. http://server.wenzibase.com.libproxy.wustl.edu/jsp/front/prodlist.jsp.

Bibliography

Editions

Baochang 寶唱. 516. *Biqiuni zhuan* 比丘尼傳 [Biographies of Nuns]. CBETA T50, no. 2063.

Baochi Xuanzong 寶持玄總. N.d. *Baochi Zong chanshi yulu* 寶持總禪師語錄 [Recorded Sayings of Chan Master Baochi Zong]. CBETA J35, no. B337.

Chaoyong 超永, comp. 1697. *Wudeng quanshu* 五燈全書 [The Complete Book of the Five Lamps]. CBETA X82, no. 1571.

Ding Peng 丁彭, comp. 2009. *Fuli ci* 扶荔詞 [Lyrics of Fuli]. Accessed online at ZJGK.

Feng Jinbo 馮金伯, comp. 1805. *Ciyuan cuibian* 詞苑萃編 [Collected Texts from the Garden of Lyrics]. Accessed online at ZJGK.

Hu Ting 胡珽, comp. N.d. *Jingtu shengxian lu xubian* 淨土聖賢錄續編 [Extended Records of Sages and Saints of the Pure Land]. CBETA X78, no. 1550.

Jiang Jingyu 蔣景祁. 1681. *Yaohua ji* 瑤華集 [The Jasper Flower Collection]. Accessed online at ZJGK.

Jin Yimo 金翼謀. 1914. *Xianglian shihua* 香奩詩話 [Toilette Case Poetry Talks]. Accessed online at ZJGK.

Jizong Xingche 繼總行徹. N.d. *Jizong Che chanshi yulu* 繼總徹禪師語錄 [Recorded Sayings of Chan Master Jizong Che]. CBETA J28, no. B211.

Lianghai Rude 量海如德. N.d. *Yingxiang ji* 影響集 [Shadows and Echoes Collection]. CBETA X62, no. 1209.

Peng Yuncan 彭蘊璨. 1909. *Lidai huashi huizhuan* 歷代畫史彙傳 [Biographies of Artists through the Ages]. Accessed online at https://ctext.org/wiki.pl?if=gb&res=569217.

Qiyuan Xinggang 祇園行剛. N.d. *Fushi Qiyuan chanshi yulu* 伏獅祇園禪師語錄 [Recorded Sayings of Chan Master Qiyuan of Fushi]. CBETA J28, no. B210.

Renhe xianzhi 仁和縣志 [Renhe County Gazetteer, 1687]. 1687. Accessed online at ZJGK.

Shen Shanbao 沈善寶. 1846. *Mingyuan shihua* 名媛詩話 [Remarks on Poetry by Famous Women]. Accessed online at MQWW.

Shenqi 沈起, comp. N.d. *Cha Dongshan xiansheng nianpu* 查東山先生年譜 [Chronological Biography of Master Cha Dongshan]. Accessed online at https://ctext.org/library.pl?if=gb&file=24799&page=48#祖鐙萱大師.

Wang Duanshu 王端淑. 1667. *Mingyuan shiwei* 名媛詩緯 [Classic Poetry by Famous Women]. Accessed online at MQWW.

Wang Yu 王豫, ed. 1821. *Jiangsu shizheng* 江蘇詩徵 [Comprehensive Poetry of Jiangsu]. Accessed online at ZJGK.

Wanyan Yun Zhu 完顏惲珠. 1831, 1836. *Guochao guixiu zhengshi ji* 國朝閨秀正始集 [Anthology of Correct Beginnings by Women of the Present Dynasty]. Accessed online at MQWW.

Wuxian zhi 吳縣志 [Gazetteer of Wu County]. Preface dated 1642. Consulted online at ZJGK.

Xu Naichang 徐乃昌, ed. 1909. *Guixiu cichao* 閨秀詞鈔 [Draft Lyrics of Genteel Ladies]. Accessed online at MQWW.

Xu Qiu 徐釚. 1688. *Ciyuan congtan* 詞苑叢談 [Forest of talks from the Garden of Lyrics].

Xu Shichang 徐世昌. 1990. *Wanqing yishihui* 晚清簃詩匯 [Anthology of Poetry of the Late Qing]. Zhonghua shuju. Reprint of 1929 edition.

Yigong Chaoke 義公超珂. *Fushi Yigong chanshi yulu* 伏獅義公禪師語錄 [Recorded Sayings of Chan Master Yigong of Fushi] CBETA J39, no. B435.

Yikui Chaochen 一揆超琛. *Cantong Yikui chanshi yulu* 參同一揆禪師語錄 [Recorded Sayings of Chan Master Yikui of Cantong]. CBETA J39, no. B436.

Yu Qian 喻謙, ed. 1923. *Xinxu gaoseng zhuan* 新續高僧傳 [The New Continued Biographies of Eminent Monastics]. CBETA B27, no. 151.

Zhenhua 震華. 1988. *Xu biqiuni zhuan* 續比丘尼轉 [Supplement to Lives of Nuns]. In *Biqiunizhuan quanji* 比丘尼傳全集 [Complete Collection of Lives of Nuns]. Fojiao chubanshe. Reprint of 1941 edition.

Zhou Kefu 周克復, ed. N.d. *Lichao Jingangjing chiyanji* 歷朝金剛經持驗集 [Anthology of Diamond Sutra Miracle Tales of Successive Generations]. CBETA X87, no. 1635.

Zhou Shouchang 周壽昌, ed. 1846. *Gonggui wenxuan* 宮閨文選 [Selected Writings from the Women's Quarters]. Accessed online at https://ctext .org/wiki.pl?if=gb&res=989701.

Ziyong Chengru 子雍成如. N.d. *Ziyong Ru chanshi yulu* 子雍如禪師語錄 [Recorded Sayings of Chan Master Ziyong Ru]. CBETA J39, no. B465.

Zukui Xuanfu 祖揆玄符. N.d. *Lingrui chanshi Yanhua ji* 靈瑞禪師嵒華集 [Chan Master of Lingrui's Cliffside Flowers Collection]. CBETA J35, no. B339.

Translations

Grant, Beata. 2003. *Daughters of Emptiness: Poems of Chinese Buddhist Nuns.* Wisdom Publications.

Grant, Beata. 2017. *Zen Echoes: Classic Kōans with Verse Commentaries by Three Female Zen Masters.* Wisdom Publications.

Idema, Wilt, and Beata Grant. 2004. *The Red Brush: Writing Women of Imperial China.* Harvard East Asian Monographs.

Secondary Scholarship

Bryne, Christopher, and Jason Protass. 2015. "Poetry: China (Song and After)." *Brill Encyclopedia of Buddhism*, vol. 1, 547–553.

Chang, Kang'i Sun, and Haun Saussey, eds. 2000. *Women Writers of Traditional China: An Anthology of Poetry and Criticism*. Stanford University Press.

Chang, Kang'i Sun, and Ellen Widmer, eds. 1997. *Writing Women in Late Imperial China*. Stanford University Press.

Grant, Beata. 1996. "Female Holder of the Lineage: Linji Chan Master Zhiyuan Xinggang, (1597–1654)." *Late Imperial China* 17, no. 2 (December 1996): 51–77.

Grant, Beata. 1999. "Severing the Red Cord: Buddhist Nuns in Eighteenth-Century China." In Karma Lekshe Tsomo, ed., *Buddhist Women across Cultures: Realizations*. State University of New York Press.

Grant, Beata. 2001. "Behind the Empty Gate: Buddhist Nun-Poets in Late-Ming and Qing China." In Marsha Weidner, ed., *Cultural Intersections in Later Chinese Buddhism*. University of Hawai'i Press.

Grant, Beata. 2008. *Eminent Nuns: Chan Masters of Seventeenth Century China*. University of Hawai'i Press.

Grant, Beata. 2010. "*Chan you*: Poetic Friendships between Nuns and Laywomen in Late Imperial China." In Grace Fong and Ellen Widmer, eds., *The Inner Quarters and Beyond: Women Writers from Ming through Qing*, 215–248. Brill.

Grant, Beata. 2012. "Dwelling in the Mountains: The Hengshan Poems of Jizong Xingche (b. 1606)." In *Hsiang Lectures on Chinese Poetry*, vol. 6, 57–74. McGill University, Centre for East Asian Research.

Grant, Beata. 2014. "Writing Oneself into the Tradition: The Autobiographical Sermon of Chan Master Jizong Xingche (b. 1606)." In Jia Jinhua et al., eds., *Gendering Chinese Religion: Subject, Identity, and Body*, 47–70. State University of New York Press.

Grant, Beata. 2021. "Women in the Religious and Publishing Worlds of Buddhist Master Miaokong (1826–1880)." In Paul W. Kroll and Jonathan A. Silk, eds., *"At the Shores of the Sky": Asian Studies for Albert Hoffstadt*, 173–184. Brill.

Mazanec, Thomas J. 2017a. "The Invention of Chinese Buddhist Poetry: Poet-Monks in Late Medieval China (c. 760–960 CE)." Ph.D. dissertation, Princeton University.

Mazanec, Thomas J. 2017b. "The Medieval Chinese *Gāthā* and Its Relationship to Poetry." *T'oung Pao* 103 (1–3): 94–154.

Renhe xianzhi 仁和縣志 [Renhe County Gazetteer]. 1687. Accessed online at ZJGK.

Rouzer, Paul, trans. 2020. *The Poetry and Prose of Wang Wei*. De Gruyter Mouton.

Su Meiwen 蘇美文. 2008a. "Fushi nüchan: Qiyuan zhi chanjiaohua yu xingbie zhi" 伏獅女禪：祇園之禪教化與性別智 [The Female Chan of Fushi: Qiyuan's Chan Training and Gender Wisdom]. *Taida foxue yanjiu* 臺大佛學研究 6: 139–204.

Su Meiwen 蘇美文. 2008b. "Nüchan hexiang: Baochi yu Zukui zhi xingzhuan kaoshu" 女禪合響：寶持與祖揆之行傳考述 [Female Zen Masters' Choir: The Textual Criticism and Explanations of Biographies of Baochi and Zukui]. *Xin shiji zongjiao yanjiu* 新世紀宗教研究 7 (1): 35–89.

Su Meiwen 蘇美文. 2009. "Meng hanshuang yueleng shimen: Yigong chanshi zhi xiuwu jiaohua yu jixi Fushi" 夢寒霜月冷師門：義公禪師之修悟教化與繼席伏獅 [The Master's Gate of Cold Dreams and a Frosty Moon: Chan Master Yigong's Cultivation of Enlightenment and Education and Her Accession to the Leadership of Fushi]. *Taibei Daxue Zhongwenxi bao* 臺北大學中文學報 2009: 37–84.

Tsai, Kathryn Ann, trans. 1994. *Lives of the Nuns: Biographies of Chinese Buddhist Nuns from the Fourth to the Sixth Centuries.* University of Hawai'i Press.

Wang Chang 王昶, comp. 1773. *Guochao cizong* 國朝詞綜 [Complete Lyrics of the Dynasties]. Zhonghua shuju.

Su Meiwen 蘇美文. 2016. "Shi wu xiashi kong cheng jian: Jizong chanshi nanyue qulaide nüchan shilu" 世武俠士空呈劍：季總禪師南嶽去來的女禪詩路 [The Knight-Errant Raises Her Sword in Vain: Chan Master Jizong's Journey into Female Chan Poetry to and from Nanyue]. *Zhonghua keji daxue xuebao* 中華科技大學學報 67: 51–70.

Works Cited

Broughton, Jeffrey L., and Elise Yoko Watanabe, trans. 2014. *The Chan Whip Anthology: A Companion to Zen Practice.* Oxford University Press.

Chen Zhuo 陳焯, comp. 1873. *Song Yuan shihui* 宋元詩會 [*Collection of Poetry of the Song and Yuan*]. Accessed at CJGK.

Cleary, Thomas, trans. 1978. *Sayings and Doings of Pai-chang, Ch'an Master of Great Wisdom.* Center Publications.

Cleary, Thomas, trans. 1998. *The Blue Cliff Record.* Numata Center for Buddhist Translation and Research.

Egan, Charles. 2010. *Clouds Thick, Whereabouts Unknown: Poems by Zen Monks of China.* Columbia University Press.

Feng Jinbo 馮金伯. 1831. *Guochao huashi* 國朝畫識 [Biographies of Qing Dynasty Painters]. Accessed online at ZJGK.

Ferguson, Andy, trans. 2000. *Zen's Chinese Heritage: The Masters and Their Teachings.* Wisdom Publications.

Fu Xuancong 傅璇琮 et al., eds. 1991. *Quan Songshi* 全宋詩 [Complete Song Dynasty Poems]. Beijing daxue chubanshe.

Haiyan xian tujing 海鹽縣圖經 [Illustrated Gazetteer of Haiyan County]. 1624. Accessed online at ZJGK.

Heng Sure. 2009. *The Śūraṅgama Sūtra: A New Translation.* Buddhist Text Translation Society. Accessed online at http://www.dharmasite.net /Surangama_new_translation.pdf.

Knechtges, David, trans. 2014. *Wen Xuan, or Selections of Refined Literature*. Vol. 3: *Rhapsodies on Natural Phenomena, Birds and Animals, Aspirations and Feelings, Sorrowful Laments, Literature, Music, and Passions*. Princeton University Press.

Ko, Dorothy. 1994. *Teachers of the Inner Chambers: Women and Culture in Seventeenth-Century China*. Stanford University Press., 1994.

Leighton, Taigen Dan, and Yi Wu, trans. 2000. *Cultivating the Empty Field: The Silent Illumination of Zen Master Hongzhi*. Tuttle.

Li Wai-yee. 2014. *Women and National Trauma in Late Imperial Chinese Literature*. Harvard Asia Center.

Luk, Charles. 1974. *The Transmission of the Mind outside the Teaching*. Rider.

Luo Dajing 羅大經. N.d. *Helin yulu* 鶴林玉露 [Jade and Dew from Crane Forest]. Accessed online at ZJGK.

Mather, Richard B., trans. 2002. *Shih-shuo Hsin-yu: A New Account of Tales of the World*. University of Michigan Press.

Mazanec, Thomas J. 2017a. "The Invention of Chinese Buddhist Poetry: Poet-Monks in Late Medieval China (c. 760–960 CE)." Ph.D. dissertation, Princeton University.

Mazanec, Thomas J. 2017b. "The Medieval Chinese *Gāthā* and Its Relationship to Poetry." *T'oung Pao* 103 (1–3): 94–154.

McRae, John R. 2004. *Seeing through Zen: Encounter, Transformation, and Genealogy in Chinese Chan Buddhism*. University of California Press.

Neinhauser, William H., Jr., trans. 2002. "The World Inside a Pillow." In Y. W. Ma and J. S. M. Lau, *Traditional Chinese Stories: Themes and Variations*, 435–438. Cheng & Tsui Company.

Pattinson, David. 2019. "Bees in China: A Brief Cultural History." In R. Sterckx, M. Siebert, and D. Schäfer, eds., *Animals through Chinese History: Earliest Times to 1911*, 99–117. Cambridge University Press.

Pine, Red, and Mike O'Connor, eds. 1998. *The Clouds Should Know Me by Now*. Wisdom Publications., 1998.

Protass, Jason. 2021. *The Poetry Demon: Song-Dynasty Monks on Verse and the Way*. Kuroda Studies in East Asian Buddhism.

Renhe xianzhi 仁和縣志 [Renhe County Gazetteer]. 1687. Accessed online at ZJGK.

Rouzer, Paul, trans. 2017. *The Poetry of Hanshan (Cold Mountain), Shide, and Fenggan*. De Gruyter Mouton.

Rouzer, Paul, trans. 2020. *The Poetry and Prose of Wang Wei*. De Gruyter Mouton.

Ruizhang 瑞璋. N.d. *Xifang huizheng* 西舫彙征 [The Virtuous Ferried on the Western Boat]. CBETA X78, no. 1551.

Sasaki, Ruth Fuller, et al., trans. 1971. *The Recorded Sayings of Layman Pang*. Weatherhill.

Schlütter, Morten. 2008. *How Zen Became Zen: The Dispute over Enlightenment and the Formation of Chan Buddhism in Song-Dynasty China*. University of Hawai'i Press.

Seaton, J. P., and Dennis Maloney, eds. 1995. *A Drifting Boat: Chinese Zen Poetry*. White Pine Press.

Tsai, Kathryn Ann, trans. 1994. *Lives of the Nuns: Biographies of Chinese Buddhist Nuns from the Fourth to the Sixth Centuries*. University of Hawai'i Press.

Wang Chang 王昶, comp. 1773. *Guochao cizong* 國朝詞綜 [Complete Lyrics of the Dynasties]. Zhonghua shuju.

Wang Chang 王昶. 1802. *(Jiaqing) Zhili Taiqiang zhou zhi* (嘉慶) 直隸太倉州志 [Gazetteer of Zhili Taiqiang County]. Accessed online at ZJGK.

Wang Qishu 汪啟淑. 1773. *Xiefang ji* 擷芳集 [Collected Fragrances].

Waley, Arthur, trans. 1996. *The Book of Songs: The Ancient Chinese Classic of Poetry*. Grove Press.

Watson, Burton. 1992. "Buddhist Poet-Priests of the T'ang." *Eastern Buddhist* 25 (2): 30–58.

Watson, Burton, trans. 2013. *The Complete Works of Zhuangzi*. Columbia University Press.

Welter, Albert. 1996. "The Disputed Place of 'A Special Transmission' outside the Scriptures in Ch'an." Accessed online at http://www.thezensite.com /ZenEssays/HistoricalZen/A_Special_Transmission.htm.

Wu Dingzhang 吳定璋, ed. 1745. *Qishier feng zuzheng ji* 七十二峯足徵集 [The Seventy-Two Peaks Verifiable Collection]. Accessed online at https://curiosity .lib.harvard.edu/chinese-rare-books/catalog/49-990102769380203941.

Wu, Jiang. 2008. *Enlightenment in Dispute: The Reinvention of Chan Buddhism in Seventeenth Century China*. Oxford University Press.

Wumen Huikai 無門慧開, 1228. *Wumen guan* 無門關 [The Gateless Gate]. CBETA T 2005.

Yu Qian 喻謙, comp. 1923. *Xinxu gaoseng zhuan* 新續高僧傳 [The New Continued Biographies of Eminent Monastics]. CBETA B27, no. 0151.

Zha Sheng. N.d. *Zha Sheng Zudeng Xuan dashi xinglüe* 查昇祖鐙萱大師行略 [Zha Sheng's Biographical Account of Eminent Master Xuan of Zudeng]. In Shenqi 沈起, comp., *Zha Dongshan xiansheng nianpu* 查東山先生年譜 [Chronological Life of Mister Zha Dongshan]. Accessed online at https://ctext .org/library.pl?if=gb&file=24799&page=48#祖鐙萱大師.

Zhiguan 咫觀, comp. N.d. *Xiuxi wenjian lu* 修西聞見錄 [Records of Things Seen and Heard Regarding the Cultivation of the Pure Land]. CBETA X78, no. 1552.

Index of Poem Sources

In order of appearance.

Wulian 悟蓮

After the Rain: Wang Duanshu 1667, 1:13b.
An Autumn Night: Written in the Moment: Wang Duanshu 1667, 1:13b–c.

Jieshi 介石

Early Morning: Wanyan Yun Zhu 1831, 1836, *fulu* 19a–b.
Qingming: Wanyan Yun Zhu 1831, 1836, *fulu* 19a–b.

Miaoni 妙霓

Spring Night: Xu Shichang 1990, 9176.

The Girl Nun from Yan 尼燕女

Gāthā: Wang Duanshu 1667, 26:11a.

Xingkong 性空

Reflecting on Myself: Wang Duanshu 1667, 26:12b–13a.

Mojing 摩淨

Going by Way of Tiger Hill: Xu Shichang 1990, 9179.

Jueqing 覺清

Poem Inscribed on a Convent Wall: Wang Duanshu 1667, 26.8a.

Wuwei 無為

Deathbed Gāthā: Ruizhang, n.d., CBETA X78, no. 1551, p. 375a5–6.

Jiyin 濟印

Dharma Hall Gāthā: Wanyan Yun Zhu 1831, 1836, *fulu* 16a.

Deyin 德隱

Early Autumn: A Distant Evening View: Wanyan Yun Zhu 1831, 1836, *fulu* 16a.
Song of Planting Bamboo: Wanyan Yun Zhu 1831, 1836, *fulu* 16b.
Lady Huang Jieling Came to Stay at My Mountain Boudoir, Written in the Moment:
    Xu Shichang 1990, 9155.

Derong 德容

Pitying the Caged Bird Who Is Just Like Me: Xu Shichang 1990, 9142.
Plum Blossom: Xu Shichang 1990, 9142.

Jingming 鏡明

Improvised Dharma Instructions to My Disciples: Xu Shichang 1990, 9179.

Jingyin 靜因

Going to See Huang Yuanjie, but Not Finding Her In: Wang Duanshu 1667, 26.11a.

Dumu Jin'gang 獨目金鋼

Gāthā: Zhou Kefu, n.d., CBETA X87, no. 1635, p. 553a23–b1.
Gāthā: Zhou Kefu, n.d., CBETA X87, no. 1635, p. 553a23–b1.
Deathbed Gāthā: Zhou Kefu, n.d., CBETA X87, no. 1635, p. 553b3–4.

Xiang'an Yinhui 象菴隱慧

Gāthā: Eating Bamboo Shoots: Chaoyong 1697, CBETA X82, no. 1571, p. 619a17.
Deshan Carries His Bowl: Chaoyong 1697, CBETA X82, no. 1571, p. 619a15–16.

Miaohui 妙慧

Passing by the Tomb of Tenth Daughter Ma: Wang Duanshu 1667, 24:19b–20a.
When Drinking on Flower-Raining Terrace, I Was Assigned "Falling Leaves" as the Topic for a Poem: Wanyan Yun Zhu 1831, 1836, *fulu* 19b.

Daoyuan 道元

Seated Meditation: Reflections: Wang Duanshu 1667, 26.9b–10a.

Sengjian 僧鑒

Early Summer: Xu Shichang 1990, 9165.
The Autumn Flowering Crab Apple Tree: Xu Shichang 1990, 9164–9165.

Shenyi 神一

A Dream Journey to Mount Tiantai: Xu Shichang 1990, 9130.
Again Crossing Mount Hengyun, Thinking of Jingwei: Xu Shichang 1990, 9130.

Zaisheng 再生

Composed in Early Spring: Xu Shichang 1990, 9137.
A Winter's Day: Zhou Shouchang 1846, 20.8b.
Narrating My Feelings on a Winter's Night: Xu Shichang 1990, 9137–9138.

Jingwei 靜維

The Emerald Sea: Xu Shichang 1990, 9166–9167.

Random Thoughts on Living in the Country: Xu Shichang 1990, 9166.
Facing the Moon on an Autumn Night: Xu Shichang 1990, 9165.
Sitting at Night: Xu Shichang 1990, 9166.

Shangjian Huizong 上鑒輝宗

Village Life: Wanyan Yun Zhu 1831, 1836, *fulu* 12b–13a.
Thoughts on Living in Seclusion: Xu Shichang 1990, 9151.
A Friend from the Inner Chambers Comes to Visit: Remembering Old Times: Xu Shichang 1990, 9152.
Heartfelt Recollections: Wanyan Yun Zhu 1831, 1836, *fulu* 12b.

Wugou 無垢

Writing of My Feelings [version 1]: Xu Shichang 1990, 9139.
Writing of My Feelings [version 2]: Jin Yimo 1914, *Xianglian shihua, xia.*
Climbing the Mountain after the Snow: Xu Shichang 1990, 6138.

Chaoyi 超一

Deathbed Gāthā: Xu Shichang 1990, 9144–9145.

Mingxuan Wuzhen 明萱悟真

Autumn Night: Xu Shichang 1990, 9157.
Falling Leaves [two verses]: Xu Shichang 1990, 9157.
Inscribed on a Ying Stone: Xu Shichang 1990, 9157.

Weiji Xingzhi 維極行致

Ode to the Honeybees: Wang Duanshu 1667, 26:6b–7a.
Living in the Mountains: Ding Peng 2009, 3:6b.
Listening to the Geese: Feng Jinbo 1805, 17:16a.

Jingnuo Chaoyue 靜諾超越

Song of the Ancient Plum Trees: Xu Shichang 1990, 9162.
Passing by Yongqing Monastery, I Came Upon Its Peonies and Wrote This: Xu Shichang 1990, 9162–9163.
For Lady Yang: Xu Shichang 1990, 9163–9164.
A Celebration in Verse of the Autumn Orchid: Xu Shichang 1990, 9160

Chaoyan Miyin 超衍密印

Encomium to Myself: Wang Duanshu 1667, 26:3b.

Yizhen 一真

Mid-Autumn: Wang Duanshu 1667, 15.6b.
Younger Sister Yuying and I Planned to Meet on the Ninth Day, but She Didn't Arrive: Wang Duanshu 1667, 15.7a.

Living in the Mountains among Falling Leaves: Wang Duanshu 1667, 15.6a.
Matching the Rhymes of "Cloud Hermitage": Wang Duanshu 1667, 15.6a.

Shangxin 上信

Ice: Wang Duanshu 1667, 26:11b.

Yuanduan Yufu 元端御符

My Study: An Impromptu Verse: Xu Shichang 1990, 9158.

Miaohui 妙惠

Dawn, Sitting at Bore Convent: Wanyan Yun Zhu 1831, 1836, *fulu* 17b.

Shiyan 石巖

Recalling a Dream: Xu Shichang 1990, 9159.
Swallows: Xu Shichang 1990, 9158.
Rising at Dawn: An Expression of Feelings: Xu Shichang 1990, 9159.
A Reply to Sixth Elder Sister Ruixian: Xu Shichang 1990, 9159.

Wanxian 宛仙

Inside the Convent: Reflections: Wanyan Yun Zhu 1831, 1836, *fulu* 18b–19a.

Lianhua Kedu 蓮花可度

Gāthā: Chaoyong 1697, CBETA X82, no. 1571, p. 447b10–11.

Yinyue Xinglin 印月行霖

In the Mountains: Wang Duanshu 1667, 26:3aˈ
The Three Blows: Wang Duanshu 1667, 26:2a–b.
A Verse Commentary: Chaoyong 1697, CBETA X82, no. 1571, p. 425a13–14.
When Sansheng Saw People, He Went Out; When Xinghua Saw People, He Did Not:
    Wang Duanshu 1667, 26:2b.

Ansheng 安生

Ode to the Silkworm: Xu Shichang 1990, 9146.
Mourning Zhanna: Xu Shichang 1990, 9146.

Zhuanzheng 傳正

Deathbed Gāthā: Wanyan Yun Zhu 1831, 1836, *fulu* 17a–b.

Zhisheng 智生

Ode to the Snow: Wanyan Yun Zhu 1831, 1836, *fulu* 8b–9a.
The Chrysanthemum: Wanyan Yun Zhu 1831, 1836, *fulu* 8b.

Deri 德日

Early Autumn: Xu Shichang 1990, 9171.
Feelings by a Rainy Window: Xu Shichang 1990, 9170.

Deyue 德月

On an Autumn Night, Listening to the Crickets: Xu Shichang 1990, 9172.

Zhiyuan 智圓

A Lament for Peng E: Wanyan Yun Zhu 1831, 1836, *fulu* 13b.

Qiyuan Xinggang 祇園行剛

The First Month of Summer Retreat: A Song of Leisure: Qiyuan Xinggang, n.d.,
    CBETA J28, no. B210, p. 429b11–19.
Dharma Instructions for Person of the Way Xu Chaogu: Qiyuan Xinggang, n.d.,
    CBETA J28, no. B210, p. 428c1–4.
Dharma Instructions for Mingyuan: Qiyuan Xinggang, n.d., CBETA J28, no. B210,
    p. 428c15–16.
Addressing the Congregation on My Birthday: Qiyuan Xinggang, n.d., CBETA J28,
    no. B210, p. 429a26–28.
Matching Jiang Yundu's "Autumn Pavilion Song": Qiyuan Xinggang, n.d., CBETA
    J28, no. B210, p. 429b08–10.
Ode to the Plum Blossom: Qiyuan Xinggang, n.d., CBETA J28, no. B210, p. 429a13–15.

Yigong Chaoke 義公超珂

Grieving for My Master: Yigong Chaoke, n.d., CBETA J39, no. B435, p. 2a20–24.
*Climbing up to a Thatched Hut on Lingyin and Gazing at Feilai Peak: An Impromptu
    Poem*: Yigong Chaoke, n.d., CBETA J39, no. B435, p. 1c23–25.

Yikui Chaochen 一揆超琛

Five Gāthās: Sitting in Meditation (To a Previous Tune): Yikui Chaochen, n.d.,
    CBETA no. B436, p. 10b3–13.
To a Previous Tune: Yikui Chaochen, n.d., CBETA J39, no. B436, p. 11a6–14.
Just Before Parting from My Elder Brothers: Yikui Chaochen, n.d., CBETA J39, no.
    B436, p. 11c19–21.
Bidding Farewell to the Lay Dharma Protectors of Meixi: Yikui Chaochen, n.d.,
    CBETA J39, no. B436, p. 9b25–28.
My Feelings after Visiting the Nun Weiji from Xiongsheng and Not Finding Her In:
    Yikui Chaochen, n.d., CBETA J39, no. B436, p. 10c29–a2.
Hymn: The Honeycomb: Yikui Chaochen, n.d., CBETA J39, no. B436, p. 11b22–25.
In Praise of the Venerable Bamboo (To a Previous Tune): Yikui Chaochen, n.d.,
    CBETA J39, no. B436, p. 12a23–26.

The Road Is Hard (To the Tune "Immortals by the River"): Zukui Xuanfu, n.d., CBETA J35, no. B339, p. 759c12–28.

Summer Rest on the East Mountain: Zukui Xuanfu, n.d., CBETA J35, no. B339, p. 759b7–9.

Song of the Twelve Hours of the Day: Zukui Xuanfu, n.d., CBETA J35, no. B339, p. 759b17–c11.

Living in the Mountains: Zukui Xuanfu, n.d., CBETA J35, no. B339, p. 760a18–20.

Living in the Mountains: Miscellaneous Gāthās: Zukui Xuanfu, n.d., CBETA J35, no. B339, p. 757a10–14.

Thoughts: Zukui Xuanfu, n.d., CBETA J35, no. B339, p. 760a21–25.

Baochi Xuanzong 寶持玄總

Matching the Ten Verses of Chan Master Cishou Huaiyin's "Cloud Dispelling Terrace": Baochi Xuanzong, n.d., CBETA J35, no. B337, p. 712a7–27.

Peonies Embroidered on Silk: Baochi

Harmonizing with Temple Manager Teacher Shao's "Mastering Yangqi's Primary Strategy": Four Verses: Baochi Xuanzong, n.d., CBETA J35, no. B337, p. 712b9–17.

Watching the Snow from Nanzhou's Rising Phoenix Tower: Baochi Xuanzong, n.d., CBETA J35, no. B337, p. 712c17–20.

Dharma Instructions for Person of the Way Liyan: Baochi Xuanzong, n.d., CBETA J35, no. B337, p. 712c3–5.

Jizong Xingche 繼總行徹

Living the Nanyue Mountains: Miscellaneous Verses: Jizong Xingche, n.d., CBETA J28, no. B211, p. 462a5–c19.

Mist and Clouds Peak: Jizong Xingche, n.d., CBETA J28, no. B211, p. 463b14–17.

Gods and Immortals Grotto: Jizong Xingche, n.d., CBETA J28, no. B211, p. 463b18–21.

Heavenly Terrace Monastery: Jizong Xingche, n.d., CBETA J28, no. B211, p. 463c4–7.

Mount Zhong's Great Illumination Temple: Jizong Xingche, n.d., CBETA J28, no. B211, p. 463c24–27.

The Great Yang Spring: Jizong Xingche, n.d., CBETA J28, no. B211, p. 463c16–19.

The Second Month of Autumn: A Parting Poem: Jizong Xingche, n.d., CBETA J28, no. B211, p. 463a2–7.

Enjoying the Snow on New Year's Day: Jizong Xingche, n.d., CBETA J28, no. B211, p. 464a6–9.

My Aspirations: Jizong Xingche, n.d., CBETA J28, no. B211, p. 464a10–13.

Written to Rhymes by the Layman of Zhoukui Hermitage: Jizong Xingche, n.d., CBETA J28, no. B211, p. 464b24–27.

Visiting the Monk of Nanyue on His Sickbed: Two Poems: Jizong Xingche, n.d., CBETA J28, no. B211, p. 464a18–25.

Ziyong Chengru 子雍成如

Entrusting Head Student Zhi with Robes and Whisk, I Composed This Gāthā: Ziyong Chengru, n.d., CBETA J39, no. B465, p. 830a23–25.

Mingxiu 明修

Seeing Off Relatives, Bowing to My Master, and Taking Vows: Xu Shichang 1990, 9177.
My Inscription for a Painting of West Lake Requested While Staying at My Convent in Jingzhou: Yu Qian 1923, CBETA B27, no. 151, p. 466a14–16.

Shuxia 舒霞

Returning to My Hometown in Deep Autumn; Standing in Front of the Chrysanthemums in Sixth Uncle's Garden Pavilion: Wang Yu 1821, 178:10b.
To the Tune "Immortal by the River," Composed While on a Boat: Jiang Jingyu 1681, 6:10.
To the Tune "Bodhisattva Barbarian": A Parting Poem: Jiang Jingyu 1681, 6:10.

Wuqing 悟情

Feelings: Wanyan Yun Zhu 1831, 1836, *fulu* 14b.

Huiji 慧機

Reply to Lady Gioro Hešeri: Xu Shichang 1990, 1980.

Lianghai Rude 量海如德

Untitled Verses: Lianghai Rude, n.d., CBETA X62, no. 1209, p. 819c14–820a8.
Written in Imitation of an Ancient Style: The Filial Girl Lu of Pinghu: Lianghai Rude, n.d., CBETA X62, no. 1209, p. 820a23–b4.
Buddha Recitation [six selections from a series of forty-eight poems]: Lianghai Rude, n.d., CBETA X62, no. 1209, p. 20b5–21c6.
Poems of the Pure Land: Lianghai Rude, n.d., CBETA X62, no. 1209, p. 819b9–c1.